Peru since Independence

Peru since Independence

A Concise Illustrated History

John W. Sherman

ROWMAN & LITTLEFIELD
Lanham • Boulder • New York • London

Published by Rowman & Littlefield
An imprint of The Rowman & Littlefield Publishing Group, Inc.
4501 Forbes Boulevard, Suite 200, Lanham, Maryland 20706
www.rowman.com

86-90 Paul Street, London EC2A 4NE, United Kingdom

Copyright © 2023 by The Rowman & Littlefield Publishing Group, Inc.

All rights reserved. No part of this book may be reproduced in any form or by any electronic or mechanical means, including information storage and retrieval systems, without written permission from the publisher, except by a reviewer who may quote passages in a review.

British Library Cataloguing in Publication Information Available

Library of Congress Cataloging-in-Publication Data
Names: Sherman, John W., 1960– author.
Title: Peru since independence : a concise illustrated history / John W. Sherman.
Description: Lanham : Rowman & Littlefield, [2023] | Includes bibliographical references and index. | Summary: "This concise, illustrated survey of modern Peru provides a narrative of the country's political history since independence. Packed with photos and illustrations, it also brings to life Peru's rich cultural history through standalone 'life and culture' chapters. The closing chapter engages recent political events, including the unusual and significant 2021 election of Pedro Castillo"— Provided by publisher.
Identifiers: LCCN 2023007443 (print) | LCCN 2023007444 (ebook) | ISBN 9781538173398 (cloth) | ISBN 9781538173404 (paper) | ISBN 9781538173411 (electronic)
Subjects: LCSH: Peru—History—1829– | Peru—Social life and customs.
Classification: LCC F3446.5 .S54 2023 (print) | LCC F3446.5 (ebook) | DDC 985/.05—dc23/eng/20230223
LC record available at https://lccn.loc.gov/2023007443
LC ebook record available at https://lccn.loc.gov/2023007444

Contents

	Preface	vii
	Map of Peru	x
Chapter 1	Independence and Uncertainty	1
Chapter 2	The Time of Ramón Castilla	13
Chapter 3	Life and Culture, c. 1780–1867	25
Chapter 4	Disaster: The War of the Pacific	37
Chapter 5	Picking Up the Pieces	49
Chapter 6	Life and Culture, 1867–1908	61
Chapter 7	The Age of Leguía	73
Chapter 8	The Challenge of Mass Politics	85
Chapter 9	Life and Culture, 1908–1948	97
Chapter 10	Waiting for Change	107
Chapter 11	The Left Transcendent	119
Chapter 12	Life and Culture, 1948–1980	133
Chapter 13	The Tumult	145
Chapter 14	The Dictatorship	157

Chapter 15	The Neoliberal Republic	171
Chapter 16	Life and Culture since 1980	183
Chapter 17	Crisis, Covid, and Castillo	195
	Suggested Readings	209
	Index	217

Preface

Synthesis is arguably my primary contribution to the history profession. I enjoy reading broadly, and then pulling together and summarizing. I also savor writing far more than archival research. Hence this—my fifth solo-authored book—is my third "text," or work of synthesis. It was partly inspired by writing *Mexico: A Concise Illustrated History* (Rowman & Littlefield, 2020). I found that exercise invigorating, so was inclined to engage another nation-specific work. This project was also facilitated by the tedium of the Covid pandemic. Stuck in isolation, and prevented from overseas travel (along with history, my other lifelong addiction), what else could I do but write?

It goes without saying that the one who surveys the skyscrapers and admires the cityscape owes everything to the architects and builders. This short book would not be possible without the rich historiography on national period Peru that has been constructed by scores of gifted historians, most either in Peru or within the mammoth historical profession here in the United States.

Summarizing a nation's history, however, is always a challenge. Part of the quest is finding the right balances—in narrative sweep versus depth, in the anecdotal versus the analytical, and in chronological complexity versus simplified periodization. On the second time around, I think that I am nearer to those ideal balances. I do know, however, that I have again had to write with more decisiveness than I would often like. But burdening the prose with words of condition—"probably," "likely," "might have been," and so forth, kills the energy of the text. Knowledge is never absolutely certain. A well-versed expert on Peru might well read multiple passages herein, and recognize that this or that is not quite so linear or concrete. Please also note: I use the term *America* on occasion to refer to the United States (and *Americans* to its citizens), even though many Peruvians and Latin Americans also refer to themselves as Americans. I do this because the anticipated readership is primarily based here in the United States.

As a political historian, of course I have placed Peru's politics front and center. But the nation has a rich literary, artistic, and cultural tradition, and so I have included five stand-alone chapters relating to *Life and Culture*. The line between cultural and social history, in turn, is of course fuzzy. Overall, there is very little social history within this book. Generally, I have touched upon it within the main chapters when it interfaces with politics (and some does appear in the *Life and Culture* chapters, especially with regard to popular culture). Social history is in vogue in the classroom today, of course, and the concept of this book is to provide a stand-alone political narrative that can be taught alongside any number of social histories, without fear of overlap or repetition. An advantage of the topical division by chapter is that readers also have the option of skipping the *Life and Culture* material if they so desire (or perhaps read only those, and forego the political history).

As with my *Mexico* text, I have included photographs with captions. I have strived for variation in photographic content. The illustrations are a mix of physical historical sites, artistic works, significant or representative personages, and portrayals of noteworthy events. Having said that, the challenge of 2021 visits to Peru during the Covid crisis altered the photographic selection. Most museums and archives were closed, greatly hampering my ability to access historical material. Hence, there are about five more exterior and physical images (i.e., buildings and the like) than I would have preferred. All photos except for two were taken by me with professional-grade equipment, and very sparingly edited (mainly for issues of shadow and light) by a very capable professional photographer, Corey Weaver.

Peru is a poor nation—the poorest one I have worked in for extended periods of time, and that grind of poverty fuels some desperation and tension. On a July 2021 visit, I saw not one but two close-up and serious fistfights within hours of arriving, as I walked the streets of central Lima—part of a megapolis that now has more people than the entire state of Michigan. But I have also found Peruvians of all stripes and classes to be affable, and I am pleased to count several as friends. It is my hope that this short survey will inspire readers to seek out more readings on Peru, perhaps via the suggested readings section at the close of the book, and to engage this fascinating country directly, with travel especially to Lima and other non-touristic regions instead of the foreigner-saturated and overpriced "Inca Trail." With this goal in mind, I have self-published a short book with historical walks in Lima, available on my Amazon author's page. I also periodically include travel-related insights and material on my YouTube account with johnwshemanhistorian in the URL.

Finally, though I will refrain from a long list, I wish to express my gratitude to several friends and colleagues who assisted in this project (though its shortcomings are my own), all helping a new Peruvianist along with grace and goodwill. In addition to the outside referees provided by Rowman and Littlefield—one of whom was marvelously thorough—I leaned on a sharp-minded and reliable Cathy Conaghan, who especially focused her critique on later chapters; the prolific and hard-driving Chuck Walker helped me, as did Susan Ramírez, an amazing scholar, who continues to be consumed by Peruvian history even in retirement. Wonderfully encouraging from the start was Iñigo García-Bryce, who knows the history of APRA and twentieth-century Peru like few others on the planet. I owe a special debt to my long-time friend Peter V. N. Henderson, who as with the *Mexico* text cautiously read and helped proof many chapters (Peter also helped inspire me to make the jump into the Andean subfield by way of his own example). Finally, I am grateful to the staff at Rowman and Littlefield, but most particularly to Katelyn Turner, a consistently polite and kind-spirited editor who amazingly always has the time to quickly respond to my emails, as well as keep us on track. It has been a pleasure to publish twice with this press.

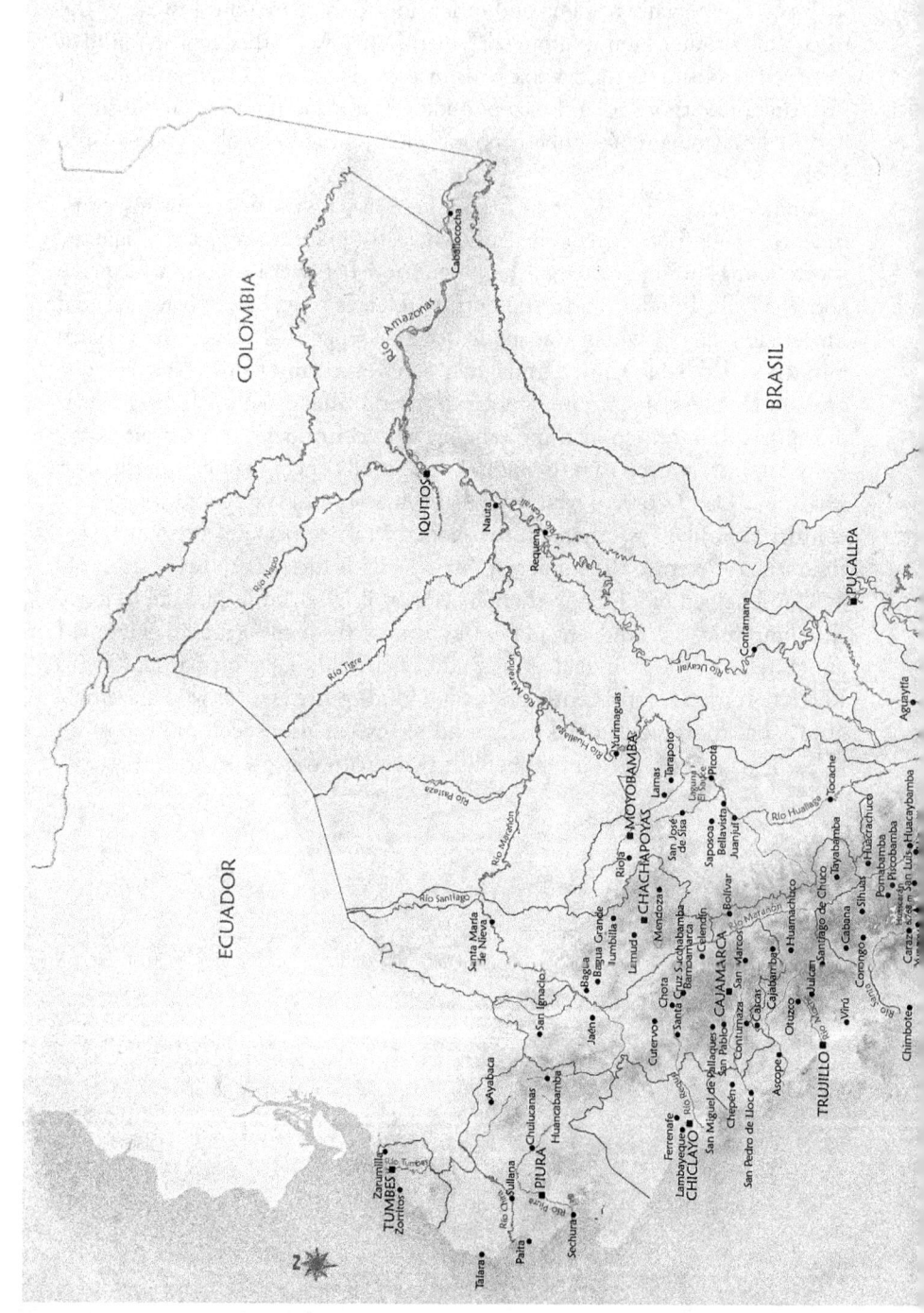

Source: Museo del Banco Central de Reserva del Peru

CHAPTER ONE

Independence and Uncertainty

The mid-eighteenth century was a time of foment and change in colonial Spanish America. Peru, the centerpiece of imperial rule over the breadth of an entire continent, faced new challenges. Its powerful, light-skinned elite living in Lima, the "City of Kings," bathed in the glories of a vast region subdued by the famous *conquistadores*. Francisco Pizarro's long-ago triumph over the great Inca Empire had made the colony first among many.

Peru's status, however, was diminishing under a new dynasty that had acquired the Spanish throne at the outset of the century. The Bourbon kings were determined to reinvent their empire. They undertook political and economic reforms to tighten administrative control and increase tax revenues. Their *viceroy*, or assistant king, based in Lima, was joined by two others— one in Santa Fe de Bogotá (present-day Colombia) and another in Buenos Aires (present-day Argentina). The regional trade monopoly of Lima-based merchants was also weakened, while newly dispatched Spaniards displaced office-holding creoles, or white-skinned residents of the New World (contrary to common perception, Spaniards themselves are predominantly white-skinned; yet multi-generational whites descended of the conquistadors now identified more with their colonial homeland than with maternal Spain).

The Bourbon Reforms were disruptive, and triggered a backlash at the very time when new ideas about self-governance were spreading throughout the Western world. In southeastern Peru, a series of small rebellions rocked the hinterlands as taxes increased in the 1770s. These culminated in a region-wide insurrection in 1780–1781. It was led by José Gabriel Condorcanqui, who claimed a noble Incan heritage and challenged royal order by adopting the nom de guerre of Tupac Amaru II. Condorcanqui was well-educated, and connected to the elite of the regional city of Cuzco. But he was frustrated in a legal battle with a rival, and became disillusioned with *Limeño* (Lima-based) authorities. Instigated by an apparently impulsive kidnapping of a popularly detested Spanish magistrate in Cuzco, his rebellion spread quickly. Many native-descended villagers perceived him as a messianic figure who would revive the great Inca Empire, and deliver them from the oppression of the whites.

The element of race helped doom Condorcanqui's cause. Authorities wooed Cuzco's well-to-do, and when tens of thousands of Natives failed to take the city under "Tupac Amaru II's" leadership his rebellion frayed. He and his logistics-coordinating wife, Micaela Bastidas, were soon captured. Condorcanqui was forced to witness Micaela's torture and execution before his own slow dismemberment. When horses failed to tear his strong body apart, he was beheaded, his severed limbs sent out to different towns as a grim warning to others. Though a cousin continued to lead the rebellion, as it rippled south into Upper Peru (present-day Bolivia), royal troops and administrators eventually regained control. Two central themes of Peruvian history were thus evident even before independence: the great divides between Lima and the interior, and between native-descended villagers and lighter-skinned town-dwellers, especially along the coast.

The Enlightenment and Subversion

At first glance the Tupac Amaru II rebellion looks like an initial step toward Peruvian independence, for colonials had risen up collectively against Spanish authority. But the trajectory twists wildly from there. Counterrevolutionary forces suppressed the insurgency and consolidated power in Cuzco, while the racial dimension of the uprising continued to loom central in popular memory. Spaniards were numerous and influential in Lima. They dominated the viceregal government, making the city a royalist bastion. Wealthy creoles, hearing reports of the dark-skinned "hordes" arising in the hinterlands, aligned themselves to Spanish institutions, including the powerful Roman Catholic Church. The Church had played a key role in suppressing the Cuzco rebellion, while even its creole clergymen were quick to celebrate the glories of Spain.

Still, in the late eighteenth century, subversive ideas emanated from northern Europe, especially France. Articulate philosophers like Rousseau and Voltaire promulgated concepts of popular sovereignty, while disparaging monarchy and questioning the authority of the Church. In 1789 the momentous French Revolution began to unfold, while just years earlier thirteen of Great Britain's North American colonies had gained their independence and set up a distinctively new form of republican self-governance. Seminal concepts about how to create a new world order based on reason were being spread through the internet of the age—books.

Spanish America and Peru were not immune to these stylish new ideas, despite the censorship of the Church. Many wealthy creoles read the latest controversial writings from Europe, and began to consider new possibilities. One such colonial was Hipólito Unanue. Born of a well-to-do Spanish father and creole mother, Unanue was privately tutored as a youth and developed an inquisitive mind. After graduating from seminary, he studied at Lima's prestigious University of San Marcos. He became preoccupied with the state of medical studies, understanding that the emerging subfield of anatomy was of critical importance. He founded an anatomy program that in time evolved into a full-fledged medical school. His students dissected cadavers and memorized body parts, while Unanue lectured on the latest breakthroughs from Europe.

Like Benjamin Franklin in the United States, Unanue was a multi-faceted Enlightenment thinker. He collected maps and studied geography; he was an amateur botanist. When he first managed and then inherited a prosperous hacienda (landed estate), he spent long days studying its natural flora and fauna. He wrote in the learned journal *Mercurio Peruano*, under the pen name *Aristo*, on a wide range of topics. He advocated free trade, "natural economies" for all nations, and argued the merits of coca leaf both for Peru's development and for its medicinal value. In his 1806 book, *El Clima de Lima*, he discussed public health and its relationship to environmental factors. He urged Spanish authorities to relocate Lima's cemeteries outside of its walls and end the unhygienic practice of burying the dead within the crypts of churches in the city's congested center. The viceroy took his advice, and dedicated a spacious new graveyard on the periphery in 1808.

Hipólito Unanue is the archetypical Enlightenment Thinker. His active mind led him to engage new ideas, and question the way things were. There were *many* Unanues throughout Spanish America by the early nineteenth century. Enlightenment ideas were a major catalyst for the independence movement in Latin America and Peru. These ideas interplayed with a series of complex events in Europe, and eventually destabilized the colonial order.

The French Revolution brought Napoleon Bonaparte to power—an ambitious military leader who rode atop the crest of rising French nationalism. In 1808, determined to punish British-aligned Portugal for violating his

Continental System, Napoleon sent his legions into both Portugal and Spain. The Spanish king was deposed, triggering a political crisis. Rebellions broke out, and a *junta*—or governing council—took form in the southwestern Spanish town of Cádiz, which sat on a small peninsula that could be protected by sea (by the British navy). The Cádiz junta was dominated by Enlightenment liberals, who sought to convert Spain into a limited monarchy. But when the Spanish king returned to power, after the fall of Napoleon, he would have none of this; he restored a strong monarchy. Later, however, liberals yet again gained the upper hand, and imposed a new constitution in 1820.

Hence, for Spain's colonials, the 1810s were a decade of confusing signals and administrative disruption. Very few orders or new appointees arrived from the motherland, while trade was increasingly conducted with the vessels of rival powers—especially those of England. Creoles took the reins of government in some places as Spanish authority weakened. This happened in peripheral areas, including Venezuela and what would become Argentina. When the king reasserted his power, these creoles—influenced by Enlightenment ideas and upset at the suspension of the Cádiz constitution—declared independence.

The creole hotbed of Buenos Aires spawned efforts to encroach on the Viceroyalty of Peru, but overland expeditions toward the great silver mining center of Potosí, in Upper Peru (present-day Bolivia), failed miserably. In the early nineteenth century, traversing several thousand miles, partly over inhospitable terrain, was a difficult proposition! Could a "liberating" army even reach Peru? Clearly the strategic effort would take many years.

In Peru itself, the rebellions to the distant north and south aroused interest, but the rich whites of Lima, proud City of Kings, declined to entertain serious thoughts of subversion. A strong-willed viceroy, José Fernando de Abascal, also helped ensure their faithfulness. But in Cuzco a pro-independence rebellion broke out in 1814, with some racial overtones that echoed the Tupac Amaru II revolt of a generation earlier. Royalist troops defeated the rebels a year later, executing their ringleaders. To the Limeño elite, the insurrection was worrisome.

San Martín and Independence

Throughout South America, the momentum toward independence ground slowly forward. In the north, "The Liberator" Simón Bolívar pressed into New Granada (present-day Colombia), capturing the viceregal capital of Santa Fe de Bogotá in 1819. He soon symbolically rechristened it simply *Bogotá*—its indigenous name. In the distant south, a former Spanish army officer named José de San Martín led a small army across the Andes into Chile, routing the few Royalist forces there with relative ease. He soon levied taxes on the Chileans, and entered into an allegiance with the British navy. Knowing that Spanish naval capacities were limited, he proposed to invade the royalist bastion of Peru by sea.

In September 1820, just months after word of a re-imposed liberal constitution in Spain had arrived, San Martín landed his army south of Lima. His arrival triggered a political revolt in the town of Trujillo, on the northern coast, unsettling the capital's powerful. Viceroy Abascal had since returned to Spain, while his replacement was a man of fickleness and indecision. He parleyed secretly with San Martín, as all Limeños could divine that the royalist cause was now on the wrong side of history. Still, unleashing popular forces from below was a disturbing proposition! The situation was delicate.

Historians have long debated the role of the underclasses in Peru's independence movement, with some on the political left claiming—not unjustly—that the lower classes were manipulated and ultimately gained nothing from the struggle. Others have countered this, emphasizing a range of popular actors, such as among rebel columns in the highlands. That San Martín's arrival in Peru sparked civil unrest across economic classes is not in doubt; the greater question is how much will, by him and the elite, was expended to control these volatile forces. San Martín was a monarchist at heart, and his political leanings were fundamentally conservative. The elite feared race-inspired revolt, and even the most progressive of its members could never accept dark-skinned persons of indigenous descent as their political or social equals.

Making the puzzle still more complex is the tension between practicality and ideology. As San Martín stayed outside of Lima, the indecisive but absolutist viceroy was toppled by his subordinate, José de la Serna. Though favoring liberalism, de la Serna was a proud Spaniard and no traitor—he would fight to keep Peru for Spain. As a cholera epidemic ravaged Lima, and royalist supplies ran out (thanks to an English naval blockade), he decided to evacuate in favor of the highlands. He arranged to do so even as elite-creole emissaries opened communications with San Martín. As the royalists departed, the rich convened a town meeting and invited in their "liberator." On July 28, 1821, San Martín, arriving without his army, entered Lima and proclaimed Peru forever free and sovereign.

All in all, it was a strange dynamic. While nearly everyone celebrated, including (with most passion) the darker-skinned lower classes, it was a transfer of political power singularly designed to preserve social order and the status quo. San Martín soon dramatically declared an end to African slavery

Figure 1.1. José de San Martín first declared Peruvian independence from the balcony of the viceregal palace on the Plaza de Armas (the present, vaguely similar City Hall is a mid-twentieth century rebuild). Cognizant of history and with a flair for showmanship, he then toured central Lima, re-declaring independence in several other plazas, generating excitement especially among Lima's darker-skinned citizens.
Photo by the author

and native tribute, but these paper declarations meant very little. He later quietly decreed that those born into slavery had to remain in the custody of their masters. Indigenous villagers continued to pay burdensome taxes and perform obligatory work for the white elite.

Ironically the supposedly counterrevolutionary Royalists, under de la Serna, were now ensconced in Cuzco, the previous heart of a pro-independence rebellion. The mid-1810s unrest there sat poorly with affluent whites, and they made their peace with the last viceroy's presence. The silver mining revenue from Potosí sustained the government, even though it was cut off from the coast and no relief from a politically divided Spain could be expected. Thus positioned, de la Serna governed and fought on for over three more years. In many ways, a more *liberal* Spanish-loyal regime was now pitted against a conservative independence-proclaiming government.

During this interim, San Martín deferred to the arriving Simón Bolívar. Again, in an awkward alliance with Lima's rich, the Enlightenment-minded Bolívar prepared to campaign in the highlands. Himself a prosperous creole, he also had predictably circumspect relations with his indigenous and *casta* (mixed race) underlings and insurgents. But at the Battle of Junín (August 1824) Bolívar scored a resounding victory, while his erstwhile subordinate Antonio José de Sucre delivered a knockout blow four months later. Spanish royalism was finished in the Americas. Peru was "free," though now all the inherent contradictions of this convoluted process had to work themselves out.

In these final battles probably more Colombians, Ecuadorians, and Venezuelans fought on behalf of independence than did Peruvians! The Royalist army, in fact, was more Peruvian in composition than that of the "Patriots." It was also collectively darker-skinned. In setting up the first "republican" government in Lima, San Martín had shunned the masses, and instead drew upon the expertise of the local elite. Hipólito Unanue, for example, was named Peru's first minister of the treasury—a post he held on three different occasions. Bolívar, too, relied on wealthy Peruvians, many of whom previously had close connections to the viceroyalty. In the countryside, supposed "royalists" still fighting in the name of the king, in the mid-1820s, abolished the tributary system with far more effectiveness than the self-proclaimed republicans.

Divisions and Disarray

Appreciating the deep contradictions of the independence era makes what followed more comprehensible. Lines between factions were never sharp; there was overlap everywhere. The contradictory sentiments of nearly everyone—but especially the creole elite—carried over into the equally confusing web of political activities in subsequent decades. Just as Patrick Henry's famous cry "Give me liberty or give me death" did not make much sense in Virginia, since he was one of the colony's largest slave owners, tidily expressed Enlightenment ideas did not neatly match up with on-the-ground realities.

As is normally the case in a successful rebellion, proponents were united in their conviction of what must go, but divided over what should follow. Even before final victory over the Spaniards in the highlands, Limeños were splintering apart. San Martín and his most trusted political advisors had sought to establish a monarchy, creating a Patriotic Society among the elite to work toward this end. But other rich creoles contended for a republic. Of these, a northerner named José Faustino Sánchez Carrión was most important. Born outside of the coastal town of Trujillo, Sánchez Carrión's father was an *hacendado* (landlord of a large estate) and local mayor, who also owned several mines. Trained in Lima's Jesuit school of San Carlos, young José had come under the influence of several Enlightenment-oriented teachers. Rejecting San Martín's monarchism, he wrote a series of political tracts. These helped shift the debate in favor of republicanism, even as the Limeños were beginning to weary of their original "liberator," and welcomed Bolívar as his replacement.

With the blessing of Bolívar, the republic-favoring elite convened a constitutional congress, with Sánchez Carrión as its secretary. Of the ninety-two delegates (all were rich males, and nearly all fully white), about a third were lawyers, and another third clergy. Unanue informally led a contingent of ten medical doctors. The congress drafted the Constitution of 1823, albeit as a centralist document—against Sánchez Carrión's wishes. In practice, this political charter went nowhere. The rich were already in political competition, endlessly feuding, and collectively refusing to pay taxes. The "government" did not exist, save for the presence of Simón Bolívar, who was sojourning in Lima but focused on defeating the Spaniards in the highlands.

After his final victories, Bolívar did not stay long. He was disinterested in the new constitution, and instead appointed a compliant junta of three ministers to manage affairs as he headed north. But after he left town, several Peruvians demanded the council be disbanded and replaced by a presidency under José de la Riva Agüero, a popular local. Riva Agüero assumed office, but then fled Lima when a resurgent army of Royalists approached. After things settled down, he was partially usurped by an arriving Bolívar sidekick, Antonio José de Sucre, who took nominal political control.

At this juncture, others became convinced that only Bolívar himself could settle things down and defeat the still-troublesome Royalists. Sánchez Carrión went north and asked that the great Liberator return. Bolívar did so, and was soon made "Protector of Peru" with absolute powers, the supposed republican Sánchez Carrión his faithful assistant. But when Sánchez Carrión died suddenly, at the age of thirty-nine in 1826, it added to a renewed sense of disarray. Rumors abounded that he had been poisoned, but an elderly Anunae conducted an autopsy and found that an aneurism had caused his death.

Bolívar's popularity waned among the elite (the only ones who politically mattered) in the mid-1820s—he was, after all (like San Martín), an outsider. In 1826 a congress reconvened and rejected his plan to incorporate Peru into a giant South American confederation. Bolívar, meanwhile, had drafted a centralist constitution for the newly named nation of *Bolivia* (Upper Peru), and brought the document back to Lima. He imposed it, as best he could, upon the congress—many liberals balking at its authoritarian features.

With criticism rising, even as troubles brewed in his Venezuelan homeland, Bolívar again left Lima, placing a Colombian named Juan Jacinto Lara in charge. Locals bought off some of Lara's own Colombian troops, and soon replaced his dysfunctional government with a local one. But another local betrayed the new president, even as congress decided to draft a third constitution. The Constitution of 1828 facilitated the presidency of José de La Mar, but rivals soon plotted to oust him. This transpired as Peruvian armies forced Sucre out of office in Bolivia, and warred in present-day Ecuador against Colombians under an increasingly demoralized Bolívar. By 1829, Peru installed its eleventh president (the count itself is disputable) in six years.

Now if readers are frustrated by the endless political confusion, how much more were the Peruvians! Thus, all can be thankful for Agustín Gamarra, an authentic *caudillo*—or regional strongman—who had considerably more political acumen then most of his peers, and managed to hold the presidency for a remarkable four-year term (1829–1833). Gamarra, a talented general, ruled with a firm hand, successfully collecting tariffs and a modicum of taxes, and using the money to preserve loyalties. He was also quick to exile his opponents—a novel and successful tactic. He had an additional weapon in his wife, Francisca Zubiaga. Eighteen years his younger, with boundless energy, Francisca worked at his side and took on administrative responsibilities. Known as *La Mariscala* (The Lady Field Marshall), she fought in battles, and on one occasion helped suppress a Limeño rebellion in her husband's absence. Her strong will and hard-driving personality helped Gamarra obtain and hold power—an unusual feat at a time when women were excluded from politics and marginalized.

Possibilities of Confederation

Agustín Gamarra played a prominent role in Peruvian politics for a long decade, returning to the presidency for two years, beginning in 1839. His accomplishments were overshadowed, however, by another formidable caudillo, Andrés de Santa Cruz. Ironically, both men studied together in their youth, in the city of Cuzco. Both also had once fought for the royalist cause, switching sides as San Martín declared Peruvian independence upon taking possession in Lima. Not surprisingly, two men of such great ambition eventually clashed; by the late 1820s Gamarra and Santa Cruz despised each other.

Born in Upper Peru (present-day Bolivia) of a Spanish father and native mother, Andrés de Santa Cruz was, like Gamarra, a smart and self-disciplined man. He was a gifted administrator, and by all accounts personable besides. Taking a page from Condorcanqui/Tupac Amaru II, he dubiously claimed (through his mother) a direct lineage to Inca emperors, and used this race-based appeal to help govern the native masses. He enjoyed some popular support. He brought stability to Bolivia by the early 1830s, and decided to extend his rule into (Lower) Peru thereafter.

Figure 1.2. One of the more conservative independence-era figures, José de la Mar had spent much of his life as an army officer fighting the French in Spain. Impressed by the monarchist San Martín, he eventually converted to the cause of independence. He served with Unanue and Sánchez Carrión in the first junta (1826), and as president for two years (1827–1829).
Source: Museo Nacional de Arqueología, Antropología e Historia

In 1836 Santa Cruz declared the Peruvian Confederation. Under his strong-armed executive were three equal regions: Upper Peru, Southern Peru, and Northern Peru. Each were to have their own legislatures and local administrators in a federalist system (that also somewhat resembled the model of the ancient Inca). In many ways the Confederation made sense: Peru and Bolivia had been one under the Spanish viceroys, and geographically and culturally had much in common. If the Confederation had survived, Peru-Bolivia would likely today be richer and more politically significant, in both South America and beyond.

But as Santa Cruz established himself in Lima, he failed to fully win over the Limeños. They were disappointed by a decentralization that reduced the significance of their city, nor were they particularly impressed by the arrival of yet another outsider seeking to exercise authority. The animosities and divisions persisted as well. Agustín Gamarra and his friends, fleeing to Chile, were ready to oppose Santa Cruz by force-of-arms.

Within a short time, the Confederation was at war. Chile, troubled by a united and potentially more powerful nation to its north, supported and later fought with the rebels. Interestingly, "South" Peruvians largely fell into line behind Santa Cruz. With Arequipa as its capital, this region saw attractive possibilities—the Arequipeños liked Santa Cruz's free trade policies, and enjoyed having roughly equal commercial status with Lima. The first rebel forays into the south were easily turned back.

Regrouping in Ecuador, an anti–Santa Cruz coalition eventually gave battle from the north. At Yungay in February 1839, armies of several thousand clashed, and late in the day the tide turned decidedly against Santa Cruz. Barely evading capture, the caudillo resigned from power and went off into exile, his dream of a Greater Peru shattered. One of the architects of his demise was of course Gamarra, who appealed to Limeños with his slogan "No More Foreigners!" But the problems besetting Peru were not solely caused by the meddling presence of outsiders (nor was Santa Cruz so terribly foreign). It remained to be seen if locals themselves could lay aside their differences and make a government in Lima work.

CHAPTER TWO

The Time of Ramón Castilla

At the 1839 battle of Yungay, which ended the confederation of Andrés Santa Cruz and his aspirations to unite the Andean region, a young Peruvian cavalry officer gained fame. Ramón Castilla executed a charge against the Bolivians that initially failed. Ordered to retire, he spotted an opening in enemy lines. Disobeying orders, he launched a second charge and exploited it, turning the tide of battle.

In the wake of Yungay, Agustín Gamarra was returned to the presidency via the electoral college. He oversaw the drafting of yet another constitution—Peru's sixth in sixteen years—but one that signaled an ideological shift. All of the previous documents except for Santa Cruz's (1837) had placed preeminent power in the legislative branch. Gamarra's second constitution moved to a strong executive, supported by a council of state that could also endow the presidency with emergency powers. A bicameral legislature had weakened prerogatives though, as always, it required officeholders to possess land or other demonstrable wealth. The franchise was extended to Spanish-literate males of age twenty-five or older, though no safeguards for clean and reliable elections were created.

Would Gamarra's Constitution of 1839 have finally delivered stability to Peru? This is unlikely. But Gamarra was its inspiration, and when he died in battle in 1841—while again invading Bolivia—any hope for stability collapsed. From November 1841 to August 1845 Peru had fourteen different presidents, with an average tenure of about ten weeks. Political infighting had reached a new high, as military officers betrayed and ousted one another in the midst of a series of mini-rebellions and constant feuding.

The most "stable" figure of this mind-boggling era was Manuel Ignacio de Vivanco—and given his eccentricities, that itself is a cold commentary on the state of affairs. Vivanco fancied himself an emperor-like figure. With his goatee and waxed mustache, he wore showy clothes and tall feathered caps. Self-proclaimed to the executive, he found the title "President" too subdued for his tastes, opting instead for a Napoleonic-like "Supreme Director of the Republic." He disregarded the constitution, prohibited congress from convening, and ordered the execution by firing squad of his stalwart adversaries. His flamboyance entertained the Limeño upper class for awhile, and his vow to bring *regeneración*—one of his favorite words—helped him stay in power for just over a year. But his personality cult eventually wore thin. A rebellion in the south gained steam under Domingo Nieto, a stickler for constitutionalism who found Vivanco's cavalier practices offensive.

Alas, Nieto died in the midst of campaigning, but his army fell into the hands of an even more capable and equally principled man, Ramón Castilla. Born of an Argentine father and an indigenous mother who claimed lineage from Incan nobility, Ramón had joined the royalist cause as a youth. He was captured at the battle Chacabuco, in Chile, and sent to distant Buenos Aires as a prisoner of war. Escaping, he made his way by ship to Rio de Janeiro, then began a months' long trek to his homeland, through Mato Grasso and the Amazonian hinterlands, across the mountains of Upper Peru, and west to Lima. He again offered his services to the crown but, like so many others, switched sides as San Martín declared his conservative expression of independence in Lima. Castilla missed the battle at Junín, but fought with Bolívar's cavalry at Ayacucho. He was an excellent and disciplined officer, as he demonstrated at Yungay.

After Vivanco's eventual fall, and another ten months of internecine strife, Castilla fully secured the presidency in 1845. Limeño elites were weary—seeking a time of stable respite, and though they were disinclined to support a *mestizo* (mixed blood—of dark-skinned native and white-skinned Spaniard or creole), they acquiesced to his rule. By nature, Castilla was an amicable and generous man. Nicknamed the "Soldier of Laws," he certainly believed in order. But he also had a positive public persona, and readily communicated his intentions. He attempted to suppress outlaws and bandits, who were operating especially along the northern coast, but he also favored leniency whenever possible. He continued Gamarra's effective policy of exiling unruly political opponents; he ordered overseas diplomats to check into their well-being, however, and to provide funds to those who were impoverished.

The Guano Boom Fuels Progress

It was Castilla's very good fortune to have funds with which to govern. While much has been written about Peru's most famous nineteenth-century president with regard to his wisdom and farsightedness, the real root of his success was bird droppings, or *guano*. This natural waste, accumulated over centuries from many varieties of sea birds, piled dozens of feet high on a series of small islands along Peru's southern coast. In the 1840s, Europeans came to understand that guano worked wonders as a fertilizer (it being high in ammonia). They were thus willing to pay significant sums for this raw material—though guano-bearing ships often prompted townsfolk to leave the port area for a few days until the stinky cargo was removed.

Castilla's government negotiated with a British banking house, and secured very large advances for the delivery of guano. In retrospect these upfront loans were ill-advised; Peru could have made much more money by a sequence of cautious agreements or, better yet, by marketing guano directly. London and Paris banks also bilked the nation financially, through compounding interest rates and many, often spurious, bankers' fees. Still, for the first time since independence, the government had discretionary funds to spend. Castilla's presidency would be fondly remembered.

Castilla's administration used guano revenues to launch a host of projects that gave citizens a taste of modernity, though almost all were undertaken in the environs of Lima. The nation's (and South America's) first railroad was constructed from the capital to the port of Callao, a distance of just nine miles, with standard-gauge track. Muleteers lobbied successfully against its use for freight, so in its first few years the single-locomotive line carried only passengers. A second stretch of track, of about the same distance, soon ran to the fishing town of Chorrillos to the south. Callao received a new lighthouse and improved docks, while the southern town of Pisco became a functional port with the installation of a long iron pier. Under Gamarra, Peru had contracted for coastal steamship service; these operations now expanded. Citizens could affordably travel up and down the coast and send mail as well. Increasing port activity helped spawn further international trade. After decades of isolation, Peru was beginning to connect with the world.

Castilla's government was administratively efficient. In his first year in office, the president submitted a formal budget to congress for the first time, the ledgers and tallying of an accounting office befuddling some of the deputies. Civil servants were required to have full literacy, and the quality of office management rose sharply. Engineers systematically studied the nation's roads, drafting plans for a coherent transportation system, while many bridges (especially around Lima) were rebuilt or repaired. Telegraph wires were installed, first along the coast—connecting Lima and Trujillo—and then slowly up into the highlands. Trails were carved out of the jungles of Amazonia, and Peru cut a deal with a Brazilian steamship company to deliver supplies to the remote region. A Peruvian-owned firm began to ply the waters of the Amazon's broad tributaries within the nation's borders.

Castilla was anxious about his country's geographic integrity. The army established small outposts in Amazonia, and sought to demarcate the distant borders with Colombia and Brazil. To the south, the port of Arica was further developed, and attempts to better link this region with the center were undertaken. It was under Castilla that the Peruvian navy came of age. Officers were sent to Europe to study new technology in ship design and weaponry. Peru purchased its first steam-powered vessels, and by the 1860s had one of the most advanced collection of warships in Latin America. The army received rifled musketry and heavy cannons. The Foreign Ministry initiated diplomatic talks with all adjoining nations, even staging a regional

Figure 2.1. In 1840, under Gamarra's relatively stable government, elites founded El Colegio Guadalupe, which quickly became one of the nation's premiere schools. It provided a Catholic education based on the French educational model for boys. Castilla's government began funding it as a rechristened Colegio Nacional in 1855. The original building was moved to its present location and expanded in 1909.
Photo by the author

conference. Castilla took note of the rising power of the United States, with its aggressive war on Mexico, and expressed concern that, in time, this northern leviathan could one day threaten the Andean states.

Social improvements in Lima were noteworthy. The beginnings of a sewage system appeared, augmented by better trash removal along some newly paved roads. Gas lighting in the center of the city encouraged nightlife and reduced crime. The government made the first substantial steps toward a public-school system. A Normal School in Lima began to train teachers, while several primary and secondary schools opened in provincial cities. The University of San Marcos was reorganized and expanded. The elite still only enjoyed full access to high-quality education, however, while tuition and fees inhibited access by the poor. Very few schools were built in the highlands, where Spanish-only instruction precluded Quechua-speaking Natives. Even by 1860, less than twenty thousand children attended public schools.

In sum, Castilla's rule was productive and benign, as money leavened the political system and softened it. Congress held eight sessions during his first term; the president lobbied and cajoled, instead of exercising power through force—not a single deputy was dismissed or exiled, much less executed. In 1847 he and the congress passed a general amnesty, allowing all exiles to return unmolested. Many did so. As Castilla's term wound down, he was committed to respecting the constitutional six-year mandate.

The Disastrous Echenique Interim

Ramón Castilla endorsed as his successor in 1851 the affable José Rufino Echenique, head of the Council of State, and his influence largely brought Echenique to power—despite the plotting of several rivals, including the power-hungry Vivanco who had returned under the amnesty. If Echenique could have just kept the ship of state on course, Peru would have progressed reasonably. Unfortunately, although a senior military officer, he was an exceedingly weak man easily influenced by the strong-willed around him.

Even worse, Echenique was blind to the brazen corruption of his cabinet officials and friends. His treasury minister executed a terribly conceived scheme to honor past debts, and accepted informal papers and testimonies as proof of monies owed. Word spread among the Limeño elite, and hundreds arrived at government offices with IOUs signed by Bolívar, San Martín, and others, though strangely their signatures hardly ever matched. The government accepted them all, and took out enormous new European bank loans, against future guano exports, in order to make payments. Some rich families more than doubled their wealth. Other well-connected middle-class families joined the aristocracy. Almost no poor, however, were privy to the scam. It was an unscrupulous season of graft at the expense of the state, which assumed a debt almost certainly several times greater than what actually existed.

Honest men, including Castilla (living in his Chorrillos home), were aghast. Several decried what was happening, often forcefully in writings in Lima's newspaper, *El Comercio*. But President Echenique was told by his advisers that these were slandering critics, who sought to destabilize the government. One of his intimate counselors was the endlessly ambitious Juan Crisóstomo Torrico, who held the post of Minister of War. A physically large and imposing man, and a political fixture over the previous two decades (he himself was briefly president in 1842), Torrico led the feeble-minded president to false conclusions.

Echenique began to again exile opponents, while censoring the press. He exiled a young Mariano Ignacio Prado to Chile, but in the port of Arica Prado dived into the sea and swam to safety. He made his way to Arequipa, where a powerful hacendado named Domingo Elías was organizing resistance to the government. Not only was Elías disgusted with the debt scam, but he was also a committed liberal, frustrated with the conservative ideology that seemed to be taking hold in the capital. Years earlier, he had helped fund a new school, the *Colegio de Nuestra Señora de Guadalupe*, to promulgate classical liberalism. Here, two brothers, José and Pedro Gálvez, taught an anticlerical brand of liberalism, along with laissez-faire economics, while advising Castilla in his first term. The Gálvez brothers joined Elías, and soon they and others prevailed upon Castilla to take political and military command of the movement. By late 1854 the liberals were ready to march northward on Lima.

Torrico prepared the army to meet them. He was aided by an alliance with Vivanco who, though he personally detested Echenique (and felt he should have again become president), saw the struggle in ideological terms. The two forces collided at La Palma, just south of Lima in the present-day municipal district of Miraflores. The battle was one of the most serious in Peru's many civil wars, resulting in several thousand casualties. Although his attacking columns appear to have taken the worst of it, Castilla prevailed. His angry partisans ransacked select buildings in Lima, including the president's own home. Echenique fled to safety in the British ambassador's residence and left for New York City thereafter. Ramón Castilla was back in charge.

A Shakier Second Term

At the outset of his longer second term (1855–1862, first as provisional, and then as elected president), Castilla encouraged the political class to craft yet another constitution. A primarily liberal document, the Constitution of 1856 forbade slavery; removed the special rights possessed by military officers, noble-titled families, and clerics (for example, exemption from certain types of civil and criminal trials); and even abolished the death penalty. Voting, however, was still restricted to the literate who possessed land or other monetary resources. The presidential term was reduced to four years, without reelection, and the previously created council of state persisted—though now, in theory, as much a check on unbridled presidential powers as a supplement. Roman Catholicism remained the state religion, one of several features designed to appease conservatives.

Conservatives, however, remained uncomfortable with the document. Their champion was Bartolomé Herrera, a figure partially lost to history, as Castilla and his brand of moderate liberalism eventually defined the age. The arch-conservative Herrera was a gifted, book-loving intellectual. Clearly prophesy was not his spiritual gift: when he conducted the funeral of Agustín Gamarra in 1841, he predicted that a season of political stability was about to unfold. In the mid-1840s he served as rector of San Carlos, converting the Enlightenment-influenced institution into a bastion of conservatism. In the 1850s he worked for Echenique's administration as a diplomat, networking with arch-conservatives in Europe, while also advising Pope Pius IX (an ardent opponent of liberalism, who later convened the Vatican I council and promulgated the Doctrine of Papal Infallibility).

Herrera's intention, as a congressional deputy, was to spearhead a complete overhaul of the new constitution. Instead, he and his cohort effectively modified it, though in doing so did eventually designate it as the Constitution of 1860—Peru's eighth in twenty-nine years. Conservatives strengthened the executive, ironically to Castilla's advantage, and centralized power by reducing regional and municipal authorities. Prefects (governing provinces) were appointed by the executive. The legislature was bicameral, with a senate able to censure the president only with difficulty. The franchise was further restricted, and the death penalty reinstated for murder. All in all, the changes were relatively modest, and Castilla accepted them. Herrera, embittered that a more rigid and aristocratic document had not been crafted, refused to sign it and resigned his congressional seat. He left the capital to become the Bishop of Arequipa.

Herrera's nemesis in the seemingly endless conservative-liberal debates was ironically another cleric, Francisco de Paula González Vigil. Born in the far southern town of Tacna, González Vigil studied at the liberal-inclined Seminario de San Jerónimo in Arequipa, under, among others, the literary scholar Mariano Melgar (see chapter 3). An exceptional student, he reluctantly agreed to ordination before teaching at his alma mater; his real calling, though, was politics. In and out of congress for nearly forty years, he worked on multiple constitutions, tending toward liberal and even sometimes anti-clerical positions. He served as director of the National Library in the late 1840s when he penned several controversial treatises, including a short booklet arguing for the supremacy of national bishops over the authority of Rome. The essay prompted his excommunication by the Vatican, yet González Vigil never retracted it and died a rather popular if contrarian figure in 1875, while still professing the Christian faith.

That Herrera and González Vigil sparred with pens and legal documents—instead of swords and armies—reflected an encouraging trend. The real significance of the age of Castilla is Peru's transition away from blood feuds as led by power-hungry caudillos. The president, courtesy of guano, was about new buildings, a stronger state, and material progress. In his second term, however, Castilla oversaw fewer public works; the government coffers were often nearly empty. The only major project was the construction of an enormous penitentiary, modeled on Jeremy Bentham's concept of a panopticon. It took years to build but, when finally completed, this symbol of state power just south of Lima's central district stood for a century—torn down only in 1961. The modest network of railroads also slowly expanded, though much of the interior remained isolated.

When he approached the capital in 1854, on a hacienda near Huancayo, Castilla had declared (like San Martín before him) the end of native tribute. This eliminated a significant portion of the state's revenue. He also decreed the abolition of slavery, as subsequently confirmed in his 1856 constitution. His commitment to recompense slave owners ensured a nearly bankrupt treasury. African slavery had been in steady decline for three decades, primarily because of manumission (especially of females), and also the ability of Black people to slowly buy their way to freedom (with freed slaves helping family members). But the final end of the institution still seriously disrupted certain economic sectors, especially sugar and cotton plantations along the northern coast.

Castilla inadvertently provided hacendados an alternative. In his first term he had passed legislation encouraging immigration—what became popularly known as the China Law. A clipper brought the first Chinese laborers to Peru in 1849, but in the late 1850s many plantation owners spent their slave remuneration on the importation of more Chinese indentured servants. Obligated by signing contracts, these *coolies* (Chinese agricultural laborers) were, in truth, little more than replacement slaves. Overwhelmingly young males from the south of China, they were packed into ships for a harrowing four month-long voyage, provided little food and fresh water on their sea journey. Many died even before, or shortly after, their arrival. Practices of abuse and even corporal punishment continued—so brazenly, in fact, that Castilla briefly retracted the immigration law.

Planters convinced him to reverse the policy again, and tens of thousands more Chinese worker-slaves arrived in the 1860s. The U.S. civil war disrupted cotton exports, spiking prices for much of the decade. Cotton production surged, with hacendados making stellar profits. Castilla's government benefited, too, from a modest export tariff. But the death rates among coolies was horrendous—upward of 50 percent died prematurely. The more fortunate ended up working on new railroads, or in shoveling guano on the southern islands, though for all life was harsh in a strange and foreign land. Suicide among coolies was not uncommon.

Trouble with Spain

In 1862, when Castilla's constitutional term ended and he finally retired, an aged if colorless independence hero named Miguel de San Román took his place. By official count the twenty-fifth president of Peru in thirty-nine years, San Román is remembered only for rechristening the currency as the *sol* ("sun" in Spanish), an appropriate name referencing the Incan cultural veneration of the sun and sunlight. When San Román died of natural causes in 1863, he was succeeded by Juan Antonio Pezet. Son of a graduate of Hipólito Unanue's medical school, with a French surname bequeathed by his immigrant-grandfather, Pezet—like San Román—had fought with Bolívar in the highlands, and in the internecine strife of the early 1840s. Sufficiently liberal in his credentials, he had served as Castilla's Minister of War in his second term.

Soon after taking office, Pezet faced diplomatic tensions with Spain. Basque-Spanish workers on a coastal plantation had been reputedly abused, with two killed in a labor conflict. This incident came at a time when European powers menaced Latin American countries. Advances in naval technology gave them an impetus, while the United States' preoccupation with its civil war opened a window of time for adventurism. Spain was interested in profiteering. It dispatched a naval flotilla into the Pacific. It decried the deaths of its citizens, and announced that Peru and other nations needed to pay on supposed independence-related debts.

Spanish warships visited the port of Callao in 1863, then outright seized the guano-rich Chincha Islands. Since Spain had never recognized Peruvian independence, it claimed that the islands were still its own territory. Pezet's rattled administration agreed to sign a treaty, and paid a very stiff indemnity. This move was immensely unpopular with the political class in Lima, and was condemned by an aged Castilla. Pezet ordered Castilla's arrest, which triggered a revolt by others. An army officer named Mariano Prado then forcibly replaced him, reneging on the treaty.

But the Spaniards did not go away. Their flotilla sailed south and harried the Chilean coast, eventually bombarding the unguarded port of Valparaiso. The Chileans took revenge. A Chilean warship, the *Esmeralda*, caught a lone Spanish vessel on the high seas. Tricking it by flying a British Union Jack, the Chileans came alongside, opened fire, and mauled their prey. The Spanish admiral was so distraught by the incident that he later committed suicide aboard his flagship.

These setbacks—and Prado's insolence—enraged the Spaniards, who now returned to Peru. In April 1865, the flotilla reentered the harbor of Callao, giving its defenders four days in which to surrender or face a bombardment. Peru declared war on Spain, while indignation fueled a surge of patriotic fervor. Thousands of military personnel and civilians rushed to Callao to aid in its defense. The Peruvian batteries at the port had been upgraded, and could hold their own against the warships, though the thirty-four-gun ironclad *Numancia* was a formidable foe.

On May 2, for several hours, the two sides pummeled one another as neutral warships watched the battle from a distance. In a lucky shot, a Spanish artillery shell struck exposed ammunition, triggering an explosion that claimed the life of Prado's Minister of War, José Gálvez. When the battle subsided, nearly three hundred Peruvians and two hundred Spaniards were dead, but the flotilla drew off. Though both sides claimed victory, Peru clearly had held its own against a European power. *Dos de Mayo* (May 2) soon became a national day of celebration.

The Spanish incursion into the Pacific in the mid-1860s prompted both Chile and Peru to invest in new warships. For a brief season, the two coastal nations had been comrades-in-arms, but the subsequent increase in naval firepower helped spawn their own competition and thoughts of war. The Peruvians purchased two state-of-the-art ironclads from Great Britain. Christening them the *Independencia* and *Huascar*, they gave the country one of the most potent naval forces in South America. This was a mixed blessing. Coupled with the heady victory of Dos de Mayo, Peru felt almost strong for once, its politicians willing to risk a more assertive foreign policy. Stability under Ramón Castilla had brought Peru up, the young nation finally standing on its own feet. Soon, however, new challenges would knock it back to the ground.

CHAPTER THREE

Life and Culture, c. 1780–1867

In economics and politics, Lima's wealthy whites have dominated Peruvian life for centuries. But when we glance at the broad contours of how people have lived, and examine the cultural expressions of Peruvian society, we find multiple layers of an intricate fabric. Yes, the rich have primarily funded and largely defined the arts, but over time unanticipated creative variation and dissidence have emerged. It is certainly true though, that in the earliest decades of independent Peru the shadow of Lima's privileged loomed culturally large.

Culture and Power

Spanish colonial society thrived under the twin pillars of church and state. There was much overlap. Clerics frequently served in government, and on many occasions, especially in the seventeenth century, the viceroy was often simultaneously a bishop or even the archbishop. With the Bourbon Reforms more Spaniards arrived to perform administrative functions of state, though in terms of material wealth creoles generally surpassed them. Scores of Peruvian-born whites dominated commerce, in particular, affording them the highest quality of life.

The rich lived in the center of Lima. They strolled and socialized on the nearby *Alameda de Acho*, a terraced promenade along the Rimac River which, by the time of independence, featured stately trees. Their typically cut-stone, two-story houses were neoclassical and austere on the exterior, but ornate within, the second-story living quarters filled with fine European furnishings, the latest in gadgets (such as clocks), and amenities like porcelain dinnerware. They wore fashionable clothes, including silk items imported from the Far East. They were served by a retinue of servants, a high percentage of African origin or descent held in bondage, some of whom worked as artisans—often in shops on the first floor of the abode.

During the course of the nearly three-century colonial epoch, Limeño architecture developed a distinctive feature, that of balconies. Many of the sixteenth-century conquistadors hailed from the region of Andalusia, in southern Spain, where balconies were common (acquired in turn from the Moors of North Africa and the Muslim world). Most typically, elite Limeño homes expanded upward, with the second floor added sometime after the mid-seventeenth century. Balconies thus flourished under the Bourbons, as it became a vogue addition for anyone who could afford it.

An entire guild of balcony builders emerged. Special hardwoods were imported from the jungles of Panamá. Resistant to dampness (with Lima in a coastal desert, drawing less than an inch of rain per year), these structures could easily last unaltered for decades. Predictably, an ornate and embellished balcony exuded status. Most were enclosed, in a style known in Spanish as a *balcón cajón* (literally, a box-balcony). But balconies collapsed by the score in Lima's devastating 1746 earthquake, and authorities discouraged their reconstruction, in part due to the concomitant fire hazard. With the guano boom, however, the upper class reengaged a frenzy of balcony-building, though most of these *balcones cajones* were more austere than those of over a century earlier. They also now often featured hinged panels that allowed for opening up the space.

At the center of nearly all things cultural in the late colonial era was the Roman Catholic Church. Its values guided society and defined social and cultural norms. At the outset of the eighteenth century, an astounding 16 percent of Lima's population lived in religious houses; large convents and monasteries dominated the heart of the city. The Office of the Inquisition ensured conformity, enforcing a morality in social affairs, civic relations, and artistic expression—such as in theater and literature. The Church nearly monopolized education. In the later decades of colonialism, however, its power was in nominal decline. The 1767 expulsion of the Jesuit Order from the Americas dealt a heavy blow. With the unfolding Enlightenment, clergy debated new ideas vigorously among themselves. The Church ultimately experienced divisions similar to those found in broader society in the era of independence.

Figure 3.1. Among the most celebrated balconies in Lima today are those of the Palacio de Torre Tagle. Made of mahogany and cedar, they are ornate in the Iberian Mudéjar tradition; even the *corbels* (supports) are embellished. Though technically dating from the eighteenth century, the Palace—home to the Ministry of Foreign Affairs—underwent an extensive renovation in the mid-1950s.
Photo by the author

Rich Limeños were proud that their city governed a vast region. They welcomed the pageantry and regal authority of their city's "kings." Bourbon-era viceroys, though Spanish-born, enjoyed their engagement and support. The crown was particularly fortunate to have assigned José Fernando de Abascal to the office shortly before the Napoleonic chaos enveloped Spain. Abascal (ruling from 1806–1816) was a self-disciplined and intelligent administrator. He carried out a series of reforms ranging from the dedication of a large cemetery outside city walls (at the behest of Hipólito Unanue—recall chapter 1), to the establishment of an Academy of Drawing and Painting, which helped incubate Peru's unusually rich artistic traditions.

Spanish authorities, however, unwittingly empowered future creole separatists by expanding civil militias in the closing decades of the eighteenth century. Thousands of Spanish troops also arrived to suppress Tupac Amaru II's rebellion; many stayed. A culture of militarism captivated the rich, fanned by the appearance of the dapper foreigners San Martín and Bolívar. Soon nearly every wealthy creole male aspired to be an officer, while adding military uniforms and paraphernalia to their wardrobes. By the 1830s, it might well be that army officers numbered at a ratio of 1:3 per enlisted, with contact between the lofty whites and lowly dark-skinned conscripts in fact very limited. What else was there to do, but plot endless intrigue and insurrection with one's closest friends? The political chaos of the early national period diminished the quality of life for nearly everyone, including the rich.

Diversities of Race, Gender, and Class

Lima was a city of wealth, but also one of great contrasts. Its population was around seventy thousand when San Martín declared independence in 1821, making it one of the largest cities in the hemisphere. In the booming United States, only New York and Philadelphia were larger. Still, compared to today, it amounted to what we would regard as a small city—roughly equal in size to Eau Claire, Wisconsin. Its public spaces drew diverse persons across lines of race and class; native-descended, mixed-blood *castas* (mestizos), and women engaged in buying and bartering. The biggest market was in its main square, the Plaza de Armas, where vendors hawked nearly everything imaginable.

In terms of assemblage, the two most important venues were the cathedral, which could hold several thousand, and the *Plaza de Toros de Acho*, or bullring. After the traumatic 1746 earthquake, viceregal authorities undertook construction of the circular ring as a means of restoring public morale. Here, over ten thousand Limeños could watch the display of machismo, though in seating there was still hierarchy, with no lowly native sitting in earshot of a wealthy creole (the rich always ensconced on the shady side of the ring). Conversely, these and other forums did feed a broader sense of community and belonging. There is comparatively little evidence of racial or class tension in Lima before the arrival of San Martín's army.

One common bond was devotion to Catholicism. Though Limeños gained a reputation by the late eighteenth century as jovial and inclined to *fiestas*, they also practiced a fervent faith. Street processions were a regular occurrence, most in honor of saints, including the city's protector *Santa Rosa de Lima*. The festival of *Amancaes* celebrated the feast day of San Juan each June, pilgrims flocking to a hillside alight with bright yellow Amancay flowers. These frequently ornate affairs were organized by *cofradías* (lay religious brotherhoods), which vied with one another to stage the most elaborate and well-attended marches. Though access to the priesthood remained difficult for dark-skinned males, many played influential roles in the cofradías.

The underclasses zestfully enjoyed the limited leisure time they could secure in their demanding lives, drinking and raucously singing in the modern-day equivalent of bars. When San Martín arrived in the city, they

Figure 3.2. In the late colonial and early national period the Cajón de San Marcos (St. Mark's Box) was common in the homes of mestizo townsfolk. This popular art featured small, painted wooden carvings, often of intricate detail, most typically representing events in the lives of Jesus or the saints. Family members knelt before these for devotions and prayer.
Source: Museo del Banco Central de Reserva del Perú

welcomed him with the popular ditty *La Chicha*, about the native drink (but also a celebration of things Peruvian): *It's tastier than wine or cider . . . it's very frothy—and I prefer it.* But for the urban poor the disruption of the break with Spain was, in practical terms, difficult. Lima was in turmoil, with refugees, increased hunger, and disease. There was great anxiety, too, and although a week of celebration followed "The Liberator's" entrance, for many 1821 was a year best forgotten.

Peru's diversity increased through immigration in the mid-nineteenth century. The arrival of Chinese agricultural workers (see chapter 2) brought the first significant Asian presence to the country. The largest of the European communities—after a post-independence exodus by Spaniards—was that of the Italians. The 1857 census showed 3,500 Italians in Lima, or 3.7 percent of the population. Hundreds of others lived in the nearby port city of Callao. The *Sociedad Italiana de Beneficencia y Asistencia*, created in 1862, provided charity for the poor among this distinctive community. Hundreds of Irish arrived in the early 1850s as part of the exodus relating to the devastating Potato Famine.

Peru was, of course, a "nation" in multiple parts but, at its simplest, a racially diverse coast and a native-dominated highland. Political gamesmanship was performed by the lighter classes in the cities, primarily Lima; Arequipa, the commercial and political center of southern Peru, repeatedly vied with the capital, and served as a frequent starting point for political countermovements. There, a formidable elite occupied its center grid of streets, as well. It is prudent, though, to note how apolitical and detached much of the rest of the population would have been at any given point in the opening decades of nationhood. Hundreds of thousands of villagers would have gone about their daily lives oblivious to the competition and antics of the distant political class.

Having said that, for the highlands' indigenous people independence was decidedly a setback. In colonial times, both state and church nominally protected communal rights. As elsewhere in Latin America, (classical) liberalism undercut those rights, most notably with regard to land tenure. Legalizing and slowly converting communal holdings into privately held titles, the new state unwittingly facilitated the deprivation of Native villages. Even worse, it failed to remove the burdensome tributary system—even after Castilla's bold 1854 pronouncement, it largely persisted (albeit to the benefit of local estates rather than the national government). Many natives migrated into serf-like conditions on coastal plantations, or to the mines, effectively increasing the tax burden on those who remained. Coupled with incessant war and banditry, many rural areas saw a net population decline into mid-century.

As with indigenous peoples, the early national period brought little positive change for women. The relative prosperity of the eighteenth century had opened some very modest possibilities, while the dominance of the always patriarchal Catholic Church at least ensured the option of nunnery, which in turn could provide a modicum of education and (collective) economic independence for elite women. The weakening of the Church, coupled with the dislocation and political instability of the early nineteenth century, made for more difficult lives, and women bore the consequences most acutely. Even elite women had few plausible roads to empowerment, though widowhood could bring some degree of economic freedom. At best, they could expect to obtain a rudimentary education—either three to four years of primary (religious) schooling, or instruction via a private tutor. In 1830 a school did finally open for creole nuns. But young women were expected to aspire solely to motherhood, with the bearing and nurturing of children as their primary life's task. Having the ability to write was seen by many men as rather unnatural or suspect.

Physically, wealthy women were restricted to the home, though they ventured out to church services in sealed carriages, heads covered. In the capital this covering was called a *tapada limeña*. A black cloth, it enclosed the head, and typically shrouded part of the face as well (inadvertently the *tapada* empowered audacious women; hidden from view, they could conduct business affairs without revealing their identity). Always under the supervision of either father or husband, many were allowed to sit in their *balcones cajones* and view street life below. More liberal-minded males sanctioned opened balcony panels and visibility, and the right to readily speak to and greet other female friends.

In contrast, poorer women were compelled by economic need to live public lives and readily interact with a variety of males. In the struggle for independence they frequently bore the same hardships as men, accompanying armies and fulfilling a range of duties, including sometimes fighting. Women spied on Royalists and conveyed secret messages, dangerous tasks that could result in a quick death sentence if captured. In the difficult decades following independence, women suffered disproportionately in terms of economic hardship. Without political rights, they were marginalized in the cities and oppressed in the countryside, their rural plight ably chronicled in the writings of Flora Tristán, who lived in southern Peru in the 1830s. Her *Pérégrinations d'une paria* (*Wanderings of a Pariah*—1838) published in Paris, reputedly triggered a burning in effigy when copies arrived in Lima. The daughter of a Spanish naval officer, she contended that Peruvian males were incompetent as soldiers.

Though women and persons of color were marginalized and kept from power, many were increasingly depicted in art. The Hispanic world beheld the phenomenon of *Costumbrismo* in the late colonial and early national era, a movement somewhere between classicism and romanticism that allowed for social criticism, political satire, and the portrayal of locals and everyday life. In Lima, the irreverence of Costumbrismo was captured in the career of José Joaquín de Larriva y Ruíz, a poet, essayist, and contrarian cleric who taught philosophy at the University of San Marcos. A friend of Viceroy Abascal, Larriva y Ruíz was ultimately on the losing side of history, as he frequently ridiculed Simón Bolívar and was slow to endorse independence. Near the end of his life he occasionally wrote for *El Peruano*, the nation's first newspaper (though it primarily convened legal and judicial information in its erratic early editions).

The modest viceregal Academy of Drawing and Painting survived into the mid-nineteenth century. Under the directorship of Ignacio Merino it trained a small cadre of artists, garnering Merino the epitaph "Father of Peruvian

Figure 3.3. *Fusilamiento de María Parado de Bellido* by Consuelo Cisneros (1929). Parado de Bellido was an illiterate woman who served the patriotic cause as a courier, until arrested by Spaniards. She was reputedly tortured for information to no avail, before being executed by a firing squad. Cisneros' representation owes an obvious debt to Francisco Goya's *El Tres de Mayo*.
Source: Museo Nacional de Arqueología, Antropología e Historia

Painting" after his untimely death at age forty-three in 1869. The nation's most prominent artist in mid-century, Merino painted portraits of political figures (see figure 1.2 for an example) and of saints, including Santa Rosa de Lima. He traveled to Paris and studied briefly with Eugene Delacroix, but showed very limited interest in Romanticism.

Some Peruvian artists were more innovative than Merino. Francisco Laso, born of wealthy Arequipeños, continued the tradition of the late colonial Costumbristas, often portraying common folk in everyday dress. Unfortunately, like Merino, he died young, in the 1868–1869 yellow fever epidemic. Luis Montero studied primarily in Florence, and shocked the elite with his nude *Sleeping Venus* (1851). In the mid-1860s he executed his most astounding work: inspired by William Prescott's account of the conquest, he portrayed *Los funerales de Atahualpa* on a mammoth canvas. In popular art, thousands of simple watercolors circulated among the working class by Afro-Peruvian Pancho Fierro. These typically portrayed everyday workers plying their trades.

Creating a National Identity

The political transition from Spanish viceroyalty to independent nation was also reflected in the arts. José de San Martín was cognizant of the potency of symbols. One of his first acts upon arriving in Peru was to craft a distinctive national flag. He chose the colors red and white for undisclosed reasons (this thus became a long topic of debate among later nationalists), and though the original banner was modified, it became the now famous tri-band by 1825. Artistic forms were also appropriated by the new state in literature, art, and music.

Independent Peru's rich literary tradition began with its first poet and martyr, Mariano Melgar. Born in Arequipa to an affluent family, young Mariano was given an excellent education in the southern city's Catholic schools. He studied law, and became a professor at San Jerónimo Seminary. He mastered both Greek and Latin and translated some ancient texts into Spanish. But his real love was poetry. His earliest works were poems of love directed to women, especially one named Sylvia. But he also began to write poetry about liberty and independence. His *Ilustre Americano* is self-evident, but a more nuanced poem was entitled *Los Gatos*, which dealt with the sensitive issue of race:

> A cat gave birth to kittens, one white, one mixed, one black;
> Soon they were but orphans, chased by a dog-turned-maniac.
> In order to fight this enemy,
> they had no choice but unity,
> and found a tender harmony . . . but who should now hold primacy?
> "It must be me—nobility,"
> meowed the lone white kitten.[1]

Melgar participated in the 1814 rebellion in Cuzco, and was captured in battle outside of his native city. The Spaniards executed him by firing squad; he was just twenty-four years old.

Independence heroes like Melgar were painted by the first noteworthy Peruvian (national) artist, José Gil de Castro. Gil was Afro-Peruvian, born of a freed mulatto male and a mother still held in bondage. A Limeño, he moved as a young man to Chile, where he trained as a painter and began to

---

1. As is nearly always the case, I have to take great linguistic liberty in order to create an English rhyme. The Spanish is: *Una gata parió varios gatitos / uno blanco, uno negro, otro manchado / luego que ellos quedaron huerfanitos / los perseguía un perro endemoniado / y para dar el golpe a su enemigo / no había más remedio que juntarse / y que la dulce unión fuese su abrigo / Van pues a reunirse / y al tratarse sobre quién de ellos deba ser cabeza / maullando el blanco dijo: / "A mí me toca por mi blancura, indicio de nobleza."*

earn commissions through portrait work. Generally he represented persons standing, often employing bright colors—though typically showing little animation or facial expression. A shield-symbol near the base of the canvas, or a banner-ribbon near the top, provided the subject's name and titles.

Gil joined the independence cause in Chile and returned to Peru in 1822. He painted dozens of portraits of wealthy creole "Patriots" who supported San Martín. He portrayed San Martín himself, several times, and was later contracted to paint Bolívar. He made many bust portraits of the Liberator designed to hang in administrative offices. Though his style was flat-line and simple, and not in league with the great European portrait artists of the time, Gil's accomplishments are remarkable, especially given the racial prejudice of his day.

José Gil's representation of José Olaya helped make the commoner famous. Olaya's story is known even today by every Peruvian school child. A fisherman from Chorrillos, he smuggled notes into Lima in 1823, at a time when the Royalists had briefly reoccupied the city. Captured and savagely tortured, he refused to divulge information, and was executed by firing squad in the Plaza de Armas. Gil painted a fully standing Olaya dressed in martyr-like white. Although the details of Olaya's personal Calvary are poorly known, and his story likely enhanced, Olaya's tale was an important expression of (and invitation to) popular identification with the *independista* cause.

José Bernardo Alcedo became independent Peru's first renowned composer, again working at the service of the Republic. Born in Lima, he studied in seminary and joined the Dominican Order, teaching music in Catholic institutions at the time of independence. Although religious music necessitated a more formal sound and frequent choral arrangements, Alcedo also had an ear for popular melodic songs, and also marches. He successfully entered a competition, sponsored by San Martín, to write a national anthem in 1821, with lyrics provided by José de la Torre:

> We are free—may we always thus be so,
> and let the sun deny its light
> before we neglect the solemn vote![2]

The hymn changed over time, though its opening line remained the same. Instrumentation greatly changed over time, too; the original composition was written for the *clave* (a keyboard, and precursor to the piano). Living into old age, Alcedo penned many songs of patriotic import. Peru's success

---

2. The well-known opening refrain in Spanish is: *Somos libres, seámoslo siempre / y antes niegue sus luces el sol / que faltamos al voto solemne / que la Patria al eterno elevó* . . .

against the Spanish navy in 1865 inspired his marching *Hymn of the 2nd of May*. Perhaps it was merciful that this ardent nationalist died shortly before Peru's vicious and cataclysmic war with Chile.

Not all art and cultural expression exuded triumphalism in the name of independence. In 1837 Pope Gregory XVI beatified Martín de Porres, a Peruvian who had lived in the late sixteenth and early seventeenth century. Gregory XVI was ultra-conservative, appalled by the Enlightenment and subsequent rise of (classical) liberal politics and thought. At a time when darker-skinned Peruvians were being wooed by art and culture into the orbit of liberal-infused nationalism, it was highly convenient for the Church to find and promote a darker-skinned saint. By timing, the beatification was politically expedient.

According to Catholic tradition, Martín de Porres was a mulatto (mix of black African and white) and an illegitimate son of a slave. Admitted to the Dominican Order—a rarity for someone of his racial composition and background—he became a Christ-like servant to his brothers. In older age he tended tirelessly to the sick, while declining to eat meat and easily befriending animals. When his monastery nearly went bankrupt, he reputedly proposed that he be sold into slavery in order to save it. After his 1837 beatification, representations of Porres multiplied and were coveted especially by ex-slaves and other citizens of mixed descent. These typically showed him as young and strong, yet humble in facial features, donning a Dominican's habit and sometimes a broom (a symbol of work and humility). Other variations portrayed him eating from a simple bowl while sharing it with an animal. Ignacio Merino painted a celebrated portrait of Porres in 1841, further enhancing his reputation as a national hero even among some whites.

Broadly, however, the economic stagnation and enveloping political chaos of the post-1825 period were not conducive to supporting the arts. There were some accomplishments, though sectarian divides were astutely avoided, while acclaimed independence themes and heroes received most artistic attention. Statues of the liberators, Bolívar and San Martín, were placed by mid-century in several of Lima's major squares, and in the main plazas of a few secondary cities. The small town of Chorrillos eventually erected a statue of its celebrated son, José Olaya, in 1865. A few years earlier, Christopher Columbus received honor with a tall statue of white marble in the *Alameda de Acho*. This symbol of whiteness and conquest clearly reflected the persistent triumphalism of the nation's creole power elite, with their European heritage.

CHAPTER FOUR

Disaster—War of the Pacific

In the mid-nineteenth century Peru's aristocracy was firmly in control of the nation's economic resources. And though the political winds blew wildly, with army officers still relentlessly vying for power, the Limeño rich also exercised much indirect control—governance was basically that of an oligarchy. In the time of Castilla, elite social clubs arose in the capital. The most important of these was the *Club Nacional*, established in 1855 by eighty well-to-do white males. Its first president, Gaspar de la Puente y Ramírez, could trace his familial heritage back to a Spanish conquistador. Though a few foreign-born whites were invited into the exclusive group, most members were Lima-born, "old money" rich.

By 1870, the capital had a population of nearly 120,000, with five daily newspapers. Several thousand Limeños thus read a steady diet of mostly local news, with rising numbers of middle-tier professionals also taking an interest in politics. Both social clubs and the interplay between the nascent middle class and the rich influenced political life. Parties began to take form, although political engagement remained nearly the exclusive pastime of the affluent. The chaotic era of the caudillos was at least passed; stable elections with more regular presidential terms became the norm, albeit with a limited franchise.

Patterns of Governance

Though respected for his successful posturing and Dos de Mayo fight against the Spanish, Mariano Prado was otherwise a mediocre president. Liberals controlled congress and much of his cabinet, and pushed for yet another new and more anti-clerical constitution. The 1867 document, unpopular in the provinces, threatened to trigger a civil war. Ramón Castilla himself opposed it, but died of natural causes while assembling yet another a revolutionary army in the south. In the north, a conservative but more conciliatory military officer, José Balta, led the opposition. Prado slipped off into exile, and after a caretaker administration Balta obtained the presidency in 1868.

There are striking similarities between the two mid-century Josés, Balta and Echenique, both in personality and in style of governance. José Balta had supported Echenique's corruption-flawed early 1850s' government, and now gave Peru a very similar administrative experience. The nation was badly in need of cautious oversight and fiscal discipline. Instead, Balta pushed ahead with reckless spending. As the debt skyrocketed, he contracted with American entrepreneur Henry Meiggs for the construction of railroads up into the highlands. Meiggs, who had already made millions with wharves, shipping, and sawmills in San Francisco (and had also constructed railroads in Chile), was glad to oblige—he made a new fortune in Peru. But while many of the railroads were marvelous feats of engineering, they cut into territories with little in the way of commercial life. Freight volume was low; it took decades before most lines began to turn a profit.

To manage his treasury, Balta relied on a wealthy, conservative, and devout Arequipeño named Nicolás Piérola. A chronic optimist filled with nervous energy—only thirty years old when he obtained the post—Piérola sought out easy money. He secured enormous loans from a Parisian commercial house, signing a deal that gave its investors exclusive rights to all remaining guano deposits. The Dreyfus contract was one of several highly questionable pacts with greedy foreign interests—though in keeping with a pattern that plagued nearly all of Latin America in the late nineteenth century. Peru's national debt quickly doubled, and ultimately increased eightfold in less than four years. The government spent lavishly on an international exposition, constructing a stately park and exposition grounds on Lima's newly broadened Avenida Colón. It doled out generously high pensions, especially to military officers. It rained millions on Henry Meiggs. The free-spending Piérola convinced investors, and himself, that the nation's natural endowments ensured that all the accumulating debits could be easily unwound.

Troubled by Piérola's lack of frugality, a businessman named Manuel Pardo formed a political organization, the *Partido Civilista* (*Civilians' Party*), to contest the 1872 elections. Pardo had made his own fortune primarily by shipping Chinese indentured servants to Peru, though he also owned prosperous sugar plantations that worked these immigrants like slaves. His apparent love of money fed a concomitant urge for frugality. Having briefly served as Prado's Treasury Minister, Pardo had work left undone. He was determined to set Peru's national finances in order. He was also weary of the role of military officers in the government—hence his party's name—and wanted to reorder the nation's political life. His ideas held significant appeal among both the old rich and Lima's small-but-rising middle class.

With only the monied citizens allowed to vote, Pardo won the election easily. But Balta's Minister of War, Tomás Gutiérrez, was unwilling to accept the results. With the support of part of the army, he staged a coup and declared himself president. He arrested his boss, José Balta, who was later murdered while in custody at an army barracks. But Manuel Pardo had fled by boat, was picked up by a warship, and soon gained the support of an influential naval commander named Miguel Grau. Far worse for Gutiérrez was the reaction of Limeños. Crowds ravaged the center of the city, as rank-and-file army units melted away. Caught hiding in a storage tank in a drugstore, the would-be president was killed, his body dragged through the streets and then unceremoniously hung naked from the bell tower of the cathedral.

The gory mob execution of Gutiérrez compelled others to think twice about usurping the well-liked Pardo, and he ruled unmolested for his entire four-year (1872–1876) term. But his was not a pleasant task: after the free-spending Balta regime, he was obliged to implement a strict austerity. Fortunately, having studied economics in France and having prospered in business, he was able to provide sound guidance. One of his most important and lasting contributions was to further professionalize the governmental bureaucracy. Building upon what Castilla had started, he saw to the hiring of administrators based on merit. A new program at the University of San Marcos began to systematically train office managers.

Manuel Pardo initiated several other reforms. He oversaw changes to the tax code, and set the stage for an eventual creation of an income tax. He further reduced the size of the army, dismissing from service thousands of underpaid enlisted soldiers. Budgetary shortfalls dogged him as he tried to facilitate the construction of more primary schools. He hoped to diversify the economy away from guano, too, and was pleased to see the nascent development of nitrate mines in the south—though unfortunately nitrate itself was fast-becoming a substitute for guano.

Despite Peru's exploitation of some of these Atacama Desert mines, positioned as they were in ill-defined borderlands territory, Pardo could not have easily anticipated the looming conflict with Chile. For many years Peru had enjoyed cordial relations with its southern neighbor—both having recently tangled with the intrusive Spanish. But as he slashed the military budget,

Pardo wagered that foreign alliances would keep the nation safe. He signed a defensive pact with Bolivia. Though ostensibly secret, it soon became widely known; Chile was offended. Plans to sign a mutual defense pact with Argentina floundered as that nation continued to recover from a bitter war with Paraguay.

It was financial duress that compelled Pardo to cancel the purchase of two naval vessels from a British shipyard. The English, who did not appreciate Peru's financial alliance with the French, were peeved. The two state-of-the-art warships were soon ominously bought by the Chileans. The cancellation annoyed Pardo's opponents within the slowly professionalizing armed forces, who also resented his slashing of the Balta administration's generous pensions and financial support. Austerity of course made the responsible Pardo immensely unpopular. At the end of his term he headed briefly into self-exile—to Chile, of all places.

Nipping at Pardo's government through the breadth of its term were both the aged caudillo, Manuel Ignacio Vivanco, and the impetuous Nicolás Piérola. Vivanco's maneuverings seemed to be primarily motivated by his endless ambition; Piérola's were more ideological, though he had come to hate Pardo with a passion, and deeply resented the government's blaming him for its dire fiscal condition. Both would-be usurpers appealed to discontented clergy, the Church upset at its relative decline and lost monopoly on education. They also repeatedly tapped into regionalism, as well. Multiple minor insurrections roiled the provincial interior in mid-decade.

In 1876, with the blessing of Pardo, Mariano Prado returned to the presidency (although perhaps to the bane of future history students—the two surnames awkwardly similar). Returning to Peru, Pardo became head of the senate, and was again intimately involved in governmental affairs. In November 1878, as he walked into the senate chamber, a sergeant in the Honor Guard drew his revolver and shot and killed him. Frustrated at his inability to gain promotion because of budget cuts, the NCO blamed the austerity-minded politician. Though likely the act of this disgruntled soul, a broader conspiracy is not out of the question. Pardo's friends launched a witch hunt—even Piérola's wife was briefly incarcerated. Political animosities rose to new heights.

By the close of the 1870s Peru was again at low ebb. Rife with internal divisions, thanks to Balta and Piérola it was—despite Pardo's best efforts—nearly bankrupt. The might-have-beens of its mid-century history are enticing. Had Peru developed the guano business on its own, it would have experienced an infusion of capital that surely would have made it the richest country in all of Latin America. Had it intelligently managed that capital, it would have likely set itself on a course to lasting prosperity. Given its mineral endowments, by the mid-twentieth century it well might have become what Costa Rica is to Central America: an oasis of strength in an otherwise enfeebled region. It is certainly true, though, that an independent-minded Peru would have also likely been checked. European powers might have seized the guano-laden islands outright, while blockading its coast and imposing political changes. Still, if Peruvians today are unhappy, they can at least partly thank their political ancestors. Castilla, Prado, Pardo, and others made mistakes; Echenique, Torrico, Vivanco, Balta, and Piérola made egregious errors that effectively ruined the country.

The War of the Pacific

Chile, in contrast—today South America's richest nation—made fairly intelligent moves, though it also became something of a lackey for a major European power. Miffed that Bolivia and Peru were attempting to tax the Atacama nitrate mines, coupled with the latter's annoying economic pact with France's Dreyfus firm, Britain generously armed the Chileans. A century of coastal shipping activity around the cape of South America had spawned lasting relations between the English and Chileans, as evident in the British naval role during the Wars of Independence. Indeed, in some ways history was repeating itself: the Chileans were again coming to Lima, and doing so (again) with the help of the English.

President Prado's sputtering government was ill-prepared to meet them. Circulating paper money, Peru was increasingly ravaged by inflation. The deep political divisions also must have enticed the Chileans; one side could perhaps be played against the other. Meanwhile, the vision of security through protective alliances (as bequeathed by Pardo) proved a mirage. A hasty diplomatic mission to Buenos Aires by Prado's government yielded nothing. Bolivia and Peru were on their own. For any hope of success, coordination between the two would be essential.

At the outset of the confrontation, though, naval operations predictably took preeminence. Since both Chile and Peru had great exposure to the Pacific coast, and the Atacama Desert was not easily traversed, warships would largely determine the victor. The failure of the Pardo and Prado administrations to update the fleet was thus a grave error. The fate of Peru ultimately rested upon just two armored vessels—*Independencia* and *Huascar*. The Chileans possessed the two newer and notably more powerful warships, one of which was named after a Briton (who had assisted San Martín in the Wars of Independence), *Almirante Cochrane*. The irony was rich. Peru did, of

Figure 4.1. Miguel Grau's ironclad *Huascar* vanquishes the Chilean corvette *Esmeralda* at the Battle of Iquique, May 1879. Many Peruvians know of Grau's magnanimous efforts to save the *Esmeralda*'s crew. The widow of the mortally wounded Chilean captain later exchanged letters with the Admiral, who expressed sorrow at his death, and saw to the return of his body.
Source: Casa Museo Gran Almirante Grau

course, have the fortified port of Callao—which was nearly impenetrable, as the Spanish had discovered.

There was by the nature of mid-nineteenth-century naval warfare an added factor of timing and luck: who found whom, when, and in what strength, among the vast expanse of ocean. In this, Peru initially fared well. Its two ironclads caught inferior Chilean warships at the southern nitrate port of Iquique. The *Huascar* vanquished one, but *Independencia*—Peru's heaviest and best ship—foolishly pursued the other into shallow waters, ripping open its hull on a reef. The loss of *Independencia* all but guaranteed Peru's eventual defeat; it was an irreversible setback.

The weight of the nation's military fortunes now fell onto Miguel Grau, the captain of the 1,130-ton *Huascar*, a taciturn man of principle and daring. An experienced seaman (he worked merchant ships and sailed the world as a teenager), possessed with a deep patriotism (his father had fought for independence), Grau demonstrated both exceptional ethics and courage. At Iquique he ordered the rescue of shipwrecked Chileans, and personally wrote the widow of the Chilean officer, Arturo Prat, commending his valor and expressing sorrow for her loss. Commanding a well-trained and motivated crew, much of which was Afro-Peruvian, Grau prowled the seas. Again, luck was repeatedly on his side: *Huascar* singlehandedly held off the greatly superior Chilean navy for several months, periodically skirting along the enemy's coastline, and even once capturing a transport filled with an array of war matériel.

Feted in Lima, as his ship was refitted in the safe port of Callao, Grau nevertheless predicted his imminent death, visiting his wife and ten children for one last time. In fact, back at sea, his luck finally ran out. Cornered by the *Cochrane* and other superior vessels, the *Huascar* was trapped. Early in the battle, a shell killed Grau and his first officer instantly, but the crew still fought against hopeless odds. Their eventual surrender gave Chile control of the Pacific, and its greatest war prize—*Huascar* was towed back to a port and put on display, to the delight of the nation (where it remains to this day). The ship's illustrious service, though, had won much regional and worldwide admiration. Grau's example inspired many others, now on land, to fight.

The first large Chilean army began to operate on Peruvian territory shortly after the capture of *Huascar*. Bypassing the southern port of Arica, it marched inland, confronting a numerically equal, joint Bolivian-Peruvian force near the town of Tacna. The fourteen thousand Chileans, however, had ample supplies, notably better small arms, and vastly superior artillery. Taking their own heavy losses, they drove their opponents from the field, in an engagement that became known as the Alto de la Alianza. The Bolivian army bore the brunt of the assaults, eventually withered, and effectively dropped out of the war thereafter. Chilean troops then sacked Tacna, an act that ensured the long-term alienation of its citizens.

The allied defeat isolated coastal Arica and, in a strategic blunder, authorities in Lima failed to withdraw its garrison. A command of 1,600 Peruvians was trapped. Under the command of Francisco Bolognesi, an elderly but gifted artillery officer, the small force declined Chilean instructions to surrender. Bolognesi hastily fortified his position, most notably on the heights of a steep hill, El Morro. Several hundred feet high, with sheer rockface on its seaside, El Morro was both a formidable fortress and a trap. Frustrated by the tenacity of their opponents at Alto de la Alianza, agitated by the hostility of civilians, and upset with Bolognesi's refusal to surrender, the Chilean commander ordered engagement without quarter. When Bolognesi's batteries mauled the bombarding *Cochrane*, the Chileans became even more enraged.

The bitter struggle at El Morro lasted only an hour, as the Peruvians—outnumbered 3:1 with inferior weapons—made a courageous last stand. Bolognesi fell mortally wounded, still reputedly clutching and firing his revolver. Another martyr was Alfonso Ugarte, a thirty-three-year old, wealthy entrepreneur, who had armed and equipped soldiers at his own expense. According to tradition, a devastated Ugarte drove his stallion over the ledge of the rockface at the end of the battle, rather than surrender to Peru's enemies. Though the circumstances of his oft-recounted death are in fact unknown, there is little doubt that Chilean soldiers massacred hundreds of wounded survivors. Arica became synonymous with national honor, and Bolognesi's name is, to this day, much celebrated and revered among the Peruvian people.

The Battle for Lima

After the first phases of the war, all advantages rested with the Chileans. To end the war and force Peru to cede territory, however, the invaders had to capture the capital. Though most of the Peruvian army and its invaluable equipment had been lost in the southern campaign, the nation determined to fight on. In December 1879 Nicolás Piérola regained the presidency, even as Prado willingly left the country on a mission to Europe, in which he hoped to secure new loans and ships, or perhaps persuade France or a European power to intercede on Peru's behalf. Encouragingly, the specter of defeat was uniting the country. Piérola made overtures to his former rivals, while Limeños broadly rallied to the cause; thousands of volunteers from the central highlands also came down and joined in the city's defense.

Peru, however, faced tremendous disadvantages. From the start, its artillery had been grossly inferior to that of the Chileans; so too, most of its small arms were antiquated. While Chilean infantrymen had standardized repeating rifles that could fire twelve rounds per minute, most Peruvian muskets fired single-shot minié balls, with a typical firing speed of three rounds per minute. Nor were Peruvian arms uniform. Different sets of guns required different types of ammunition, creating a logistical nightmare for quartermasters. Though defenders appear to have slightly outnumbered the nearly twenty-three thousand Chilean invaders, the quality of their training was generally poor. Most were recent volunteers or conscripts; some had never fired their weapons before the outset of battle. Shopkeepers, merchants, artisans, and other civilian trades comprised entire units. There were semi-trained Reservists, and naval contingents—including Marines—that were hastily converted into mobile infantry commands.

Leadership shortcomings for Peru were also great. Piérola distrusted his remaining senior military officers, and endlessly tampered with their assignments. A military novice, he readily fell to Chilean strategic deception.

Landings north of the capital convinced the president that the attack would come from that direction. For much of 1880 Limeños dug earthworks on the ridges facing north, and carefully positioned their heaviest and best batteries there. But then, with full control of the sea, the Chilean army embarked and redeployed to the south, advancing with ease from the port of Pisco.

The Peruvians now hastily constructed two defensive lines facing south: one from the coastal village of Chorrillos to the hills of Monterrico, through the town of San Juan, and another in the vicinity of a small town named Miraflores. The outer line was too long, at seven and a half miles, to be adequately defended. On January 13, after a vigorous artillery bombardment, the Chileans easily overran it. The only substantial fighting ensued later, near Chorrillos, where hundreds of Peruvians tenaciously resisted atop a seaside ridge known as El Morro Solar. The commander here, Miguel Iglesias, was compelled to surrender; one of his sons, Alejandro, died in the fighting. Decades later, Peruvians installed a monument and buried their symbolic Unknown Soldier atop the dramatic Morro Solar.

In celebration of their victories, Chilean soldiers sacked Chorrillos. Venting their disgust for the local inhabitants—most of whom were darker-skinned than themselves—drunken Chileans raped women and stole anything of value. Their officers sanctioned this orgy of violence, and allowed similar atrocities to unfold later in Miraflores and Lima itself. To many Chileans, the refusal of the "inferior" Peruvians to readily surrender was an offense. They were weary of living on army rations in a distant country for months on end, and wanted to go home.

Peace negotiations, through the auspices of observing European naval missions, appeared to deliver an armistice. But as the Chilean army maneuvered and positioned itself in front of the better-designed Miraflores defensive line, fighting unexpectedly erupted midday on January 15. Nicólas Piérola himself was on the scene, sanctioning an attack by select units near the coast. Initial charges went well, but ammunition shortages doomed them, while Chilean artillery soon took its toll. Within their Miraflores line, the defenders held a series of seven strongly fortified redoubts. But as the weight of the Chilean army fell on the three closest to the coast (along with bombarding fire from Chilean naval vessels), the rest of the Peruvian army sat idly, failing to engage. Even worse, units in the fifth redoubt withdrew completely, vacating their key position. By the end of the day, though their own losses were considerable, the Chileans had broken through the defenses. Some house-to-house fighting in Lima only delayed the evitable; Peru had lost the war.

In the throes of defeat, however, Peru found its greatest fighter. Andrés Avelino Cáceres was the son of wealthy land-owning parents in Ayacucho.

Figure 4.2. War damage in the town of Miraflores. The Chilean Army proved itself ill-disciplined from the start of its operations in Peru. Property destruction was commonplace. In the first few days of occupation in Lima, Chilean soldiers pillaged property with mob-like abandon, their officers indifferent or sometimes even participating. Rape of especially darker-skinned, young single women was frequent.
Source: Museo Metropolitano, from Coleción Rengifo, Biblioteca Nacional del Perú

In 1854 he had joined Castilla's Liberal Revolution, and subsequently served with the famous caudillo-president at La Palma and elsewhere. He was a military attaché at Peru's embassy in France, studying military tactics at the academy of Saint-Cyr. He might well have learned about counterinsurgency strategies there (the French were bogged down in an occupation of Mexico), but his real knack for warfare lay not only in strategy, but also in his relentless determination and stubborn resolve. He played a key role in a preliminary (and victorious) engagement at Tarapacá during the southern campaign. At Tacna, he had two horses shot from under him. At Miraflores, Cáceres commanded the critical right flank and fought with abandon—until he fell gravely injured with a wound to his right leg. To his vexation, in the defense of the capital, Piérola and his commanding officer repeatedly dismissed his intelligent tactical advice out of hand.

Cáceres was a man who did not give up. Fleeing to the city center, he hid in the Convent of San Pedro, nursing his wounds. He then took flight from Lima to the highlands, determined to continue the war there. Utilizing his knowledge of native culture—and fluency in Quechua—he organized guerrilla resistance columns in his native Ayacucho. With his wife Antonia Moreno in support, he gathered supplies and reengaged the enemy. Cáceres's hit-and-run attacks flustered the Chileans, and turned the highlands into a new, final front. The frustrated invaders dispatched more and more troops, who abused the locals and further incited the insurgency. At the town of Concepción, in July 1882, Cáceres's forces annihilated a seventy-seven-man garrison of Chileans who fought to the death. For two years his well-paced attacks wearied the occupiers.

For all his efforts, however, Cáceres could not alter the war's outcome. The weight of the Chilean occupation was ultimately overwhelming. The invaders extorted money from the Limeño rich, while keeping their city under a harsh martial law. Chilean troops, with their officers' blessing, visited wanton destruction upon Lima and towns all along the central coast. Peru had clearly lost the war, and was compelled to sue for a final peace. The terrible mismanagement of its finances over the previous decade, and subsequent political infighting, had critically weakened it. A lack of coordination with the hapless Bolivians also helped ensure the victory of an opportunistic Chile. The War of the Pacific was a defining and bitter chapter in Peruvian national history; full recovery would take decades.

CHAPTER FIVE

Picking Up the Pieces

When the Chilean army withdrew from Peru, in August 1884, it left a traumatized nation. The humiliating defeat had wrecked the feeble country's infrastructure, shattered its already decrepit finances, and destroyed its self-confidence. It was hard to see how Peru could again rise to its feet. In fact, the nation was entering a prolonged period of malaise, marked also by political infighting.

Having arranged the peace, Miguel Iglesias still held the presidency. He immediately faced opposition, which only increased as the daunting task of reconstruction inched forward. Adversarial political groups circled him like vultures. The *Civilistas* regrouped under Aurelio Denegri, one of Peru's wealthiest individuals at the outset of the war. Nicolás Piérola formed a new Democratic Party, but then watched its fortunes ebb as it competed with an upstart Constitutionalist Party under Andrés Cáceres. The tenacious Cáceres, the most successful of Peruvian resistance fighters, had captured the admiration of much of the populace. He demanded Iglesias resign, and brought his guerrilla forces to the gates of the capital to ensure he did so. Seeking a savior, many wealthy Limeños backed Cáceres, and he secured the presidency in July 1886. He would dominate Peruvian political life for the next decade.

Cáceres in Control

Cáceres's most immediate challenge was to rebuild the nation, which in turn required he address its insolvency. His government entered into talks with a group of British investors led by Michael P. Grace. Grace, and his brother William, had long operated in Peru, and had often prospered via government contracts. They had delivered munitions during the war. Concerned that his business interests might collapse, the Irish-born Grace organized a cadre of lenders from among London's banking community. He signed a lucrative deal with Cáceres's government, in which his investors acquired ownership of all the railroads for sixty-six years, obtained rights to a million acres of land, enjoyed privileges in trade and banking, and could claim some of the remaining guano deposits. As Peru would also make interest payments for thirty-three years, it seemed to some that Cáceres had nearly turned the nation into a vassal of British banks. Congressional opposition to the "Grace Contract" was so stiff that Cáceres had to forcibly replace many deputies in order to pass it.

In fact, the package made the Grace family very rich, and facilitated the eventual rise of the powerful W. R. Grace & Company. But there were redemptive features to the deal: It restored Peruvian fiscal credibility almost instantly, providing access to further investment and loans. The British also quickly improved and expanded the nation's railroads at their own initial expense. Later, Peru evaded the forfeiture of most of its remaining guano reserves by employing a contractual provision that gave domestic needs priority. Fortunately, too, the British ultimately did little in terms of exercising land acquisition rights.

British investors, however, benefited from the exploitation of new silver mines in the highlands. The British built the Central Andean Railroad to access the Oroya region, which lay some 110 miles northeast of Lima. When the line opened in 1893 it was the highest in the world, later passing through the Ticlio Pass at an astounding 15,800 feet. Ernest Malinowski, a Polish-born engineer who had lived in Peru for most of his life, oversaw the project. In both capital and engineering, Europeans were possessing Peru's rich natural endowments. Cáceres's government had passed a law in 1890 that gave foreigners tax-free mining concessions for a quarter-century. In the medium-term, Peru received nothing from the extraction of these ores.

State revenue was thin on Cáceres's watch. His administration continued the practice of native tribute, which had been reinstituted (yet again) under Iglesias. The government levied new, popularly resented taxes on alcohol and tobacco. Its tariffs were low and ineffectually collected, even as exports raced ahead of imports. Peru did receive its first insurance agencies, courtesy of investing foreigners, and the *Banco Italiano* opened its doors in Lima. The government had enough fiscal integrity to more adequately back the *sol*, as it removed inflationary paper currency from circulation. Cáceres's government was, in sum, a fusion between laissez-faire economics and political dictatorship. True, it often bargained poorly in the postwar years, but one must bear in mind the weak hand it held; foreign capital would have fled had not the Peruvian state yielded to its demands. After the Panic of 1890, investment in all of Latin America had become unappealing, especially among Europeans.

Cáceres faced relentless critique by his political rivals, and his government slowly calcified into a dictatorship. Nicolás Piérola, who had returned to Peru, edited the opposition newspaper *El País*, and sought to rupture the alliance between Civilistas and Constitutionalists that had brought Cáceres to power. With the presidential elections in 1890 he had his chance. The Civilistas backed Francisco Rosas Balcázar, a trained physician and long-time senator committed to displacing an emerging pattern of military rule. The product of Domingo Elías's *Colegio de Nuestra Señora de Guadalupe*, Rosas insisted that the generals relegate themselves to the barracks. But Cáceres orchestrated the campaign of his longtime sidekick, Colonel Remigio Morales Bermúdez. Rosas and his followers were harassed; Piérola was arrested and thrown in jail. Though Cáceres headed to Paris to assume a diplomatic post, it was understood by all that he exercised keen influence over Morales's subsequent administration. Erstwhile civilians fled the Constitutionalist ranks, and opposition to the government mounted.

Within a short time Cáceres returned and announced his intent to again run for president. This galvanized his detractors, who rallied to the candidacy of Mariano Valcárcel. Having recently served as Minister of the Interior, prime minister (a largely symbolic post), and president of the Chamber of Deputies, Valcárcel was an unlikely opponent; but as a former regime insider, he was well-informed and formidable. Piérola, meanwhile, had escaped from prison. Disguised, he boarded a foreign vessel at Callao and sailed to a safe exile in Ecuador, soon decrying the military dictatorship.

The mid-1890s saw Peru's political dynamics briefly fall into a pit reminiscent of the long-ago age of the caudillos. President Morales Bermúdez contracted a fatal illness and died one week later. His constitutional successor, Pedro Alejandrino Solar, was disliked by a number of senior military officers who replaced him with the second vice president, Justiniano Borgoño. At Cáceres's behest, Borgoño's administration rounded up Civilista opponents, preparatory to the *jefe*'s own, strangely unanimous reelection. Following in the footsteps of Piérola, Valcárcel snuck aboard a German ship at Callao and went into exile. He and Piérola conferred, made their peace, and announced to Peruvians their unified call for a decisive return to civilian rule.

Rebellion broke out in the south, along the coast, and in Lima itself. There was widespread frustration with Cáceres, whose governance had ultimately

Figure 5.1. Andrés Avelano Cáceres and his family. This portrait was taken shortly before he became President. Strong-willed and domineering, so too was Antonia Moreno Leyva, his spouse of forty-six years. In the 1881 fighting in the highlands she managed logistics and on occasion took to battle. As Peru's First Lady, she raised funds for war widows.
Source: Museo Marina Núñez Del Prado

failed to answer Peru's economic and social needs. Dubbed *montoneros*, the rebel forces coalesced and brought the fight to the capital, where Cáceres himself took command. The struggle within Lima was brutal—the worst internal fighting that the city proper has ever seen. Presidential forces positioned machine guns in major squares and near the palace; hundreds of assaulting rebels were mowed down. But still surrounded and cut off, Cáceres recognized that his time was up. After accepting a truce to care for the wounded and bury the dead, he agreed to depart into exile. The brief and bloody Revolution of 1895 had brought his decade-long dominance to an end.

A fair assessment of the rule of Andrés Cáceres necessitates weighing its context: taking the helm of a defeated and demoralized nation is a daunting task. Besides great economic challenges, Peru faced nearly insurmountable geopolitical and diplomatic barriers. The victorious Chileans gave the nation no quarter. A case in point is the status of the Arica and Tacna Provinces. The Treaty of Ancón provided for an 1893 plebiscite to determine their fate. The Chileans spent lavishly on these regions in the intervening years, yet when it was apparent that the locals would still vote in favor of reincorporation into Peru, Santiago evaded and delayed the plebiscite. For all its efforts, Cáceres's regime had little to show in terms of accomplishments. And yet in this era of reconstruction, it also arguably laid the groundwork for subsequent progress.

The Aristocratic Republic

"Progress" was a celebrated word in the mid- and late-nineteenth century, which harkened to the ideas of French philosopher Auguste Comte. Comte and his followers believed that humanity had entered a new era of rationality and metaphysical triumph with the outset of the Enlightenment, and that scientific breakthroughs were about to usher in a utopian age. Comtean thought, or *Positivism*, enraptured many well-read elites around the world—Brazilians even emblazoned a Positivist slogan on their national flag. But there was a simultaneous and darker concept also emerging in the closing decades of the nineteenth century: Social Darwinism. Drawing on the evolutionary theories of Charles Darwin, Social Darwinists accepted the notion that the "survival of the fittest" was a natural law of selection that applied to the human race. If primitive peoples died out—so the argument went—it was a natural, inevitable process. These two seminal ideologies sometimes blended together.

Nicolás Piérola's presidency initiated an important period that has been termed the *Aristocratic Republic* by Peru's most famous historian, Jorge

Basadre. Positivist ideas came to the fore, but with an important caveat: both their major proponents at Lima's University of San Marcos, and Piérola himself, rejected the premise of Social Darwinism. Why this is so is something of a puzzle—after all, racism was deeply engrained in Peru's white elite. But certainly the sheer size of the indigenous population was a factor. Though early Peruvian census data has proven dubious, about 60 percent of the country was native around 1900. If Peru was to thrive, it had to incorporate its native population into the state-building project. If primitive peoples naturally die out, Peru's future was inherently bleak.

Piérola viewed the indigenous masses in a patriarchal vein, but also aspired to improve their lot and increase their role in politics and society. He (again) abolished tributary taxes, and legislated a universal draft, in part to discourage the forcible abduction of indigenous males into military service. He created a Ministry of Development that sought to improve the highlands through infrastructure and public works. Scores of municipalities received new city halls, and local elections began to more frequently determine officeholders. Piérola believed that more people should have access to the vote, and thus reformed Peru's electoral system with the creation of an oversight council and direct balloting for the presidency (instead of via an electoral college). Myriad public primary schools were built on his watch, too, both in provincial capitals and secondary towns. The systemic changes were haltingly slow and uneven, but there was a modicum of genuine progress.

Still, the label "Aristocratic Republic" is apropos. As it entered the twentieth century, a powerful white oligarchy based in Lima continued to rule the country. In financial matters, Piérola was cautious. Though the national budget rose by 70 percent during his term, he adhered to strict budgetary limits and rarely ran deficits. Tariffs became a major source of revenue, as exports surged further and collection improved, but the rich still largely evaded taxes. Many spent more betting on horse races in a single week than what they paid into the coffers of the always lean government in a year. Foreign companies continued to also operate largely tax-free. The state played a more active economic role than in many other Latin American countries around the turn of the century, but by modern standards it was miniscule. The only significantly developing city was the capital, feeding the popular adage among the well-to-do at the time that "Peru is Lima, and Lima is Peru."

Piérola attempted to professionalize the army and remove it from politics. Key to this effort was the enhancement of the military academy near Chorrillos. The government integrated more educational features into officer training, while the army began to distinguish between commissioned and non-commissioned officers. Peru welcomed French military advisors, who oversaw strategic and tactical instruction; engineering became a major component in the school. But despite these efforts, and the universal military service law, the army continued to employ dubious practices. Even in the early twentieth century, poor indigenous males in the highlands were kidnapped into military service, where physical abuse and racial discrimination were common.

Piérola loudly proclaimed his allegiance to democracy, but in 1899 chose his own successor. In the highlands, because his electoral reforms had not provided for secret ballots, workers on large estates were typically lined up and told for whom they would vote. Powerful hacendados arranged their own election to congress, where the rich often debated nonsensical policies while the nation lurched forward in fits and starts. Piérola's imposition of his successor agitated the Civilistas and the two major parties feuded more, while other elite launched a new Liberal Party in the spirit of Domingo Elías and José Gálvez. A Liberal-Civilista and former protégé of Gálvez won the presidency in 1903. The might-have-beens with Manuel Candamo are intriguing, but this agile-minded and adaptable man died of natural causes shortly after his inauguration. Special elections in 1904 saw the return of Piérola intercepted by Civilista leader José Pardo, son of Manuel—the president in the mid-1870s.

Despite the rivalry, Pardo's presidency built on the accomplishments of Piérola. In particular, he extended efforts at building primary schools. The government's education budget nearly doubled, as did the number of children in free public education. Still, only about half of Peru's youth were enrolled by the end of his term, with the rural poor woefully underrepresented. Higher education also received more support, allowing for some access by Lima's small but growing middle class. A National Polytechnic School was established, and the University of San Marcos received increased funding. It was organic growth in the nation's economy, however, that was even more readily improving the lives of many citizens.

Turn-of-Century Development

Demand for commodities—raw materials that drive the world's economy—soared in the 1890s and early 1900s, creating new sources of income for Peru. Oil was an important emerging commodity. Tar pits along the northern coast, at La Brea and Pariñas, had long been known, with tar from here used since late colonial times in shipbuilding. In 1890 the London & Pacific Petroleum Company began drilling for oil near the pits. Easily finding crude, it soon built a short-line railroad to the coastal town of Talara, along with storage tanks, docks, and later a small refinery. Production rose sharply. By 1913, when British owners sold their operation to Rockefeller's Standard Oil of New Jersey, they were annually exporting nearly 1.7 million barrels of oil.

The invention of the automobile brought explosive growth to the oil industry, but also triggered a boom in rubber—which was used primarily for (both car and bicycle) tires. Tapping rubber trees in the jungle, and then boiling the sap, yielded latex. The renowned rubber rush in Brazil had a smaller but still dynamic counterpart in Amazonian Peru. At its peak in 1902–1906, rubber exports were nearly ten times the value of Peru's still-rising oil exports. It made many Peruvians millionaires, and enriched the few British commercial houses that monopolized the trade.

Rubber production was highly exploitative, however, with extreme and even genocidal practices. The worst abuses were visited upon the primitive tribes living in the Putumayo River basin, at the time under Peruvian territorial control, though presently in southern Colombia. Here, the Amazonian Rubber Company coerced Natives into slavery, using whip-wielding overseers brought in from Barbados. Natives who failed to meet quotas were tortured, their family members held hostage. Many thousands died. Waves of epidemics also simultaneously ravaged these remote tribes. British investors, delighted with their profits, turned a blind eye—until a 1910 investigation revealed the truth about the operations.

The Putumayo practices enriched one Julio César Arana, the "Rubber King," though others became rich by overseeing primarily mestizo workers held in debt peonage. Several hundred suddenly wealthy entrepreneurs thrived in the Amazonian town of Iquitos, center of the Peruvian rubber boom. They built lavish houses, threw sumptuous parties, and even shipped caviar and fine French wines up the Brazilian Amazon. The ostentatious Malecón Palace Hotel sat among European consulates in this Wild West–like town of twenty-five thousand. The rich even aspired to build a great opera house—a saga recaptured in the classic 1982 Werner Herzog film *Fitzcarraldo*. But alas, the rubber boom subsided as quick as it rose, in the mid-1910s, as more efficient British plantations in the Far East captured the global market.

Foreign capital poured into metallurgy around the turn of the century. In 1902, a group of American investors began what would become Peru's most important industry one century later: copper mining. When a rich vein was accessed at Cerro de Pasco, investors built a spur railroad line and coal-burning smelter, while opening feeder coal mines nearby. Pollution from the plant killed miles of grassland and sickened animals and villagers. Hence, a concomitant tradition of localized protest began with Peru's earliest mining industry—a pattern that continues to the present day. As copper demand rose, with industrial uses and piping, production steadily climbed into the late 1920s. Silver production, long important in Peru, soared for a season too, doubling between 1903 and 1913.

In agriculture, the availability of rail transport dramatically increased exports of sheep and alpaca wool, especially in the southern provinces. Though alpaca fiber is slippery and difficult to work with, it was coveted by select British textile manufacturers. Native villagers wove cloth and sold it to British agents, who set up collection points along the railroad. Sheep herding and wool production soared around Arequipa, integrating an otherwise insular regional economy into global trade. Not insignificant amounts of coca leaf left Peru for the United States and Europe, too, the powerful natural stimulant used in the carbonated drinks of a new company called Coca-Cola. Along the northern coast, while cotton exports flat-lined, sugar production rose steadily. Peru produced 172,000 tons of sugar in 1910, four-fifths of it for export—to Britain, Chile, and even Japan. But as they made healthy profits, the so-called Sugar Barons declined to modernize the industry, instead relying on labor-intensive methods and a cheap, semi-coerced workforce.

Although the commodities-based economy percolated to life in the time of Cáceres and the Aristocratic Republic, its benefits for Peruvians were skewed and limited. Most commodity investments overwhelmingly served foreign capital; local entrepreneurs often did get very rich, but the wealth rarely trickled downward. The lack of labor rights and protections ensured ample exploitation, mostly of indigenous peoples. Government revenue was also limited. Oil companies never paid more than 10 percent on their profits, and the rubber and sugar barons paid considerably less. Export tariffs did rise, but their collection—although improving—was still often evaded. Rubber producers received enormous concessionary tracts of public land for very modest fees.

With the temporary exception of Iquitos, money and government spending gravitated toward Lima. A series of improvements in the opening decade of the twentieth century made urban life more pleasant—especially for the rich. Inspired by photographs of Paris, Limeños constructed broader and longer *avenidas*, such as Avenida Colón, on the edge of the historical downtown. Under a popular and innovative mayor, Federico Elguera (1901–1909), the city fathers began serious sanitation efforts, laying the first sewage lines under newly paved streets. Free bath houses improved public hygiene as well. Plazas were built or fixed up, while a new municipal theater competed with private houses for entertainment and social events.

The Outspoken Contrarian

Although Peru was making visible material progress at the turn of the century, a few raised their voices and questioned the accomplishments of the Aristocratic Republic. Far and away the most important of these was Manuel González Prada, who in the late nineteenth century laid the groundwork for the early-twentieth-century rise of the Peruvian political left. Ironically, González Prada himself was scion of one the aristocracy's most illustrious families, with a lineage stretching back to the viceregal Spanish court. His father, in the mid-nineteenth century, sided with Vivanco and Echenique, obligating the family to self-exile to Chile when Ramón Castilla returned to power in 1855. In the city of Valparaíso, young Manuel received an excellent education at an English-run private school.

Into adulthood, González Prada embraced the sciences and eventually repudiated his Catholic upbringing, to the chagrin of his mother. Successful in business and finance, he made money while writing romantic poetry on the side. But then the Pacific War erupted, profoundly altering his perceptions of politics and life. While serving in the Reserves he saw limited action in the defense of Lima, then resolutely avoided contact with the occupying Chilean forces thereafter. In isolation within his mansion, he brooded and bemoaned the fate of his country. He later married Adriana de Verneuil, a French woman twenty years his younger. When the couple lost two of their three children in youth, it seemed to have further embittered him.

In the 1880s, González Prada took to writing and public speaking. He drew large crowds into Lima's theaters, where he denounced the very aristocracy of which he was a part. He blamed Peru's rich for producing three generations of self-serving politicians, and argued that the entire Republic was a farce and failure. In a spirit akin to that of Nietzsche (though also with a Positivist edge), he turned over the tidy tables of conventional political thought, and shocked his listeners by damning the oligarchy's "corrupt" political parties. He condemned the Cáceres government, with its Grace contract, which he termed a sellout to foreigners. He heaped scorn, often with an acerbic wit. The old, he said, should simply go off and die, and make way for a Peru recreated by energized youth employing real patriotism and science. González Prada was more than anti-clerical: he hinted at atheism, a shocking premise in this orthodox land.

At the time of his tirades González Prada served as president of Lima's Literary Club, comprised of luminaries, including Ricardo Palma. His furious denunciations predictably triggered a backlash from his own kind—Palma openly broke with him and published editorials refuting his ideas—but won

Figure 5.2. A generation after its horrific defeat, Peru began to elevate two men to nationalist sainthood: Miguel Grau and Fernando Bolognesi. Gonzalez Prada participated in this endeavor, especially glorifying Admiral Grau. Juan Lopiani's 1899 painting *El Último Cartucho* (*The Last Cartridge*), meanwhile, romanticized the sacrificial death of Bolognesi in his defense at El Morro.
Source: Museo Bolognesi

him the devoted allegiance of many idealistic, especially middle-class students. He became something of an icon at budding San Marcos University, where followers joined him in creating a new rival club, the *Círculo Literarío* (Literary Circle). Many also joined his upstart *Unión Nacional* (National Union), a political party nominally aligned with the Radical Civic Union in Argentina. Its program called for decentralization, land reform, and other changes that would—according to its members—place Peru on a path to true modernity.

In 1891, just when it seemed that González Prada was converting his hot rhetoric into action, he surprisingly left Peru for France, partly at the behest of his French-born wife. The couple spent the next several years in Europe where they intermingled with politically active outsiders to power. González Prada began to embrace anarchism and more radical ideas that would challenge not only the dominant sociopolitical order, but overturn economic structures as well. When he returned to Peru, he pronounced himself an anarchist. Doors closed, and he had less influence than before; newspapers, in particular, shunned him, refusing to publish his editorials.

It was in this period of his life that he promoted the participation of the indigenous population in the highlands, and called on them to lead—if necessary—through armed revolution. In 1904 he published an essay titled "Nuestros Indios" ("Our Indians"), celebrating the noble "race," while vigorously condemning both the Spanish and the subsequent republic that gave them nothing. It was a somewhat strange argument, coming as it was from a white man who once made money as a youth managing one of his family's haciendas. And despite his ever-increasing radicalism, González Prada made little progress in shedding his own considerable wealth, though he did financially support some workers' organizations, and occasionally even spent time with workers themselves. He was the first of a series of prominent Peruvian leftists who called Natives to action without learning their languages, embracing their culture, or interacting with them in their villages.

The lasting significance of González Prada is that he challenged political norms and made it acceptable to question the domineering role of the aristocracy. His influence on a generation of especially younger Peruvians was great. As Peru fully entered the twentieth century, many in its rising middle class were prepared to challenge the elite's grip on political power. Some workers, having listened to González Prada, were ready to envision a different and more equitable society. By around 1910, a quarter-century after its brief occupation by a victorious foreign army, Peru was entering a stormy season filled with internal tension, new possibilities, and dissent.

CHAPTER SIX

Life and Culture, 1867–1908

The political stability of the mid-nineteenth century was good for Peruvian cultural expression, as subsequent decades produced one of the nation's most illustrious men of letters, Ricardo Palma. Though the rural hinterlands evinced a timelessness not far removed from the late colonial epoch, cities began to see significant physical and technological change as a global Age of Progress took hold. In both literature and art Peruvians continued to wean themselves from Spanish influence, though in architecture and other areas they continued to follow Europe's lead.

Glimpses of Urban Life

Peru's wealthy dominated both city and country in politics and economics, while their social and cultural tastes resonated power and exclusivity. As before, the rich continued to live in the center of Lima, still typically within only a dozen blocks of the Plaza de Armas. The plaza, set as it was in the midst of the palace, archbishop's mansion, cathedral, and city hall, was by this time effectively off-limits to the underclasses. Its decades-long service as a market venue now ended. Now, a manicured garden featuring a wide variety of lush semi-tropical flora occupied the very center of the square. In the evenings the rich came here for socializing strolls, wearing their finest silks and courtly suits, still imported from Europe. The nearby terraced *Alameda de Acho* was increasingly surpassed by a newer promenade that bore the unlikely name *Avenida de los Descalzos* (Avenue of the Barefoots—a reference to a colonial order of friars). This wide, well-ordered park was decorated with statuary representing the Zodiac, and was also meticulously landscaped and maintained in the late nineteenth century.

Until the 1870s, Limeños still lived within the confines of the viceregal capital's enormous adobe walls. Built in the mid-colonial era to stave off English pirates, the walls rose and fell in line with the terrain, but were generally about fifteen feet high. They featured dozens of periodic, large, and triangular ramparts, and though various gates had been added they were nevertheless a major hindrance to movement. An American contractor was hired to demolish them in the early 1870s, a task completed shortly before the war with Chile (improvements in artillery would have made them of negligible use, though their removal was still badly timed). Flat stones from walls were used to pave streets on the edges of the city center, and these later took the names of various war heroes, such as Avenidas Bolognesi and Grau.

When the rich left the core of the city, it was most typically to attend the horse races at the hippodrome, which was constructed on the southwestern outskirts of Lima in 1877. Here, again in their finest clothes, the wealthy bet large sums on their favorite mounts, and impressed their peers with feigned indifference when their money disappeared. As the decades progressed, and more affluent foreigners arrived in Lima for diplomacy or business, they too were welcomed into the Jockey Club and at the races—provided, of course, they were white-skinned. Near the turn of the century affluent Limeños, and the slowly emerging professional middle class, increasingly took short outings to the Pacific. A hydraulic incline was installed on the cliffs at Barranco, providing spectacular views and access to an oceanside bath. Farther out, to the northwest, the town of Ancón also became a weekend destination for seaside play.

By the end of the nineteenth century, the upper classes numbered roughly eighteen thousand, or 12 percent of the urban population (within this number a few hundred were truly super-rich). Marriage ensured that the distinctive classes perpetuated; it was unacceptable for children to socialize, much less bond, with anyone from the lower classes. The rich began to build more houses on the edges of the historical center, many architecturally influenced by *beaux arts français*—indeed, anything French in the late nineteenth century was the rage. But there were very few French actually living in Peru, while the proportion and significance of the Italian presence (see chapter 3) was in decline. The British community, though not large, was disproportionately influential. Englishmen formed cricket and tennis clubs that eventually drew in Peruvian elite, as did their *Club Regatas* (Sailing Club) in Chorrillos, begun in 1875. The British-invented passion of *fútbol* (soccer) was also beginning to take hold, with the earliest clubs well-established by the end of the century (see chapter 16).

All was not leisure, however, even for the rich. Devout Catholics, they practiced the religious conviction of charity, with wealthy women prominent in the Society of Benevolence. This organization oversaw the construction and maintenance of many facilities for the less fortunate—two orphanages, a facility (with primitive practices) for the mentally ill, and multiple clinics and hospitals. Throughout the nineteenth century these Church-linked activities also received funds from the government; even liberals did not readily question the appropriateness of this kind of public expenditure.

Lima was the center of Peru, boasting a population of approximately 150,000 by the first decade of the twentieth century. It was the first city to receive electric lighting and street cars. Its stately buildings, including a majestic post office and the two-thousand-seat Politeama Theater, reflected Limeño confidence. Thousands of literate inhabitants connected with the world, and engaged long gossip columns about the lives of the elite, in several daily and weekly newspapers, led by the oldest and most respected *El Comercio*. By 1905 Peru also had 6,800 miles of telegraph lines connecting the capital with every major secondary city, all of which also had regular mail service via railroads or the coastal steamers.

The second largest city in Peru was the primary port of Callao, which many visitors found dirty and unattractive, though a turn-of-the-century sewage and sanitation system made it a much healthier place. Callao was divided into old and new quarters, the former marked by narrow, twisting streets and congested housing. Its port was far and away the best, and always busy, with typically a half dozen or more seafaring vessels at anchor, though most were slowly loaded and unloaded via lighters—small boats that conveyed cargo to and from the shallow-water docks.

Arequipa, with thirty-five thousand inhabitants in 1900, was a distinctive city about to surpass Callao in size. Long known as *La Ciudad Blanca* (The White City), it was built on a Spanish colonial grid of tidy right-angle blocks, making it orderly and easy to navigate. At its heart were many stately white-limestone mansions, most dating from the eighteenth century. Its churches, convents, and university gave it a cosmopolitan air, the backdrop of four volcanoes providing a spectacular setting. Arequipeños exuded a sense of purpose and regional pride, many convinced that the nation's course would be far better if they governed Peru instead of the haughty Limeños. Although a railroad now linked the city to the coast, its life and economy were a world apart. The region's fertile valleys provided an ample foodshed; southern Peru rarely suffered famine. Rollicking creeks and waterfalls generated enough electricity for the small city by the early 1900s and, like Lima, it soon had a system of electric-powered trolleys.

The country's fourth city, Cuzco, was a further contrast, lacking the modern amenities especially evident in Lima-Callao, and the prosperity and cleanliness of Arequipa. A more primitive city and region, seemingly lost in time, Cuzco still had great stone walls and plazas bequeathed by the Inca, though not much else. While small workshops and some modest textile enterprises took root here, it remained largely detached from the broader commercial world. Few foreigners visited, though in 1911 an American named Hiram Bingham did arrive, and asked locals to show him the abandoned Incan fortress at Machu Picchu.

Intellectual and Artistic Pursuits

The name Hiram Bingham is of course famously associated with Machu Picchu, as he spent the rest of his life promoting and studying the site that he had supposedly "discovered." Though an amateur archaeologist, whose theories proved badly flawed, Bingham's curiosity reflected an important feature of the era; in the mid-nineteenth century geographic societies emerged, and exploration of the "unknown" continents flourished. Peru, with its remote valleys amidst the magnificent Andes, attracted its share of international attention.

One of the first geographers of note was himself Peruvian. Mateo Paz Soldán, an Arequipeño born of wealthy parents, spent much of his life absorbed in curiosity about land, surveying, mathematics, and astronomy. He traveled widely, and accumulated an important collection of records, data, and documents about the national territory. In 1865 he published the first significant topographical map of the country and, after his death, his brother compiled much of his opus and folded it into a tome titled *El Diccionario geográfico del Perú* (1877). That brother, Mariano Felipe, studied both geography and history. With Mateo he published *El Atlas geográfico del Perú* (1861), during a time when he was Ramón Castilla's director of public works and busy overseeing construction of Lima's enormous penitentiary. But it was in history that Mariano Felipe left his larger mark. Writing a three-volume study of Peru, he was the first to synthesize and reflect upon the early national period, finding glimmers of hope amidst the chaotic 1820s and 1830s while justifying the break with Spain.

Though no formal geographic society formed in Peru, fraternal (male-only) organizations connected to various emerging professions proliferated in the 1860s and 1870s. Reflecting the need for engineers with the advent of large mining operations and the railroad, the National School of Engineering was established in 1876. A graduate of Hipólito Unanue's late colonial medical school, José Casimiro Ulloa was integral to the formation of the *Sociedad Médica de Lima* (Lima Medical Society) in 1864. The Society intermittently published *La Gaceta médica*, Peru's first medical journal. Casimiro Ulloa also helped introduce psychological care in Peru, as director of a major hospital, and affiliated his nation with the International Red Cross in 1879.

The new field of photography began with the arrival of a Frenchman, Eugène Courret, in 1860. With a brother, Courret opened a studio in Lima years later, but was financially secure enough that he did not let portrait photographs of the rich consume his time. He avidly photographed buildings and streets in Lima, before focusing on the destruction and aftermath of the war with Chile. Unfortunately, neither the hinterlands nor highlands held much appeal to Courret, but by the time his studio went bankrupt in the mid-1930s it had amassed nearly 150,000 negatives, many of which eventually ended up in the National Library (see figure 4.2 for an example).

Other inquisitive foreigners did venture throughout Peru in an attempt to grasp the significance of its remarkable natural endowments. Though Charles Darwin neglected the country in his famous regional travels, British botanist Richard Spruce spent years studying flora in Amazonia. German photographer Charles Kroehle wandered among the lowlands' peoples a decade later, providing scholars with important turn-of-the-century ethnographic material. In the early twentieth century several European and U.S. universities established various scientific missions. Harvard University, for example, built an astronomical observatory in the southern highlands.

Ironically, the writings of a man who never saw Peru are what shaped much of the industrialized world's late-nineteenth-century perception of it. New Englander William Prescott penned epic historical accounts of the Spanish and their conquests. His *A History of the Conquest of Peru* (1847) was widely read in the United States and Europe over subsequent decades, and it familiarized three generations with the names *Pizarro* and *Atahualpa*, as well as stimulating much general interest in the ancient Inca and fate of their descendants into the early twentieth century.

As with many fields of intellectual inquiry, artistic expression for the period reflects both foreign and domestic influence. The relative ease of international travel (at least for the rich), and better means of communication, increased the natural interplay of the well-established European art scene with that of Lima. Yet despite this, Peruvian art all but missed the Romantic Age; most mid-century artists were still neoclassical. Besides religious art, the other financially viable exercise was painting portraits of the

Figure 6.1. Daniel Hernández's *La muerte de Socrates* (1872) is an important work in the classical tradition. The great teacher is dying, yet the young man to the right—with a facial resemblance to Hernández himself—is clearly ambivalent. Trained in Europe, later in life Hernández helped found Peru's Fine Arts Academy and pioneer distinctively local artistic themes and expression.
Source: Museo del Banco Central de Reserva del Perú

rich. Francisco Masías, raised in the northern town of Piura and trained in French and Italian academies, made a comfortable living for himself doing this into the 1870s. But in death, alas, the wealthy favored the Europeans. Limeño elite contracted Italian sculptors, and imported marble sarcophagi and statuary for their final resting places in the Presbítero Maestro Matías cemetery. Other major sculptures in Lima were also of mostly Italian origin. The great bronze equestrian work of Simón Bolívar, installed in the early 1860s and still standing in front of Congress, is the work of Adamo Tadolini.

Despite the rising artistic interface with Europe, Peruvians also largely bypassed Impressionism. Teófilo Castillo was the noteworthy exception, though he came later and used sharper lines than true Impressionists. In 1906, he opened a small studio in Lima's Barrios Altos district, from where he also taught classes. After reading Palma (see below), he painted a series of colorful paintings of Limeño religious processions. Albert Lynch, born in Germany to a Peruvian father, studied art in Paris and also flirted with Impressionism, favoring the mediums of watercolor and gum-like gouache over oil in his many portraits of women.

The Writings of Ricardo Palma

Despite the relatively limited and somewhat imitative (of European) cultural life of the mid-nineteenth century, the epoch did produce one of Peru's most illustrious literary figures in Ricardo Palma. Born to a provincial family who moved to Lima, Palma received an excellent education with other sons of the rich at the Colegio de San Carlos. As a young man he obtained a bureaucratic position in the Ministry of the Navy, and thereafter engaged in politics. Writing for the upstart newspaper El Comercio, he networked with various competing political factions, but eventually ended up on the wrong side of an anti-Castilla plot in 1860. Exiled to Chile, Palma ventured to Europe and then to the United States. He returned years later and secured a seat in the senate, pressing for new schools and educational reform. When he left off politics in 1872, he turned his attention solely to writing.

In the same year the first edition of his famous Tradiciones appeared. Repeatedly revised and expanded over the next four decades, this multi-volume project is the classic literary work of national-period Peru. It is an unusual blend of history and fiction, with countless short stories, many culled from oral tradition. Palma provides masterful insight into mid-nineteenth-century life and thought, and offers an engaging prose that matches that of many great contemporary novelists. There is hardly anything that is not covered in Tradiciones, from food and folklore, to festivals, customs, medicinal practices, and religious beliefs. Observant, Palma was an insightful historian. His writing engendered a national pride at a time when nationalism was just beginning to take root.

One of the enticing features of Tradiciones is its periodic blend of reality with the supernatural. Admittedly, many of its mysterious elements are of a religious orientation, but there is a bit of Halloween-ish spookiness in select passages. Many of these fables have wrongdoers punished. Such is the brief account of the Cuzco noble, who lives in the "Admiral's House" and beats anyone who dares to take water from his fountain. When he is later found hanging from gallows in his front yard, the culprits are revealed as none other than goblins! Widely known among Peruvians is the short yarn titled La procesión de ánimas de San Agustín. When a strong-willed judge wrongly convicts a Native boy of murder, he is visited in the middle of the night by this chanting column, dressed in monks' habits and carrying candles. He is terrified to discover only skulls under the hoods—they are the walking dead of purgatory.

Palma's Tradiciones is most readily associated with Lima's Miraflores neighborhood, where the author lived. Unfortunately, when the Chileans attacked the capital from the south during the War of the Pacific, this area was badly damaged and Palma's house completely destroyed. In it was one of the finest libraries and archives in Peru, with hundreds of colonial documents lost to posterity. After the war, Palma became director of the new National Library, and served in this capacity for twenty-eight years. By the time he retired in 1912, he had made the library one of Latin America's very best. He even befriended a Chilean president, and convinced him to help collect and return thousands of books from his own home. Though proudly Peruvian, Palma also accepted membership in Spain's Royal Academy, and traveled to Madrid in 1892 to honor the 400th anniversary of Columbus's voyage. He networked with many great literary figures of his age, and encouraged Spaniards to embrace their former colonials in cultural life. He inspired his son Clemente to become a writer, too, in a haunting style similar to that of Edgar Allen Poe.

One of Clemente Palma's literary friends was José Santos Chocano, a prolific writer who ultimately became one of Peru's most celebrated poets. Born in Lima in 1875 to an army officer and a devout and devoted mother, Chocano as a youth endured the trauma of the Pacific War (his family's home was

Figure 6.2. The Ricardo Palma house in Miraflores, today a museum with updated interpretative displays—it underwent renovation during the Covid pandemic. This is the house where Palma resided after the War of the Pacific. He died here in October 1919, his large funeral marked by the solemn pageantry befitting a national hero. Palma is buried in Presbítero Maestro cemetery.
Photo by the author

just two blocks from the National Palace). He was thus predictably imbued with a fiery patriotism, augmented by his own combative personality. As a young man he pursued a career in journalism, penning articles critical of the Cáceres dictatorship under the pseudonym *Juvenal*. Arrested, he languished in prison for several months, fearing execution. The Revolution of 1895 saved him, and he suddenly became an insider, working for and promoting Piérola's government. He also published his first poems, including long and patriotic works such as *La Epopeya del Morro* (Epic of the Knoll—1896), a romanticized tribute to General Bolognesi and his troops. His passionate verse appealed to Spanish-reading Peruvians and—even more than Palma's works—fed their budding nationalism.

Women Seek Basic Rights

The late nineteenth century saw the tepid beginnings of women's emancipation in Peru. A regimen of severe limitations began to at least be questioned, though Peru's hyper-conservative society was even farther behind that of other Latin cultures in creating space for women to think and work. Directly challenging the basic dual premise, that women were to fulfill a maternal role and otherwise remain naturally subservient to men, was still unacceptable; hardly anyone was yet envisioning women as professionals, let alone as participants in political affairs.

Still, among the Limeño upper class there were stirrings. An Argentine couple living in the center of the city provided an important forum for educated, wealthy women. Juan and Manuela Gorriti routinely held *tertulias* (drinking socials) in their home, with Ricardo Palma often among the guests. These gatherings revolved around literature, with a clique of aspiring female writers in regular attendance. Many became involved with *El Album*, the first magazine written specifically for women. When the prosperous Gorritis funded Peru's first private primary girls' school, it further raised the specter of change.

Among the Gorritis' regular attendees was Mercedes Cabella de Carbonera, the most visionary and outspoken of the group. Writing newspaper articles under a pseudonym, Cabella called for greater female access to education, the opening up of the professions and, later, the right to vote. She was decidedly ahead of her time. On one occasion, a unit from the National Guard tried to burn her house down. Cabella was one of the first women to publish novels in Peru, penning works in rapid succession in the 1880s and 1890s. Her boldness and courage inspired others.

Another outspoken pioneer was Clorinda Matto de Turner, who revived the Gorritis' tradition of literary socials in her own home after the disruptive War of the Pacific. In her first novel, *Aves sin nido* (*Nestless Birds*, 1889), she criticized the Catholic Church and society's marginalization of indigenous peoples—a position decades ahead of the *Indignismo* (celebration of things native) of the mid-twentieth century. Purchasing a printing press, she began a modest tabloid called *Los Andes*, though by supporting Cáceres she ran afoul of political currents and was eventually forced into exile.

More cautious in her approach, but also highly effective, was Teresa González de Fanning. Born to wealthy landowners in the north, González received private tutoring and a solid education in her youth. She married a naval officer, Juan Fanning, who thereafter maintained the inherited estate. Despite their liberal proclivities, the Fannings practiced a traditional, feudal-like dominion over their workers—which eventually triggered a revolt. As they lost control of their land and relocated to Lima, their two children fell ill and died. Juan himself then perished in the War of the Pacific, mortally wounded in the battle at Miraflores. Tragedy could have thus easily broken and silenced Teresa.

Instead, González de Fanning became exceedingly active as a middle-aged widow. As the war wound down, she raised funds and helped manage hospitals tending to wounded veterans. She then solicited donations and organized the first private secondary school for girls, the Liceo Fanning. In her administration of the school she insisted that young girls be afforded an education equal to that received by males. In content, she emphasized practical disciplines of a liberal and quasi-secular vein (though like all the early advocates of women's rights in Lima, she adhered faithfully to Catholicism). Many of Peru's most prominent women of the early twentieth century were educated at Liceo Fanning.

Among the school's graduates was Laura Rodríguez Dulante, whose mental dexterity prompted her well-to-do parents to lobby for her admission into San Marcos University. She became one of the university's first female students and, though all kinds of barriers were set up against her, she passed special examinations and obtained entrance into Peru's School of Medicine, which by this time had been expanded and incorporated into San Marcos. Again excelling, in 1900 she became the nation's first female medical doctor, though social dictates all but required that her specialty be gynecology. She taught for many years at Liceo Fanning, and later trained nurses, dictating a rigorous study of anatomy and physiology. Rodríguez greatly outpaced her time; Peru would not produce its second female doctor for over two decades.

Figure 6.3. The Liceo Fanning is long gone—even the street where it was located no longer exists (both the building and short street were near present-day Plaza San Martín, and were lost in 1920s' urban renewal). Its legacy, however, remains. The visionary school produced a first generation of educated women who initiated the slow, still ongoing process toward gender equality.
Source: Museo Metropolitano de Lima

Other determined women pressed their way into San Marcos. Trinidad Enriquez earned a degree in law, though discrimination prevented her from practicing as an attorney. Margarita Práxedes Muñoz was the first Peruvian woman to earn a university degree in the sciences. Afterward she migrated to Santiago de Chile, where women enjoyed greater socioeconomic mobility. Assisting in instruction at the School of Medicine, she later worked in clinical psychiatry, even while reading prolifically. Her autobiographic novel, *La Evolución de Paulina* (1893), exudes the Positivist thought that so influenced her, Matto, Cabella, and others.

The accomplishments of these and other pathbreaking women in the late nineteenth century were themselves long neglected in the historical record, but have been fortuitously rediscovered in recent years. Given the nearly insurmountable odds women faced, each triumph came only through great perseverance, and often at considerable personal cost. The barriers that restricted Peruvian women were at least finally being challenged in the late nineteenth century, however, if not fully breeched. The groundwork was laid for greater gains in the future.

CHAPTER SEVEN

The Age of Leguía

The Aristocratic Republic, around the turn of the century, saw Peru enjoy relatively stable government while experiencing significant economic diversification and growth. A powerful clique of Limeño elite effectively held the reins of power, but both in the capital and in select provincial cities a budding middle class was beginning to insist on having a political voice. Entrepreneurial professionals found a sympathetic figure in Augusto Leguía, the Minister of the Treasury whom President José Pardo had supported as his successor in 1908. Leguía would dominate Peruvian political life for much of the next two decades.

The Politics of Change

As a youth, Leguía studied at the same British-run private school in Valparaíso, Chile, that had educated a young González Prada. He mastered the English language—a rarity for Peruvians in the late nineteenth century. Leguía worked at a Lima trading house after his schooling, and fought fleetingly in the capital's defense during the War of the Pacific. With the postwar economy in tatters, he left his homeland for an extended time, carving out a prosperous career in the United States at the New York Life Insurance Company. He was instrumental in bringing the insurance business to the Andean region, and became a millionaire in the process. He married into additional money after his return to Lima. He traded again in commodities, most notably sugar, before his stint in Pardo's cabinet.

Leguía's transition into the presidency was rocky. The rival Democratic Party backed a failed coup attempt in May 1908. Another competing faction kidnapped the new executive on an eventful day one year later. Hauled to the base of the statue of Simón Bolívar, in front of congress, Leguía was ordered at gunpoint to resign. He refused to do so, even as a detachment of police arrived to confront his abductors. In the gun battle that ensued dozens were killed, but Leguía escaped unharmed. The incident appeared to have convinced him that a firm hand must be used to govern in such an intractable environment.

Leguía subsequently attempted to apply *la mano dura*, but with little success. It was a difficult time to rule. Like elsewhere in Latin America, political life was opening up to new societal forces and players. The nation's first labor organizations were forming, and strikes periodically erupted, especially in Lima's multiple textile factories. An anarchist-infused movement surfaced with the founding of the *Federación Obrera Regional* (Regional Workers Federation). Students at San Marcos, now numbering over a thousand, were taking an interest in politics too. After the government meted out harsh penalties to the president's 1909 abductors, a student-led protest movement arose and had its own violent confrontations with the police.

Despite some strong-arm leanings, in its policymaking Leguía's first administration was hesitant, even disengaged. While he initiated a few reforms, such as a law that held employers liable for many types of work-related injuries, Leguía still practiced very limited government, believing as a businessman that laissez-faire economics would pull the nation out of its backwardness. He spent many long days at the racetrack, gambling on steeds and socializing with the upper class. He liked and favored foreigners, especially Americans. The Seventh Day Adventists began Lake Titicaca–area missions under his watch, as led by Michiganders Ana and Ferdinand Stahl. The Young Men's Christian Association (YMCA) was also welcomed into Peru, and Leguía made an Indiana Hoosier, Harry E. Bard, his de facto Minister of Education.

A Briton living in Lima at the time observed: "The average native is by no means as dull or stupid as some people imagine, nor as dense intellectually as several writers upon Peru have audaciously asserted."[1] In keeping with this implicitly racist assessment, reflecting the sentiments of many white foreigners, Bard ordered that English be taught in public elementary schools in the highlands—an unfathomable policy supported (at least on paper) by Leguía. In contrast, Stahl and his missionaries launched many Native-language

---

1. Percy Fackle Martin, *Peru of the Twentieth Century* (London: E. Arnold, 1911), 98.

schools in the southeast, with considerable success, especially among the Aymara-speaking peoples.

In economics, the administration played one particularly adept hand. Utilizing an obscure clause in the Grace Contract, it facilitated increased domestic usage of guano, engendering gratitude from especially the landed elite. Sugar and cotton plantations along the northern coast particularly prospered, and exports of these two commodities soared. There was another, darker reason for this success, however: the continued use of slave-like imported Asian labor. Alongside Chinese coolies, the coastal estates began to use Japanese worker-slaves. The first Japanese immigrants arrived in 1899, many from the impoverished interior of Okinawa, with most signing four-year contracts of indentured servitude. But although subjected to often heartless abuse, the Japanese persevered. Their numbers soared. By 1923 eighteen thousand had arrived, 89 percent of them adult males. Many of these married poor Peruvian females, yet still rigorously sought to preserve their language and distinctive cultural traditions. In time, unlike the brutalized (and largely unmarried) Chinese, the Japanese-Peruvian community would come to prosper.

By 1912, however, much of Peru's underclasses were seeing little in the way of progress. In Lima, always the political and economic heart of the nation, disparate groups yearned for a faster pace of change. They turned to an unlikely champion: a nitrate-mining magnet named Guillermo Billinghurst. Of English extraction and born in Arica—the southern port town seized by Chile during the Pacific War—Billinghurst was a bit of a demagogue. Outspoken and polemical, he led a revived Democratic Party which made populist appeals to the masses. For the first time in Peruvian history thousands attended open-air political rallies.

Once in office, Billinghurst accelerated the pace of reforms, especially with regard to labor. These efforts, coupled with his unconventional, bombastic personality, unsettled the aristocracy. With their blessing, in 1914 the army ousted the president, then transitioned the government into the hands of the *Civilista* leader, José Pardo. Pardo's return to office seemed to augur stability, but myriad forces tugged at Peru's body politic and pulled it in different directions. Ironically, persistent calls for labor reform compelled Pardo to implement many of the very initiatives that had inspired the rich to oppose Billinghurst. Various safety regulations were legislated (though enforcement remained erratic), and child labor was finally abolished. Pardo mandated a controversial minimum wage law, though he ignored calls for rent and price controls. The long-sought eight-hour workday was granted in January 1919, when an enormous general strike unsettled the capital, and news of a near-revolution in Buenos Aires spawned fear among the upper class.

Pardo's second government pleased no one. The aristocracy was unhappy, and the underclasses still dissatisfied. Periodic general strikes shut down Lima. Some, such as those in May 1919, were marred by excessive police violence. After Catholic mobs attacked the Seventh-Day Adventist missions in the southeast, the government passed a religious tolerance law (at the urging of the United States) that distressed devout Catholics and upset the Church. Student demands for university reform went unanswered, triggering resentment among the intelligentsia toward the political class.

The rupture between intellectuals and the establishment is particularly significant. In time, it gave rise to combative ideologies of the far left and right. One of the most important figures in both political and intellectual life at the time, though now somewhat lost to history, was José de la Riva Agüero. Riva Agüero was born to one of the nation's oldest and richest families, his colonial childhood home just three blocks from the National Palace. Given the best in a Catholic education, he entered San Marcos University with a disciplined mind, and wrote a brilliant treatise on Peruvian history for his doctoral dissertation. Teaching at San Marcos, he led the student strike against Leguía (for the amnesty of his opponents). Then, a still-young Riva Agüero undertook an unusual adventure: he trekked through the south, east into Bolivia, and back across the highlands, often traveling on foot or by mule. His subsequent *Paisajes Peruanos* (*Peruvian Landscapes*) provides an insightful account of the remote countryside. When he returned to San Marcos, Riva Agüero taught classes on the ancient Inca, and advocated the incorporation of native society into national life.

José de la Riva Agüero, like many of those around him, is not easily pigeonholed by political grouping or ideology. Part of what has been called the Generation of 1900, he and other disenchanted intellectuals wearied of the constant infighting of the Limeño political class. Many helped form an upstart National Democratic Party in the mid-1910s, though this effort at creating a new path ultimately floundered. Riva Agüero joined others in launching Peru's first private institution of higher education, the Catholic University of Lima, in 1917. This later evolved into the Pontifical Catholic University of Peru, and in time came to rival San Marcos as the country's premier educational institution.

Riva Agüero despised Augusto Leguía who—during the Pardo administration—had gone overseas, reengaging his international business interests. As Pardo's second term wound down, the Civilistas splintered, even as many conservative rich sought to revive an elitist party and install

Figure 7.1. The Leguía government built this house for an elderly General Cáceres, who died before he was able to occupy it (the mural above the portico shows Leguía handing Cáceres the deed). Today it serves as the home of the *Sociedad Fundadores de Independencía*, a club for those who can trace their family lineage back to the struggle for independence.
Photo by the author

an anti-reformist administration. A conglomeration of popular and middle-class forces would have none of this, and looked for an alternative. They found it, somewhat surprisingly, in a returning Leguía. Winning a decisive electoral mandate, the businessman prepared to again wear the presidential sash. He allied with Andrés Cáceres, the now elderly army general and war hero, who forcibly seized power on his behalf when rumors of an intended counter-coup emerged. Now, it was Riva Agüero (among many others) who headed overseas to Europe. Leguía's time was at hand.

The Leguian Oncenio

For eleven years, from 1919 to 1930, Augusto Leguía held the reins of power—the era thus known as the *Oncenio*. The minefield that Peruvian politics had become gave no quarter to the returning magistrate. For his part, he was a different political agent. Time in the United States in the 1910s had introduced him to progressivism, and he was now prepared to engage the state in social and economic matters for the betterment of society. One consistency in Leguía's personality, however, was the commitment to the firm hand: he would still brook no significant opposition.

Opposition was not slow in coming. San Marcos University was quickly evolving into a political machine, with a combustible mix of middle-class youth and contrarian intellectuals. Leguía largely answered demands for university reform, including quasi-autonomy (freedom from direct governmental oversight), but for many these changes were not enough. Students aligned with the rising workers movement pushed further labor demands, and assisted in organizing general strikes. Lima and the port of Callao were frequently shut down by these work stoppages, and a frustrated Leguía soon moved to curtail the university-empowered activism. He suspended classes—San Marcos was closed more than it was open between 1921 and 1925—and forced many faculty members into exile. Unruly students were given scholarships that also sent them overseas. Anarchists were arrested, often brutalized while in custody, and forcibly exiled.

The tensions that rocked Peru in these years were reflective of worldwide events. Although not directly involved in World War I, Latin America felt its aftershocks. Peruvian workers and anarchists found inspiration in the Russian Revolution. So too, the 1910–1920 political and social upheaval in Mexico seemed to many a harbinger of things to come. When Leguía produced a new constitution in 1920, it was keenly influenced by Mexico's longwinded 1917 social contract—featuring all kinds of promises with regard to education, labor, and social reform. He christened the era that of the *Patria Nueva* (New Fatherland). But as was almost always the case in Peruvian history, the gap between paper reforms and action was great. In some ways, things went backward. Leguía resorted to the old tributary system, exploiting indigenous peoples by obligating them to work for free on road construction projects (albeit with an objective of integrating native communities into the national economy). He disregarded his own constitution's rules on presidential terms, arranging for reelection twice.

The regime fostered goodwill in the early 1920s by endlessly celebrating Peru's independence. This was possible by marking the multiple centennials that fell within the 1921–1925 period courtesy of the convoluted break with Spain. Drawing on his international connections, Leguía solicited various gifts from foreign governments: Germany constructed a stately clock tower, France sent a miniature statue of liberty, and Italy provided an entirely new (albeit modest) museum of art. Spain built a Moorish arch, which was quietly torn down soon thereafter—anti-Spanish sentiments persisted, while some elite regarded the structure as an eyesore. Public squares saw myriad formal ceremonies, typically officiated by the president himself, and many informal late-night festivities attended by Peruvians across lines of class and race.

Public celebrations could only go so far in cloaking great socioeconomic challenges. The commodities boomlet of the world war years had made the upper class even richer, but little progress had been made in the 1910s otherwise. Now, Leguía initiated extensive public works. He expanded Peru's railroad network by nearly 40 percent, improved its ports—especially at Callao, undertook the nation's first major irrigation projects, and laid ten thousand miles of new roads (with the coerced help of the indigenous population). The government bureaucracy trebled, tax revenue doubled, and debt soared. Massive loans from New York banks kept the statist project afloat for a decade. Foreign mining interests expanded, but paid very little in the way of taxes. A new lead smelter was built in Oroya, 110 miles northeast of Lima, aggravating already serious environmental damage. The capital benefited greatly from increased commerce and the government's bureaucratic rise, its population surging to nearly four hundred thousand by 1930.

During the Oncenio, Leguía's government addressed longstanding border disputes with Peru's neighbors. Two of these were resolved. In the northwest, the rubber boom had, years earlier, created great tension with Colombia, as the jungle-covered Amazonian region never had clearly demarcated boundaries. By the 1920s, rubber tapping having greatly subsided, the region was of little economic use. Leguía's business-trained mind told him that ending the tussle with Colombia was more helpful than worrying about lost tracts of marginal land. Strongly encouraged to do so by the United States, he ceded an area the size of the state of Iowa to the Colombians. The agreement was unpopular with nationalistic army officers, and also drew much public scorn when it was finally implemented near the close of the decade.

The second feud was with Chile. Much more serious, on several occasions it threatened to trigger another war. Under the Treaty of Ancón, that ended the 1879–1883 conflict, Peru ceded the province of Tarapacá, while transferring two others—Arica and Tacna—into a ten-year Chilean stewardship. After this period, locals were to vote by plebiscite in order to determine their national identity. Chile rained money and improvements upon the provinces, but when it was apparent that they would still vote to return to Peru, the occupiers evaded and then cancelled the required vote. By the early twentieth century the Chilean presence became militarized and abusive, with local newspapers closed and civil society heavily censored. Outspoken locals were arrested and beaten, their homes sacked, and their lives threatened. In 1921, ten thousand *Taceños* (nearly the entire provincial town) conducted a silent march to protest the occupation.

In 1922 the United States offered to arbitrate the dispute, and both parties accepted. Much of Leguía's foreign policy was aimed at retrieving Tacna-Arica (the settlement with Colombia must be understood in this context). A 1925 U.S. mission, led by famed army general John "Blackjack" Pershing, found conditions impossible for the long-delayed plebiscite. It also recognized the duplicitous nature of Chile's policies and the presence of paramilitary forces, who were by now selectively assassinating resistant locals. Leguía thus opted for direct talks, and personally facilitated their advancement. Eventually he engineered a partition, whereby Peru regained Tacna but permanently lost Arica. Though again much criticized for this, it was not an unreasonable compromise; it ended nearly a half-century of animosities.

Settled territorial disputes and noteworthy state-led economic growth suggest relative success by the Leguía government, but—as with Pardo and Billinghurst in the 1910s—no one was satisfied. Leguía's policies resonated most with the middle class, which fared well in the 1920s as it filled the administrative jobs created by his government. The aristocracy, however, was alienated by a rising state, and by the usurpation of their long-dominant political parties. Labor endured significant repression, especially its anarchist-influenced wing, and bemoaned its political limitations. Faculty and students at San Marcos were sullen and angry.

When the U.S. stock market crashed in 1929, triggering the outset of a worldwide depression, Augusto Leguía had few true friends. He was hounded from office and placed in a dingy cell in the national prison, ironically among many of his own long-incarcerated opponents. Suffering a prostate infection, he lost weight, his health failing him. Small of stature and always physically frail, he died in a naval hospital weeks later, his body reduced to a mere seventy pounds. Embittered Civilistas ransacked his house, destroying in the process invaluable archival records about his government.

Those documents would have helped historians understand and reconstruct this important period. Augusto Leguía is one of Peru's most controversial leaders. Was he a dictator, or did he lay the foundations for economic and political modernization—as he himself believed? That the old order of elitist political parties had passed, there is no doubt, but Leguía's role in this transition can be debated (much suggests that it would have happened without him). Whatever the ultimate place of the Oncenio, by the late twenties new ideas came forth, especially from Manuel González Prada (see chapter 5), and were now bearing fruit. Peru was entering a distinctive era, still contentious, but with only two major camps and sharper ideological lines.

The Rise of the Peruvian Left

The shadow of the contrarian González Prada looms large in the early twentieth century, enveloping a generation of youth who embraced the outspoken thinker's rebellious spirit and questioned the domineering conservatism of the aristocracy. Indebted to González Prada are the two luminaries of the Peruvian political left: José Carlos Mariátegui and Victor Raúl Haya de la Torre. Both knew the aged self-professed anarchist well. Early in the Oncenio, González Prada encouraged students to create "Popular Universities," whereby freely offered teach-ins would educate the underclass to facilitate social and political change. Both men edited *Claridad*, the journal of the Popular Universities movement.

José Carlos Mariátegui is one of Latin America's most famous intellectuals. The much-celebrated writer and activist had an empathy-evoking early life. Born in the provinces, he suffered acute poverty. His father abandoned his mother and two siblings when he was very young. He likely suffered from tuberculosis in childhood. At age eight, while playing in a schoolyard, he ripped open his left knee. Slight and sickly, Mariátegui almost died from the injury, spending much of the next four years bedridden, primarily in a French-run children's sanatorium in Lima.

Mentally inquisitive, young José read prolifically. He mastered French; he loved to write. Working at a newspaper office as a teenager, he befriended reporters and columnists, among them González Prada. Maturing into adulthood, he socialized with a cadre of bohemian social contrarians. When a group of these friends proposed performing a midnight dance in Lima's illustrious Presbítero Maestro Matías cemetery, the elite were aghast—and the authorities prosecuted. Mariátegui penned a scathing critique on the false morality of the rich. His *La Razón* magazine further antagonized the powerful, and Leguía's government arranged for the writer to spend some time in Europe, providing him with a travel scholarship.

The Leguía regime's practice of sending troublemakers to Europe was arguably ill-advised (the United States would have surely been a safer ideological bet). As with his mentor, Mariátegui fully discovered anarchism and socialism on the continent—and especially in the cities of northern Italy, where he also married, and fathered children. In 1923 he returned to Lima, engaged in the Popular Universities project, and again befriended cultural bohemians. The Mariátegui house on Washington Street became the premiere venue of Peru's counterculture. From here, Mariátegui launched and edited *Amauta*, an avant-garde journal of both political and cultural ideas. Here, too, he wrote his *Seven Interpretative Essays on Peruvian Reality* (1928), the definitive expression of his political analysis and a classic in leftist political thought.

For Mariátegui, the move toward socialism was both a political and cultural journey. It could not be purely materialist, or follow the lifeless dictates of a formula. Mariátegui believed that a natural and organic socialism (or communism—he blended the two concepts) would emerge in Peru. He also believed that it would be bequeathed by the brilliance of the native culture, and would have distinctively American origins and features. Like González Prada, Mariátegui lauded the Inca and their descendants. More than his mentor, he explored their language and ways, albeit only in measured doses. *Amauta*'s representations of the Incan imperial system are rather romanticized, and at times exude considerable historical and anthropological naïveté.

In 1928 Mariátegui and his associates organized the Socialist Party of Peru, which in turn began to build connections with labor unions. Increasingly harried by the authorities—periodically placed under house arrest and occasionally thrown into jail—the thinker left on an extended tour of southern Latin America. His always precarious health deteriorated further. He died just a couple of years later at age thirty-five, having made a rich contribution to Latin American political theory. Thousands, both workers and students, attended his funeral. Soon thereafter, his Socialist party redefined itself as Communist (some ties with the Soviet Union having already been made), and formally associated with the Communist International.

If Mariátegui was the creative mind of the Peruvian Left, Víctor Raúl Haya de la Torre was its organizational motor—a man of boundless energy who spent a lifetime searching for political change. Born in Trujillo to middle-class parents, his father a newspaper publisher and one-time accountant for a sugar plantation, Víctor Raúl received an excellent private education before his matriculation into San Marcos. Ambition defined him. He rose into the leadership of the student federation, and engineered support for Leguía's 1919 return before reversing course in his nascent dictatorship. Deported in 1923, Haya de la Torre began to travel the world. Most influential was his time in postrevolutionary Russia and Mexico, though he enrolled at London's School of Economics and also traversed much of the United States. In Mexico City and Paris, he planned revolution for Peru, and called upon all of Latin (or what he called Indo-) America to reject both Yankee Imperialism and Soviet dictates. He and a small cohort of supporters created the American Popular Revolutionary Alliance (APRA, with *Apristas* as its adherents), a political movement that would, in theory, transcend national borders.

Figure 7.2. The grave of José Carlos Maríategui, who is ironically buried in Presbítero Maestro, cemetery of the rich (though away from the main section). Even in death Maríategui followed the lead of González Prada. Like that of his mentor, the tombstone is in the shape of a mountain—symbolizing the Andes and the ancient Incan culture that both men so admired.
Photo by the author

Important in the lives of both Haya de la Torre and Mariátegui was the charismatic and gifted Magda Portal. Born of modest means in Barranco, along the coast, Portal obtained admission to the University of San Marcos and became active in the student movement repressed by Leguía. She wrote eloquent poems, and drew other young women into the budding counterculture, while later helping Mariátegui edit and publish *Amauta*. Obliged to go into exile, she was with Haya de la Torre in Mexico and joined the newly created APRA. This decision came as a great disappointment to Mariátegui, who had hoped that she would unite with his Socialists. At one time, Portal and Mariátegui may have been lovers.

The divide between the upstart Socialists and Apristas widened rapidly. Strong personalities were at play in this process as much as ideas. At first it seemed that the more famous Mariátegui would watch his party ascend—he once dismissed APRA as nothing more than a fancy name on stylish letterhead. Battling for the loyalty of Magda Portal and others spawned deep distrust. But as Mariátegui's health failed him, it was Haya de la Torre who obtained political stardom. While living in Berlin in 1929–1931, he saw the early rumblings of fascism and, unlike Mariátegui, was not entirely repulsed by it. He perceived the benefits of promoting a cult of personality around himself.

Haya de la Torre's abundant self-confidence helped make him a political lightning rod, and when he finally returned to Lima in 1931 he filled the old colonial bullring, rousing twenty thousand with impassioned oratory. Speaking just before him to the massive crowd (this was one of the first uses of amplifying microphones in Peru) was none other than Magda Portal. Great excitement gripped the mostly youthful political outsiders of the capital. Mariátegui was dead by now, and proponents for sociopolitical change began to orbit around Haya de la Torre. His APRA Party would play a dramatic role in Peruvian politics over the next several decades.

CHAPTER EIGHT

The Challenge of Mass Politics

Many political forces were at play in Peru in the early twentieth century, ensuring that the nation would have a tumultuous mid-century history. A multitude of actors and factions coalesced to bring down the Leguía government in 1930, but then frayed after the strongman had been toppled. The left, centered in Haya de la Torre's APRA movement, was most notably in ascent.

The coalition that ousted Leguía predictably included army units, the majority of which had gathered around Luis Miguel Sánchez Cerro, an officer stationed in Arequipa. Sánchez Cerro, though only forty years old, had already lived a full and reckless life. Born to a low-level government official in the far north, with at least some native ancestry, he had fought audaciously in the 1914 overthrow of Guillermo Billinghurst, suffering serious injuries as he led his charging men into the National Palace. He had survived two duels, loved to gamble, engaged in many amorous adventures, and in sum "lived for the day," as a worldly man who did little in the way of thoughtful calculation or careful planning. He had also led an early anti-Leguía insurrection that failed, landing him briefly in jail and then into exile to Benito Mussolini's Italy where he underwent further military training.

After the dictator-president's ousting, Sánchez Cerro arranged for a grand entrance into the capital, clearly coveting the presidency for himself. But as he motorcaded into central Lima, the wealthy were appalled by what they beheld—a wiry, dark-skinned "Indian." In contrast, the lieutenant colonel received considerable adulation from the underclass. When he spoke on the radio, he used vernacular wording and idiomatic phrases that convinced "average" Peruvians he was one of them. Sánchez Cerro was the first politician to truly use radio to great effect—proving far more adept at it than the aloof and formal Leguía. He was the first man (besides Bolivian-based Santa Cruz) with native-descended darker skin to hold the presidency.

Unfolding Civil Strife

At the time Sánchez Cerro arrived in Lima, Peru was entering the perfect storm. The aftershocks of the 1929 stock market crash had rippled through the global economy and commodity prices were plummeting. Unemployment soared, and the specter of hunger overshadowed much of especially rural Peru. Fascism continued to rise in Europe, while a broad disillusionment with liberal democracy slowly spread throughout the West. If there was ever a difficult time to govern, this was it. The fall of Leguía unleashed previously seething popular forces. The elitist parties of the late nineteenth century were now past, and Peru was in uncharted political waters. At first, it seemed that popular expectations could only be met through elections. To the uneasiness of the elite, Sánchez Cerro clearly had mass appeal. Yet the alternative was Haya de la Torre's APRA, which frightened the rich even more, with its anti-imperialist and Marxist-infused rhetoric.

Though Peru had experienced some popular mobilization in the 1910s, nothing resembled what transpired in mid-1931, when both Sánchez Cerro and Haya de la Torre used microphones, speakers, and periodic radio broadcasts to play to large crowds. Both men traversed much of the country in the weeks preceding the October election, with new rules and oversight allowing for broad voter participation. In all of Peru's previous contests, at best only low tens of thousands of citizens had cast ballots; in 1931, several hundred thousand adult males went to the polls in what was a reasonably clean contest. Though few native villagers engaged in the process, secondary cities saw rallies and incendiary rhetoric draw enthusiastic responses.

Ironically, both men's platforms proposed similar agendas. Both spoke of a need to develop the interior and incorporate indigenous Peruvians into the nation-building project. The far north and Arequipa-centered south leaned toward Sánchez Cerro, while the developed northern coast favored Haya de la Torre. APRA had a mix of appeal otherwise, though the small, mostly Limeño middle class was split. The aristocrats recognized Sánchez Cerro as (from their perspective) the proverbial lesser of two evils, and some even funded his campaign, though many favored centralist candidates who were easily marginalized in this crisis-ridden and polarized environment.

The final results favored Sánchez Cerro by roughly 39 to 27 percent, with other candidates splitting the remainder. It was most unfortunate that the votes took over a week to tabulate. Tensions ran high; street fights erupted in cities. Itching for power, the losing Haya de la Torre cried foul, claiming widespread fraud. The weight of the historical evidence suggests that, in fact, Sánchez Cerro won, though his robust margin might well have been cushioned by some manipulation. Acrimonious debate continued as congressional deputies gathered in an assembly that was also tasked to draft a new constitution. Once installed, the government received emergency powers, as the economy deteriorated further and strikes, led by the Communist Party–affiliated *Confederación General de Trabajadores Peruanos* (General Confederation of Peruvian Workers, or CGT), shook major industries.

Sánchez Cerro's regime aggressively suppressed labor and student unrest, shutting down San Marcos University, while its hostility with APRA deepened. On Christmas Eve, army troops raided APRA's headquarters in Trujillo, expecting (incorrectly) to find Haya de la Torre there. They killed and wounded several in the raid. A few weeks later, the government expelled the party's twenty-three-member congressional delegation, with many thereafter arrested and others fleeing overseas. In March, an enraged Aprista shot the president as he emerged from a parish church in Lima's upscale Miraflores neighborhood, gravely wounding him. In May, a pro-APRA revolt among sailors stunned the navy, though the *putsch* was quickly suppressed. Haya de la Torre was soon captured at a Lima safe house and jailed, the government hoping that the worst was over. But at this juncture, a bloody uprising took place in Haya de la Torre's hometown.

The details of what happened in Trujillo have long been contested, with many years of silence, and only a few polemical Aprista accounts published over several decades. The basic contours, however, are not in dispute. For months, resentment had been boiling up in Trujillo, ever since the army's botched attack on the local APRA headquarters. The capture of Haya de la Torre fueled rumors of his torture and pending execution, while repeated delays in launching a planned national uprising bred frustration. On July 7 impassioned Apristas attacked the local army barracks, where a vicious hours-long firefight resulted in over a dozen deaths on both sides. Parading thirty-five captured soldiers through the city, the attackers effectively compelled party leaders to commit to a rebellion. Haya de la Torre's brother, Agustín, took control of Trujillo, while Apristas soon erected barricades in the streets.

The government predictably rushed both troops and naval vessels up the coast, while a few airplanes began to indiscriminately bomb the small city of about forty-five thousand. Three days of fighting ensued, with Apristas falling back on a series of ad hoc barricades, while slipping into mind- and body-numbing fatigue and despair. Overwhelmed by numbers, low on ammunition, and no match for the high-caliber weapons aimed at them from land and sea, they surrendered. Shortly before they did so, however, some—perhaps rogue elements—massacred the thirty-five previously captured soldiers held in the town's jail. This cruel act triggered a merciless revenge: scores of Apristas and presumed supporters (though likely many innocents) were summarily tried by the army, taken out to the nearby ruins of Chan Chan, placed against its centuries-old adobe walls, and shot. Many more were killed extra-judicially, the final tally numbering in the hundreds. As time passed, many Apristas came to believe that thousands had died; among the military, lurid stories circulated of desecrated soldiers' corpses in Trujillo's jail.

The bodies of the soldiers were carried by naval vessel to Lima, and received in the city with great solemnity and fanfare. After a mass in the Cathedral, the dead were interred in Presbítero Maestro, the cemetery of the aristocracy. *El Comercio* and other pro-government newspapers reflected the conviction of the rich: that an insidious communist insurrection had been successfully crushed. Sentiment, especially among the well-to-do, turned solidly against APRA. The events in Trujillo set the stage for many more years of hatred and distrust.

Within APRA, rigorous persecution created a culture of martyrdom. Young and idealistic Apristas were jailed or driven into exile. Such was the case of novelist Ciro Alegría, whose works celebrated past and contemporary native society. Obliged to leave his homeland, Alegría gained literary acclaim while he lived overseas, in Chile, the United States, Cuba, and Puerto Rico. In custody, party members were often subjected to beatings and other forms of abuse. But in April 1933, one took his revenge: as Sánchez Cerro inspected twenty thousand volunteers for a possible war with Colombia, at the San Beatriz racetrack, Abelardo Mendoza sprinted toward the president's open touring car and fatally shot him. Plastered with gunfire by bodyguards, Mendoza died instantly, leaving many unanswered questions about the attack, and if behind it was an orchestrated conspiracy.

The Benavides Dictatorship

Shocked by the assassination, congress quickly followed the provisions of the newly minted constitution, which strangely did not provide for a vice presidency. The legislature thus elected Óscar Benavides into office—an army general who had played a significant role behind the scenes in Sánchez

Cerro's government (he had also been the lieutenant colonel's commanding officer on several occasions, including during the 1914 overthrow of Billinghurst). Benavides quickly opened communications with a newly released Haya de la Torre, likely prevented his execution in the immediate aftermath of the assassination, and briefly restrained the repression against APRA. Some saw in the sequence of these unlikely events the possibility that Benavides had played a nefarious role in Sánchez Cerro's untimely death; unfounded rumors flourished.

In fact, the low-key and levelheaded Benavides was caught amidst a whirlwind of political forces. He certainly had connections and support from the aristocracy, but a fascistic far right badgered him from the start. Many of these were Sánchez Cerro partisans, but others came from an ultra-Catholic political fringe that largely orbited around the well-known historian José de la Riva Agüero (see chapter 7). During his long exile in 1920s Europe, Riva Agüero had become enamored with the Mussolini regime in Italy. He served as Benavides's prime minister, and urged him to renew the crackdown on the Apristas. He resigned when Benavides signed into a law a measure legalizing divorce in 1934.

Broadly, the Benavides regime *was* decidedly on the right, linked to the still-powerful Catholic Church, the vested elite, and peppered with elements (mainly from within the army) that qualify as fascist. Benavides himself at times expressed an admiration for Mussolini, and later for Spain's Francisco Franco. He was well aware that Peru's neofascists were being assisted, funded, and encouraged by the Italian embassy in Lima, and he did nothing to stop this. His government welcomed an Italian military mission into Peru, and accepted Rome's technical assistance as it set up the beginnings of what would become the air force. Of course, fascism itself was a part-stirring of the masses, and segments of APRA also embraced a fascistic orientation and tone, especially in mass rallies and a glorifying personality cult of Haya de la Torre.

The multi-sided political life of 1930s Peru can be sliced in many ways, but at its core the issue of elite domination versus mass participation is still central. Benavides was acceptable to the rich; Haya de la Torre was not. APRA became even more of an anathema after May 1935, when an Aprista assassin gunned down Antonio Miró Quesada, the owner-editor of El Comercio, the nation's premiere newspaper long aligned with the upper class. The persecution of the "People's Party" again picked up. Women were now more frequently targeted; Magda Portal, the outspoken feminist, was imprisoned for several months in a filthy dungeon, like scores of other, mostly younger women. Haya de la Torre, however, evaded recapture, though he remained effectively trapped in a safe house on the south side of Lima for several years.

In 1936, when Benavides's mandate as Sánchez Cerro's stand-in expired, new elections again threatened to light the political powder keg. On the right, the remnants of Sánchez Cerro's party, the *Unión Revolucionaria* (Revolutionary Union), came under the spell of Luis Flores, a Sánchez Cerro supporter born and raised in Piura, near the Ecuadorian frontier. The party openly engaged in fascist imagery and rhetoric, complete with black shirts, the Nazi arm-salute, and a publication called *Acción* (Action) that not infrequently engaged in Jew-bashing—even though the Jewish presence in Peru was miniscule. Still mostly on the left, APRA held widespread potency, but was banned from electoral participation. It openly supported the candidacy of a San Marcos historian, Luis Eguiguren, who led the October results with 37 percent (to Flores's 29 percent, with various less and centrist parties holding the remainder). These results being unacceptable to vested interests, Benavides nullified the election and, with the blessing of the aristocracy, announced that he would remain in office for another three years.

Under constant political duress, Óscar Benavides and his cohorts gave Peru a frugal and relatively efficient government, and certainly one far less corrupt than Sánchez Cerro's, which had been plagued by nepotism. Peru's economy slowly awakened in the mid-thirties, with rising exports and tax revenue. The government initiated several noteworthy public works, among them irrigation projects and road-building. A central highway now wound its way up into the highlands from Lima, where it then ran north and south. Two thousand miles of the coastal Pan-American highway were paved. Inspired by Franklin Roosevelt's New Deal, the state launched a social security program, and tried to initiate a public healthcare system, though both efforts were ultimately very modest. New schools were also built, but the education system was broadly stagnant, with the reopened San Marcos University smaller than it had been in the 1910s.

The Politics of Moderation

The aristocracy again comfortably in control, 1939 saw the election of Manuel Prado, scion of an elite political family (his father was Mariano Ignacio Prado, president in the 1870s—he fathered Manuel at age sixty-three). His six-year tenure in office corresponded with World War II. Unlike Benavides, who declared Peruvian neutrality but quietly admired the fascist regimes, Prado wholly aligned with the United States. He shut down the Italian military mission and invited American trainers into Peru instead. After the attack on Pearl Harbor he signed an economic pact, accepting a large loan that, in exchange, locked Peru into the exportation of raw materials at ultimately below-market prices.

Encouraged by the United States, the Prado government curtailed the liberties of Peruvians of Italian, German, and especially Japanese descent. Japanese-Peruvians (see chapter 7) had made great advances in the 1920s and 1930s. Pooling their resources and organizing themselves into myriad civic associations, while exuding a remarkable work ethic, they had come to own many shops and small businesses all along the coast. Scores were barbers. In Lima, their Japanese Society ran a cultural center and school that worked to preserve their culture. In 1942, the government closed the school and cut off credit to Japanese-owned businesses. As the press portrayed them as treacherous subversives, locals ransacked their workplaces and homes. Eighteen hundred Japanese-Peruvians were rounded up and shipped to internment camps in the western United States. Neither the United States nor Peru's government have ever formally issued apologies or recompensed descendants for this brazen violation of basic liberties, which occurred when the Allies were professing to fight tyranny in order to preserve freedom.

The persecution of Japanese-Peruvians reflected the rising influence of the United States. In other, practical ways a new American presence was felt. With the help of U.S. contractors, Prado's administration began the regulation of air traffic. It soon opened the Limatambo Airport, which featured the country's first commercial-grade runway. But the government was otherwise plagued by economic shortcomings. The war greatly disrupted imports of finished products, primarily from the United States. An inflationary cycle ensued and was aggravated by the printing of money. The *Sol* (Peru's currency) lost nearly three-quarters of its value during the war years, with financial hardship especially acute for the underclasses.

Prado won popular acclaim by successfully prosecuting a short war with Ecuador in July 1941. The boundaries of the two nations had never been firmly set, and opportunistic politicians in both countries advocated war. Ecuador claimed a massive swath of land to its east, including portions of remote Amazonia, where it had established modest outposts. Prado, for his part, lived with the familial shame of the long-ago war with Chile. President-General Benavides had overseen a modernization of the armed forces and, when presented with the opportunity, Peru was ready to fight. Using two dozen aircraft and newly trained paratroopers, the army captured rear positions with ease, while the navy's six warships sealed off Ecuador's coast. Quickly suing for peace, the Ecuadorans relinquished their outlandish territorial claims in peace talks facilitated by annoyed Americans—preoccupied

Figure 8.1. Prado's government built this public hospital in east-central Lima, in an area thick with workshops and small factories. Dubbed the Workers' Hospital, it provided free medical services. In 1981 it was renamed after Guillermo Almenara Irigoyen, Prado's first Minister of Public Health, who labored to eradicate tropical diseases and expand Peru's modest social security system.
Photo by the author

with world war, Washington was displeased with the poorly timed fracas south of the border.

Prado's government was overall, however, highly responsive to the Colossus of the North. It was his administration that dramatically upgraded Peru's diplomatic mission by purchasing a twenty-five-acre estate atop a hill near Washington, D.C.'s Rock Creek Park. The mansion, standing on the site of an important U.S. Civil War redoubt, was then filled with artworks and ancient Incan artifacts. Down to the present day, relatively impoverished Peru thus has one of the better ambassador's residences in the U.S. capital. Needless to say, aristocratic diplomats have generally been delighted to receive postings here.

In 1941 Peru tallied the results from its first census since 1876. It found that 65 percent of the population still lived in the highlands, most in small villages; 30 percent resided in cities, especially along the coast, while only 5 percent resided in the Amazonian lowlands. Data revealed that nearly half of the residents of Lima originally hailed from the provinces. Although lagging behind most of the rest of the world, a process of urbanization was clearly underway. Census data also revealed great socioeconomic shortcomings. Population growth was racing past the very limited capacities of the nation's educational infrastructure. In mid-century less than a quarter of Peru's children attended even the first years of primary school. Sixty percent of the population was illiterate, while only 0.6 percent had studied at a university. The educational statistics for indigenous persons living in the highlands were far lower than for the general populace.

Still, Prado's presidency was relatively successful politically, and marked a time of comparative internal peace. While it is true that the president tempered the persecution of Apristas, the main reason for the newfound tranquility was a surprising policy shift by APRA on the orders of Haya de la Torre. His proto-Marxist theories always quirky, the party chieftain (still nominally in hiding) began to praise various aspects of Western capitalism, disparage revolution, and even periodically commend the United States. While APRA's new positions came from the tightly controlled party's boss, a multiplicity of reasons undoubtedly lay behind them: weariness of persecution, the desire to appeal to a rising middle class, recognition that the Depression-era crisis of capitalism was lifting, and fears that the Communist Party would surpass APRA with its overt support of the popular Allied cause. But ultimately, Haya de la Torre's own ambition for power likely dictated the new direction. In the present course he was getting nowhere. The 1944 death of his long-time rightist critic, Riva Agüero, perhaps also helped inspire the shift.

The Bustamante Opening

For the United States, APRA's change of heart was refreshing. By the mid-war years, the party distinguished between the "imperialist" Republican Party, and the "reasonable" Democrats of Roosevelt. It also began to intimidate Communist Party–aligned labor unions. As Prado's government let APRA operate above ground, party enforcers—picturesquely called *Bufalos*—muscled unionists, and took control of segments of organized labor. APRA tempered wartime worker demands, to the great pleasure of both business owners and the United States. Its rhetoric increasingly emphasized anti-communism, and after the war ended in 1945 Haya de la Torre returned to the United States, where he received a warm welcome at the State Department. For Washington, a tightly run and disciplined party—even if it supposedly represented the toiling masses—would be fine, if its leadership was trustworthy.

The closing of the war introduced a short season of heightened democracy in Latin America. In several smaller countries, such as Guatemala, long-time oligarchic dictators were overthrown. Talk of liberty and freedom by U.S. leaders during World War II resonated, and though these professions of principle ultimately proved hollow, at the time they were believed and embraced by many. Some U.S. officials saw Peru's hyper-conservative aristocracy as backward, and favored a broader base for governance. The "new" APRA fit nicely into this vision. Its conservative reincarnation encouraging, many Peruvian elite also began to accept the idea of an APRA-led government. The party was allowed to participate in 1945 elections, winning handily in legislative contests. While not ready to accept Haya de la Torre as chief executive, an elderly Benavides orchestrated the election of a distinctively middle-class lawyer and diplomat from Arequipa.

The largely unknown José Luis Bustamante was, in some ways, a stand-in for APRA. He and Haya de la Torre made an informal arrangement, through which the new president and the powerful People's Party would mutually govern. Or so, at least, the Apristas thought. To their chagrin, Bustamante shunned party officials as he named his first cabinet, and steered a more independent course. As he did so, tensions arose between his government and the party.

An impatient APRA soon resorted to strong-arm tactics, its semi-clandestine Buffalos carrying out targeted attacks and select assassinations. The murder of Francisco Graña Garland, gunned down in his car in January 1947, triggered a crisis. An aristocrat who had acquired great wealth in pharmaceuticals, Graña edited *La Prensa*, the leading conservative newspaper at the time. A thorough investigation, conducted with the help of Canadian detectives, pointed to Apristas. Arrests in June were followed by an APRA general strike in August, which in turn led Bustamante to declare a state of emergency. The rifts were becoming too great to sustain the political opening.

Within APRA itself, another division was breaking into the open. Since its inception, the party and its popular aspirations had drawn the participation of many women, most notably the activist-poet Magda Portal, who had sided with Haya de la Torre instead of Mariátegui in the late 1920s. But Portal and her friends longed for a more democratic internal party structure. In 1946 they convened a raucous and energized Aprista Women's Convention—mindful, of course, of the role of Evita in the Argentine Peronist movement. This progressive feminist impulse was too much for Haya de la Torre and, two years later at a critical party meeting, he and an all-male leadership squelched it. A disgusted Magda Portal, with scores of other influential women, stormed out of the session and soon quit the party. Years later, in an interview, Portal revealed some of the inner workings of APRA under an often despotic, control-obsessed Haya de la Torre.

While that view of the party is undoubtedly realistic, APRA's boss did not have total control, nor did the unwieldy organization have uniformly tight discipline. As with the Trujillo revolt in 1932, an unauthorized and preemptive revolt in October 1948 triggered political chaos and repression, when scores of mostly junior naval officers attempted a coup on behalf of APRA in the port of Callao. Several ships were commandeered, while on land the old colonial fortress, Real San Felipe, and the Naval Academy both fell to the rebels. A coordinated Aprista uprising in Lima failed to materialize, however, and the army suppressed the rebellion, though at great cost—an estimated three hundred military personnel died. Bustamante quickly banned APRA, but that was not enough for the generals. An anti-Aprista coup followed within a month. Conservative forces, wary of volatile mass politics, and were determined to turn back the clock. Peru was about to enter a harsh season of direct military rule.

CHAPTER NINE

Life and Culture, 1908–1948

Peru underwent dramatic change in the early twentieth century, as the staid Aristocratic Republic gave way to the politics of mass participation. A similar transition took place in the cultural realm, as pathbreaking artists, writers, and musicians began to celebrate the lives of common folk, and the most daring challenged the constraining societal expectations as set by the elite. For women, barriers barely moved, but efforts and accomplishments in the period laid the groundwork for much greater freedom in the second half of the century.

Art and Architecture

In art and architecture, the early twentieth century saw Peruvians break molds and experiment. Given their ongoing infatuation with Europe, the rich predictably continued to favor an imitative form of art. Coupled with the fact the nation's poverty and instability greatly inhibited artistic production after independence, there is little to excite the art enthusiast during an entire short century, when various Peruvians followed the lead first of European Romantics and then the Realists. Daniel Hernández Morillo, however, proved himself a gifted—if not entirely innovative—oil-on-canvas painter by the 1890s, having trained and worked primarily in Italy and France. He was the logical choice to direct the National School of Fine Arts, which the government established in 1918.

Fortunately, an elderly Hernández was open to new ideas (see figure 6.1). Those came primarily from a young instructor named José Sabogal. In turn, Sabogal found a talented protégé in Julia Codesido. As a young girl, Codesido had been raised in Europe by her art-loving father, a diplomat who served as Peru's counsel in Liverpool. She had traveled widely, visiting nearly all of Europe's great art repositories. She also had opportunities to interact with her father's friend, French impressionist Edgar Degas. Entering the new School of Fine Arts at age thirty-six, she soon distinguished herself, and held her first exhibition in Lima one decade later. Friends with Mariátegui, she produced covers for his journal *Amauta*.

Both Sabogal and Codesido were keenly influenced by the *Indigenismo* movement, which celebrated the accomplishments and legacies of native peoples. In time, Sabogal became Peru's foremost advocate of *Indigenismo*. Both spent time in Mexico City and befriended the famous muralist Diego Rivera and his innovative partner Frida Kahlo. The Mexicans helped Codesido in particular gain international exposure; she held exhibitions in the late 1930s in both Mexico City and New York. She was soon most

Figure 9.1. Julia Codesido's 1938 work, *Cabeza de Criolla* (**Headshot of a Native Woman**—in Peru "criolla" denotes native), is typical of her mid-career representations. By exaggerating black features she affirmed their beauty, in a society that was still fundamentally racist. This painting has traveled widely. In 2019 it was displayed at the Fine Arts Museum in Santiago de Chile.
Source: Museo del Banco Central de Reserva del Perú

content to celebrate indigenous culture. She painted scores of images of highlands towns and especially their people, in processions and activities of everyday life. She often made portraits of native women, though she also enjoyed producing representations of animals—a hallmark of her earlier work. Her mix of colors broke bounds beyond the pastels favored by the first two generations of Impressionists. After Sabogal became director of the art school in 1932, she worked for the next decade by his side. Her own style, however, continued to evolve. Given the limitations placed on women at the time, Codesido's accomplishments are remarkable.

In architecture, the extended centennial celebrations during Leguía's rule generated a historic nostalgia for Lima's magnificent colonial past. A movement dubbed *Neo-colonialism* thus flourished from the 1920s into the 1940s, the hallmark of which was construction of new *balcones* (see chapter 1), the often-ornate wooden balconies that had once adorned major public buildings and residences. In 1924, enormous dark-wood balcones were added to the Archbishop's Palace on the Plaza de Armas (main square). These set the trend, and hundreds of wealthy families subsequently funded their own balcones over the next two decades, which became common in the capital's moneyed mid-century enclaves of Jesús María and San Beatriz.

The architect who modified the bishop's residence was Ricardo de Jaxa Malachowski, a Polish-descended, Crimean-born migrant who found easy favor with the Limeño upper class after arriving in 1911 (his subsequent marriage to María Benavides Diéz, daughter of the two-time president, certainly helped). A graduate of Paris's École des Beaux-Arts, Malachowski designed the neo-baroque National Palace, which was built during Benavides's second term in the mid-1930s. The architect stayed active for three decades thereafter, designing mansions and resort hotels, while teaching on occasion at the National School of Engineering.

Literature: From Chocano to Vallejo

In literature, José Santos Chocano—the 1890s patriotic poet of note—began roughly sixteen years of overseas travel in 1901, and his outlook broadened accordingly. He served in diplomatic posts in Central America and Spain, and ventured to Mexico in the throes of its revolution, associating with luminaries Francisco "Pancho" Villa and Venustiano Carranza. Next, in Guatemala, he befriended a strongman—just before his fall in a coup. Imprisoned, for the second time in his life the poet faced possible execution; letters from writers, diplomats, and presidents saved his life. He returned to Peru in 1921 as a national hero.

In a strange ceremony in downtown Lima, Chocano was crowned Poet Laureate of the Americas, President Leguía himself present and heaping praise. Over the previous two decades he had endeared himself to Latin Americans with sweeping epics in a spirit similar to that of Walt Whitman. The most famous of these, *Los caballos de los conquistadores* (*The Horses of the Conquistadors*), romantically recounted the exploits of the Spaniards who subdued the Americas, yet equally glorified their native adversaries. His poem "El Cantor de América" ("The Singer of America"), also famously celebrated the region and its history.

Ultimately, Chocano's volatile personality led to personal tragedy. His fondness for dictatorial leaders, including Leguía, alienated the literary and intellectual left. Sparring with his critics in articles and letters, he took great personal affront to their verbal assaults. He too gave no quarter, penning vitriolic charges. In 1925 he confronted one of his most outspoken opponents in the lobby of the newspaper *El Comercio*. Drawing a revolver, Chocano shot his adversary in cold blood. Taken into custody and tried, he admitted nothing. He later improbably claimed that he was defending the nation's honor. His three-year prison sentence was suspended, but an embittered Chocano left the country for—of all places—Chile. In 1934, while aboard a city tram in Santiago, he was knifed to death by an assailant who may have had political motives.

The ever-patriotic Chocano was too conformist for some youthful Peruvian literati, especially those influenced by the great contrarian Manuel González Prada. The champion of this rising cohort was Abraham Valdelomar. The sixth of eight children, Valdelomar was raised in the fishing town of Pisco, 130 miles south of Lima. A precocious child adored by his mother, he later migrated to Lima to attend San Marcos University, where he became a social and political lightning rod, organizing students in support of the 1912 presidential candidacy of Guillermo Billinghurst. Rewarded with the editorship of the official newspaper, and then with a diplomatic post in Italy, Valdelomar launched his literary career in earnest. In Rome, he penned his renowned *El Caballero Carmelo*, a short story about a boy whose beloved rooster dies in a cockfight. This and other works—most set in Pisco—defined a genre known as *cuentos criollos* (creole stories), or localized fictitious stories that revealed of the lives of average, working-class Peruvians. When Billinghurst's government fell in a coup, Valdelomar lost his overseas post and returned to Lima, employed as a personal secretary for the aristocratic José de la Riva Agüero. Under the historian's tutelage, he wrote *La Mariscala*, a fictionalized biography of Francisca Zubiaga, the strong-willed wife of the caudillo Agustín Gamarra.

Valdelomar was undoubtedly attracted to the historical personage of Zubiaga through his own unconventional flamboyance. Not since Manuel Ignacio de Vivanco had wealthy Limiños beheld anyone as colorful as Abraham Valdelomar, who was fond of wearing yellow suits, bizarre hats, and stylish rimmed glasses. The life of the party, he "held court" at the Palais Concert, an art nouveau confectionary and bar that opened in central Lima in 1913. He wrote prolifically in the late 1910s, as a poet, satirist, and budding dramatist—while living a decadent lifestyle marked by heavy drinking, in the vein of Irishman Oscar Wilde. Into self-promotion, he lectured in provincial cities throughout Peru, charging admission while using newfound advertising techniques. In 1919 in Ayacucho, he fell from a second-story window—apparently drunk—and died two days later at the age of thirty-one.

By the time of his death, Valdelomar had befriended and cultivated the talents of a young poet of note, César Vallejo. Born in a northern town, the mestizo Vallejo weathered poverty as he worked his way through school. He endured grueling physical labor in a mine, and witnessed the routine abuse of Natives while working on a hacienda. Taciturn to the point of shyness, he was in personality the exact opposite of Valdelomar, who nevertheless took a liking to him. Associating with a young Haya de la Torre, Vallejo questioned Peru's racial and economic power structures, and longed for a more just world. Accused of instigating property damage in his hometown, he spent four months in a squalid jail cell, and was thereafter bedeviled by the authorities. Contact with Mariátegui only further radicalized Vallejo, who eventually fled his homeland for another life in Europe.

In Paris, César Vallejo again faced hardship, at times sleeping on the streets. He fell ill and nearly died. The angst of lifelong suffering echoes through his works. His poems, however, are absolutely brilliant—in structure, with artificially created words, they presaged the modernism and surrealism of the mid-twentieth century. His 1922 collection titled *Trilce* (a non-word likely from the combination of *triste*—sad, with *dulce*—sweet) is widely regarded as one of the great poetic masterpieces of the twentieth century. In Peru, however, it barely sold one hundred copies. In Lima he was instead noted for his journalistic reports in Mariátegui's *Amauta*.

Life slowly improved for the mournful poet. He lived with and then married a French woman, traveled around Europe, and visited communist Russia in trips that gave him great political inspiration. An avowed Marxist by the 1930s, he was expelled from France but thrived in Spain, where he associated with the fluorescent artistic community—his friendship with Pablo Picasso most readily known. He witnessed the unfolding civil war there, and saw in

Figure 9.2. No poet is more celebrated in Peru than César Vallejo, whose name is attached to a university, scores of schools, and hundreds of streets. Yet ironically, he was all but ignored in his native land while living. This statue, in Lima's District of Lince, shows a typically brooding and pensive Vallejo.
Photo by the author

it an apocalyptic struggle between good and evil, between freedom of the human spirit and a lasting enslavement to technology and power. Falling ill, he died in 1938, a feeble and broken man. Much of his work was published postmortem, when friends and associates like Pablo Neruda celebrated his memory. What Mariátegui is to Peruvian politics, Vallejo is to its culture. Yet, like Vincent Van Gogh, the gifted Vallejo obtained very little in the way of public recognition during his lifetime.

The Rise of Popular Music

From the time of independence into the early twentieth century, the boundaries of "culture" were set by Lima's aristocracy. From the vantage point of the rich, the underclasses had no culture. But as the decades passed, elite Limeños looked more and more to Europe—especially France—for cultural inspiration. This obsession with things European created space, in the form of a chasm between them and the indigenous masses, who continued to practice local traditions. In music, this divergence produces the awkward term *Música Criolla*. Criollos (creoles) were, of course, the Spanish-descended white elite. But Música Criolla refers to Peru's own music, that is, that of the (common) people. The term emerged in the early twentieth century, and has been used with this inherently confusing definition ever since.

Música Criolla itself is ill-defined. At its most basic meaning, it denotes any music originating from Peru. But any Peruvian will tell you that there are many *types* of Música Criolla, most of which are distinguished by rhythmic patterns, timing, and instrumentation. To complicate matters further, most genres of Música Criolla picked up foreign influences. In the late colonial era, foreigners in ports along the coast introduced locals to various musical styles and instruments. Germans and Austrians, for example, brought the waltz, giving rise to *Vals Criollo*, performed in 3/4 time. Polka and many other subgenres emerged. Rhythm was also influenced by percussion introduced from the Caribbean, and by Afro-Peruvian antecedents. Peruvians developed the *cajón* or box-shaped drum, for example, slapped by the musician sitting atop it—perhaps an evolution from dock workers, singing while slapping wooden crates, as they waited to load the next ship.

Given its nebulous nature, pinning down the "start" of Música Criolla is problematic. But convention largely holds that it began with the singing of a Limeño street bard named Felipe Pinglo Alva. Relatively little is known about Pinglo Alva, and interviews and recordings of his hundreds of songs have been lost—the improper storage of archived material resulting in their destruction. He was born to a family of modest means in the historic but rough working-class neighborhood of Barrios Altos, in Lima. He sang and played guitar with finesse, at first on street corners but then in cafes and theaters. He made several radio appearances and recordings before his untimely death in 1936 at the age of thirty-six. But he was largely ignored by that rising medium (see below), and his most famous song was banned by the government. Much like Pete Seeger, whose career fell victim to the (Second) Red Scare in the United States, Pinglo Alva was breaking too many social taboos; he was ahead of his time.

Almost without exception, Pinglo Alva's lyrics chronicled and celebrated the lives of the poor (though conversely, a product of the city, he was not attuned to the culture or plight of highlands Natives). He talked of childworkers and street life, of love and affection in the midst of grinding poverty. His most famous song, the banned "El Plebeyo" ("The Commoner"), was openly subversive. A yarn of denied love between a poor man and a rich woman, its most devastating stanza asks:

> She's of noble birth, and I, a humble worker,
> yet our blood is alike,

    and our hearts are the same;
    so why, oh Lord, are we not equal?[1]

When General-President Óscar Benavides banned the song, he and others probably took note not just of its condemnation of class discrimination, but of its reference (in an earlier phrase) to the color red. There was speculation, and much suspicion among officialdom, that Pinglo Alva was an Aprista, though his politics are in fact unknown.

Dovetailing on Pinglo Alva's career was that of Alicia Lizárraga, arguably the most famous of all Música Criolla singers. A pioneer who blazed a cultural trail for women as well—because of her accomplishments many other women were able to enjoy success by way of Música Criolla. There is a longstanding dispute about Lizárraga's birthplace, but the best evidence now points to Cuzco, though both of her parents were Arequipeños. Her golden voice was complemented by appealing youthful looks, and she soon received the affectionate but condescending nickname *La Cholita Linda del Perú* (The Cute Gal of Peru). During World War II her male handlers took her to Buenos Aires, which had the best recording facilities in Latin America at the time, and oversaw the production of many distinctively Peruvian songs. Radio stations played these constantly, enrapturing the nation in a Música Criolla frenzy. As a result, ceding to popular urges, President Prado in 1944 declared October 31 forever known as "El Día de Canción Criolla" (Creole Song Day). The last day of October is now a national holiday, with Peruvians fond of singing popular songs to family members, to one another, and even sometimes to strangers.

Lizárraga sang multiple songs in Peru's first major film, *Gallo de mi galpón* (*My Barn Rooster*), though she did no acting. This 1938 movie, produced by the appropriately named Amauta Studios, reflected the aspirations of the artistic community as bequeathed by José Mariátegui and his generation of bohemians. Set on a cotton hacienda in the north (though it was actually filmed just south of Lima, near Surco), *Gallo de mi galpón* presented a plot eerily similar to the Mexican masterpiece, *Ahí en Rancho Grande*, that had appeared just two years earlier. Two males compete for the love of a young peasant woman, Isabel. One, an overseer named Andrés, is malicious—he tries to take advantage of Isabel and molest her. She is defended by the noble Miguel, so an enraged Andrés plots to have Miguel unjustly charged for stealing. The good hacendado, Don Francisco, gets wise to Andrés's scheme and consigns him to punishment, as Miguel and Isabel live happily ever after.

---

1. For those who read Spanish, the entire stanza is: *Mi sangre aunque plebeya / también tiñe de rojo / el alma en que se anida / mi incomparable amor. / Ella de noble cuna / y yo humilde plebeyo / no es distinta la sangre / ni es otro el corazón / Señor, ¿por que los seres no son de igual valor?*

Gallo de mi galpón is a morality play with religious overtones, but it was also mildly subversive, most notably with the mid-film performance of Pinglo Alva's *El Plebeyo*, as performed by Jesús Vásquez (a female—her full name being María de Jesús). The song helped define Vásquez's own career. As with many criolla singers, she was rarely able to access radio (until after 1944)—which favored opera and other forms of European music preferred by the aristocracy. But she had ample opportunities to perform in Lima's booming mid-century theaters. In the late 1940s, she became a regular fixture on radio, while following Lizárraga's lead and recording in Buenos Aires. Like Lizárraga, Vásquez acquired a transnational fan base, and became one of the most famous Peruvian women in South America, forever known as the Queen of Criolla.

The Advent of Radio

Radio came to Peru in 1925, just a few years after its debut in the United States. The first station, with the call letters OAX, was owned by a new enterprise called the Peruvian Broadcasting Company. It launched its airtime with an address by President Leguía, who briefly spoke with regard to political matters. Receivers and speakers were positioned in nearby downtown plazas, allowing locals to hear his voice, to their astonishment. Opera and classical music followed, as OAX catered to an educated and wealthy clientele. Very few Peruvians had receivers, however, and the station struggled to turn a profit. After it fell into bankruptcy, the British-owned Marconi Wireless and Telegraph Company bought it, eventually expanding and popularizing its programs.

Years later, in the early 1930s, several companies established rival stations in the capital. One of the most important was Radio Miraflores, a station destined for prominence. Just a few stations cropped up elsewhere in Peru, those with the largest transmitters in Lima and Arequipa. In 1937, the national government took control of the again struggling OAX. Building it a new home, with state-of-the-art recording studios, it rechristened OAX as National Radio of Peru (RNP).

The heyday of radio came thereafter, as both RNP and private stations pioneered new forms of entertainment. RNP used its studios to create *radioteatros*, or theater-like dramatic broadcasts. *Radionovelas* followed, with romantic storylines similar to those found in modern-day *telenovelas*—though many of the earlier productions were imported from prerevolutionary Cuba. In the world war years, U.S. influence played out in radio, too, with newscasts and political messaging favorable to the Allied cause. The creation of the first privately

Figure 9.3. The 1937 home of National Radio. This little building, tucked away behind the National Stadium, had a far greater impact on Peruvian life than any great estate house, baroque church, or modern office tower. Into the 1960s its studios conveyed everything from critical political messages to popular music, and *radioteatros* that captivated millions.
Photo by the author

owned radio network, in 1942, facilitated distribution of a more uniform political message, with several key owners again sympathetic to the Allies.

Radio broadcasts generated new enthusiasm for music, introduced Peruvians to new forms of music from other countries, and created high-publicity careers for a select few performing "stars." The most significant imported musical sound was that of *bolero*. Bolero has Spanish origins, its name originating from the verb *volar*—meaning to fly, or fly away. This suave, dreamy genre first arrived in the Americas in Cuba, where locals blended it with Afro-Caribbean rhythmic percussion. From there, it spread to Mexico, at first because of the powerful transmitters of Cuba's Radio Martí. Mexico in turn conveyed bolero southward in the 1930s and early 1940s, into the Andean region and Peru. Radio was not the only means of dissemination, however; Mexican *ranchero* movies also served as a key conduit, with Peruvians soothed especially by the melodic voice of Pedro Infante in his myriad films. Although in its infancy in the 1940s, bolero was destined to blossom and find its place in Peruvian popular culture (see chapter 16), which itself had entered something of a golden age in the mid-twentieth century.

CHAPTER TEN

Waiting for Change

The Aprista coup attempt of October 1948 was a turning point in Peru's mid-century political history. Over the seventeen previous years, a struggle between aristocratic and mass politics had nearly descended into civil war. Conciliation, engineered by Oscar Benavides in the context of the new post-war global order, had opened space for middle-class aspirants to political life. Enraged army generals, with the blessing of the rich, now slammed the door shut. It would be fourteen more years before another window would allow for the possibility of real change.

The Odría Ocenio

Manuel A. Odría was the army officer who, with the blessing of the Limeño elite, ended the experiment in middle-class democracy under José Luis Bustamante. Born of a land-owning family in the central highlands, Odría entered the Chorrillos Military Academy as a young man, and thereafter spent much of his life in army schools as an instructor and officer. He trained on U.S. military bases during World War II and developed connections with U.S. officials. While some in Washington still favored the idea of an APRA-led government, in the context of the unfolding Cold War Odría's strong-arm rule gained the tacit support of the United States.

His was an eight-year dictatorship thus known as the *Ocenio*. More than any regime up to this time, it was an exercise in brute force. Promptly suspending civil liberties, the army rounded up and jailed Apristas and other perceived "subversives" by the thousands. Many languished in jails for years, without trial or due process. Unlike his more tolerant predecessors, Odría also pursued Haya de la Torre himself. The hunted APRA chieftain reached the Colombian embassy, however, where he lived a miserable hermit's life for five and a half years (the Peruvian army dug trenches around the building and effectively locked it down). Eventually a diplomatic deal was struck, by which the famous leader was removed from the country.

The Odría regime passed a series of security laws, via a compliant congress, that gave the police and army sweeping powers. Private residences could be searched at will, without warrants; free speech and the right of public assembly for political purposes ceased to exist. Elections became a joke: Odría "won" a full term in office in 1950 as the only viable candidate. At every symbolic opportunity, the regime celebrated the army and glorified its history. It staged elaborate annual commemorations of the "Trujillo Martyrs" (the soldiers murdered during the 1932 uprising), portraying them as innocent patriots slaughtered by godless Apristas.

But there was another side to Odría's rule that made it more palpable: using Juan Perón's government in Argentina as its example, the regime cultivated relations with select unions and strategically employed leftist rhetoric. Some limited wage and benefit concessions were granted, creating thousands of satisfied workers who were periodically bussed into Lima to attend mass rallies. Here, they cheered Odría, who often spoke of a workers' revolution. The ploy was largely a façade, but it held a certain appeal and undercut the aura of APRA.

Odría had the good fortune, too, of governing during a commodities boom. Though the first couple of years of his governance were lean, in 1950 the Korean War drove mineral prices sharply up. Peru's lead mines prospered, while U.S. corporate giants Phelps Dodge and ASARCO began to develop open-pit copper mines. Government revenues rose, even while Peru received generous loans from the World Bank and other international funding agencies. In one of his few authentically nationalist stances, Odría extended coastal sovereignty from three to two hundred miles, creating a resource monopoly for long-important fisheries.

In the wake of Odría's move, the fishmeal industry began to flourish. Fishmeal, used as livestock feed, was a rising industry worldwide. Peruvians soon harvested enormous schools of anchoveta fish, carried to the coast by the cold-water Humboldt Current. A group of innovative Spanish and Italian entrepreneurs led the upstart industry, foremost among them Luis Banchero Rossi. Banchero employed marine biologists and used pathbreaking technologies—including state-of-the-art steel ships, nylon netting, echo sounders (to draw the fish), and sophisticated processing procedures. He eventually linked up with the U.S. tuna giant StarKist and—despite a modest background and limited education—by the 1960s was one of Peru's most successful businessmen.

Banchero based his enterprise in Chimbote, Peru's best natural harbor, located two hundred and fifty miles northwest of Lima. French banks had anted up funds for the development of Chimbote under Odría's government. With technical help from Europe and the United States, a modest steel mill was constructed here, while a large energy-supplying dam and hydroelectric system was built just to the east, in the mountains at Duck Canyon. Other foreign loans funded a new highway from the central plateau down into Amazonia. In the incipient postwar heyday of the global economy, Peru appeared to be dutifully "developing."

Figure 10.1. American aid workers inoculate alpacas in the highlands. Alpacas frequently suffered from internal parasites, but this could be easily prevented through vaccination. This effort was part of the Truman Administration's Point Four Program, which delivered technical assistance to poorer countries. Needless to say, this kind of activity fostered good will toward the United States among rural inhabitants.
Source: Harry S. Truman Library and Museum

Under Odría, however, development had severe limitations. The *sol* was sharply devalued to cheapen exports and make the nation more attractive to investors. While major projects like that of Chimbote stood out, the interior stagnated in the 1950s—Odría had little interest in the plight of agriculture or the highlands' native population. In fact, he readily allowed feudal-like labor obligations to revive and persist. Though select urban unions and workers received special treatment and even profit-sharing bonuses, other groups were vigorously suppressed and strikes rarely tolerated. In Odría's Peru, the army stood first in line. Its budget rose sharply year-over-year, with officers paid well and new equipment acquired steadily (most now coming from the United States). By the end of the Ocenio, the military budget was larger than that for all of Peru's social programs combined. Many colonels and generals served in Odría's cabinet.

General Odría loved to wear his uniform and associate with other senior officers. He also took great pride in his network of military connections. One of his former students at Chorrillos, Marcos Pérez Jiménez, became the strongman of Venezuela, where he set up an even more sophisticated and repressive police state. Odría visited or hosted him frequently, both emphasizing their anti-communist credentials, to the pleasure of Washington.

Finally, Manuel Odría was spectacularly and brazenly corrupt. He amassed a personal fortune, with several large houses around Lima and robust bank accounts besides. He was fond of big automobiles and wore dapper clothes. He and his cronies cut secret deals in real estate, but also took kickbacks from public works contracts. Funds for the rebuilding of Cuzco, which was struck by an earthquake in 1951, inexplicably disappeared. Foreign interests also often benefited from underhanded deals. The U.S. firm Anderson and Clayton, hired for an irrigation project in the highlands, was able to expropriate land from native villagers without compensation as it greased the wheels with Odría and his friends in the capital.

Ousting a Dictator

There is little doubt that General Odría intended to extend his time in office past the 1956 election cycle. But while much of the army and a good portion of the aristocracy were content enough under his iron-fisted rule, nearly everyone else was dissatisfied. The middle class had tasted political power under Bustamante, and wanted to do so again. APRA sought relegalization, while most labor unions and urban and rural underclasses also longed for change. The United States clearly liked Odría, but he had unwittingly made an erstwhile enemy who stood between him and the great hispheric power.

Pedro Beltrán was an entrepreneurial businessman in the mold of Augusto Leguía, albeit without the bottomless political ambition. Educated at the London School of Economics, Beltrán turned his family's relatively modest estates into a highly successful cotton-exporting enterprise in the 1930s. Appointed ambassador to Washington in 1944, he used the embassy's graceful new residence to good effect, throwing parties and networking widely with U.S. policymakers and bankers. He participated in the critical postwar conference at Bretton Woods. Back in Lima, in 1953, he married a wealthy American heiress seventeen years his junior—Miriam Kropp was the first female diplomat ever assigned to Lima.

Beltrán had libertarian inclinations, and he expressed those convictions in his editorship of *La Prensa*, a newspaper he had bought and greatly improved in mid-century. *La Prensa* took aim at Odría and his security laws, and the dictator insisted his henchmen shut it down and arrest Beltrán. Thrown into the notorious El Frontón prison, located on an island near Lima, Beltrán and his case attracted international attention. It did great damage to Odría's standing in Washington, even as the economy slowed in the mid-fifties and the middle class pressed hard for a second political opening.

Some of the outsider rich, who were not privy to the Odría clique's networks of graft, also favored change. They sought the return of an elderly Manuel Prado, an aristocrat warmly liked by the United States. Prado had spent the Ocenio in Paris, but expressed a willingness to return. Beltrán's influential *La Prensa* also backed him. The exiled Haya de la Torre, realizing the improbability of immediately coming to power, dialogued with these pro-Prado forces and envisioned a deal that would see Prado, once elected, re-legalize APRA.

But as APRA remained sidelined on the ground, a new player emerged: Fernando Belaúnde was a former congressman, nephew of a distinguished diplomat, and son of a senior member of Bustamante's government. An architect by training, he launched an anti-Odría movement that began to catch fire. Alarmed, the dictator arranged for the national election board to prohibit his further participation. But when police aggressively repressed a large rally in Lima's San Martín Plaza, the candidate himself rushed forward. Carrying a Peruvian flag, the tall and charismatic Belaúnde reached the election board's members, and forced the issue in his favor.

May–June 1956 was a weeks-long political thunderstorm in Peru. Unions staged large strikes in the capital, while Belaúnde relentlessly toured the hinterlands in a bid to pull the rural poor into the political mainstream. Women, who had finally been franchised in 1955, organized largely on behalf of the upstart Belaúnde, many prominent Aprista feminists having bolted from the party. The ego-driven Haya de la Torre, perceiving Belaúnde as a potential long-term rival, pressed forward with his pact to back Prado, while Odría—obviously unable to stay in office—first threw his support to a third candidate, whose efforts soon floundered. On the eve of the vote, Odría met quietly with Apristas, both agreeing to back Prado in a strategy to stop Belaúnde. The dictator's own concern was to escape the presidency without facing corruption investigations.

Prado Returns

An elderly Manuel Prado returned to the presidency with much of the nation politically melancholy. His wartime administration had accomplished relatively little, and though nearly all Peruvians were pleased to see the departure of the other Manuel—expectations for the new government were low. The door to outsider mass politics, closed during the Ocenio, was only halfway open. In one of his first acts, Prado pushed through Congress an amnesty that blocked prosecution for wrongdoing in the previous government. Odría and his cronies would get to keep their millions. Another measure quickly repealed the hated security laws. APRA was promptly re-legalized, and in 1957 Haya de la Torre made his second triumphant return to Peru, though he continued to spend much time overseas. The party's congressional delegation was in lockstep with the government, in an arrangement termed *convivencia*, or cohabitation.

Fernando Belaúnde, for his part, was determined to remain in the political game. He converted his 1956 electoral base into a new grassroots party called *Acción Popular* (Popular Action). He and a new Christian Democratic Party played the role of the opposition and, despite the amnesty law, tried to at least document some of the gross financial mismanagement of General Odría's rule. Coupled with a surging population, Peru's political players were multiplying, and new movements and parties were muddling the bilateral, decades-long divide between the aristocracy (as allied with the army) and the outliers of APRA.

Other players included unions and an array of related labor organizations. The CGT saw new unions form and join it in the late 1950s, many of these coordinated by APRA, which the government favored over the activities of the still-outlawed and more belligerent Communist Party. APRA tried to restrain the urge among workers to strike, but labor unrest persisted into 1957 and beyond. Prado's administration gave ground, in contrast to the heavy-handed police tactics of the dictatorship.

Unfortunately for the elderly Prado, Odría left office after launching a series of new public works projects, mandating wage increases for government bureaucrats and the military, and otherwise bankrupting the treasury.

A mild worldwide recession in 1957–1958 saw commodity prices slump, while Peru's trade imbalance festered—the nation continued to import much more than it exported. When the U.S. Congress moved to impose tariffs on select minerals, including lead and zinc, Peru faced a potentially damaging new economic hurdle. Tense diplomatic exchanges perhaps helped persuade Washington to delay the measure into 1958, and then quietly abort it. A second point of dispute, however, was exploitation of Peru's fisheries by large U.S.-owned tuna trawlers (albeit typically registered in Panama or other secondary countries).

These issues partly explain the most memorable diplomatic episode of the 1950s, Vice President Richard Nixon's ill-fated tour of Latin America and his May 1958 visit to San Marcos University, where nearly the entire campus turned out to stone his limousine and drive him away. But the other subtext of this incident is the movement of Peru's intelligentsia away from APRA and into a more belligerent revolutionary leftism. Few could take Haya de la Torre's convoluted explanations of APRA's ideological shifts seriously. It was increasingly obvious that the party's *jefe* simply wanted political power. Educated Peruvians were turning to the precepts of the traditional left, a trend that would only accelerate with the successful 1959 Cuban Revolution.

The Prado government's difficulties were myriad, and its failures stark. During its term, the nation's population crossed the ten-million threshold. As immunization programs, carried out primarily by U.S. philanthropies, reduced child mortality rates, annual population growth accelerated to over 3.5 percent. But the most essential policy need, that of agrarian reform, went unanswered. Large and unproductive estates persisted throughout the central highlands, amazingly still compelling labor obligations by indigenous peoples, as sanctioned by the state.

Sporadic and sometimes effective organizing by idealistic leftists challenged this abusive system, most notably in the Convención Valley north of Cuzco. The government answered it with police and army repression. The number of landless peasants soared while—except for dispatching police to trouble spots, along with some limited road-building—the government was all but absent. A grim multi-year drought in the late fifties worsened conditions. The government was forced to open a line of credit with the Import-Export Bank in order to annually import tens of thousands of tons of wheat from the United States.

After floundering for half his term, Prado decided to invite one of his most outspoken critics, Pedro Beltrán, into the government. While most Peruvian presidents set policy themselves, and have wholly subservient prime ministers (technically called Ministers of State), Prado opted to give

Beltrán significant powers in this role, along with the additional portfolio of Minister of Finance. In July 1959 Beltrán took control and quickly imposed fiscal discipline upon Peru. He eliminated price controls on such items as meat, and increased gasoline prices by three hundred percent, from eight to twenty-four U.S. cents per gallon. This in turn drove critical bus and taxi fares up in urban areas. At the same time, he slashed social spending and reigned in still out-of-control deficits.

Beltrán's harsh economic medicine, urged by the International Monetary Fund and U.S. technical advisors over the previous two years, created new hardships for especially lower-class citizens. Taxes on the rich and corporations did not significantly increase. The government, if possible, became even more unpopular. In the first three months of 1959 alone, there were over sixty significant strikes, including a two-month walkout by bank tellers and staff that disrupted financial transactions. Prado, who had his car pelted by tomatoes on one occasion, made fewer public appearances. At Beltrán's urging, he undertook trips overseas, including one to Japan in search of investment and economic aid.

Foreign assistance did come, in part through Beltrán's own past diplomatic connections. The United States anted up money, the IMF extended a credit line to support the currency, and other nations funded new private and public works. Among these were the first major hydroelectric projects on the Mantaro River, which flows from the central highlands down into Amazonia and can easily generate electricity via its dramatic descent. One of the few bright spots of Prado's term was the doubling of electrical power to over 2.4 million kilowatt hours in under six years, allowing for a host of new industries, including a Japanese-owned chemical plant in the northern city of Piura. In 1959, a $40 million investment doubled the capacity of the lone steel mill at Chimbote, though a strike there in 1960 left bitter feelings and several workers dead. Other investments fizzled; no foreign companies struck oil in late-fifties test drilling in Amazonia.

Though Beltrán's economic policies pleased foreign interests and wooed some new aid and investment, most Peruvians still viewed Prado's second term as a thorough disappointment. The approaching 1962 election again inspired hopes for change. But now the political landscape was altered by the recent positioning of APRA. The decades-long "outsider party" had tied itself to the Prado administration, supporting its policies and passing its agenda in congress.

When Apristas held festivities in February 1960 in honor of the increasingly vain Haya de la Torre on his sixty-fifth birthday, they announced his candidacy for 1962. But now their leader was something of an insider. The true outsider was, in many ways, Fernando Belaúnde. When he tried to stage a rally in Arequipa early in the Prado's term, the government outlawed it, arresting him and other Popular Action leaders. Many idealists took note. It was no longer a given that a plurality of Peruvians wanted Haya de la Torre to come to power.

Fraying APRA and the 1962–1963 Crisis

Even within APRA, many saw cohabitation with the conservative Prado administration as a betrayal of the party's founding, once-revolutionary principles. Haya de la Torre had answered these critics with disingenuous semantics, explaining that his call for "socialist revolution" meant only significant social change, and that confronting Yankee "imperialism" entailed rejecting hemispheric military adventurism—not shunning corporate capitalism. This double-speak made the party an accessory to aristocratic and global power. When Adlai Stevenson visited Lima in June 1961, students greeted him with large protests similar to those that had stunned Richard Nixon three years earlier. But APRA actually staged pro-U.S. counter-rallies to welcome Stevenson.

Figure 10.2. In mid-century APRA established a headquarters near downtown Lima dubbed "The People's House." Here, the party faithful gathered for intimate rallies, and young cadre received training in political organizing and oratory—as they still do today. A billboard image of Haya de la Torre looms over the facility, which now includes several adjoining buildings.
Photo by the author

Students and labor unions were increasingly operating beyond (or ahead of) the party. APRA lost control of the Peruvian Student Federation in 1960, with widespread youthful enthusiasm for the dramatic Cuban Revolution. Despite its control of most of the organized labor, through the CGT, APRA struggled to steer individual unions and rein in the rank-and-file. The last year of the Prado government again saw much labor militancy, with several large strikes. These were often opposed by the party's leadership, which was well aware that unruly labor in 1948 had helped trigger the military coup. The big Federation of Textile Workers was most tightly linked with the CGT (it provided much of its leadership), and dutifully remained calm, putting twenty thousand cheering and subservient Apristas on the streets when needed. Other unions, however, rocked the political boat.

In June 1961 the Construction Workers' Federation struck, demanding major wage concessions. Conflict with strike-breakers and police triggered intermittent unrest around the capital, with sympathetic coverage by the anti-Prado newspaper *El Comercio*. The union won, with the Labor Ministry acquiescing to a nearly 15 percent wage hike. In October, public teachers went on strike. Protestors overran the congress building, guards killing one in the fracas. Thousands attended the funeral, and rallied again in a nearby park without further bloodshed. Concessions again followed, but the belligerence of various unions unsettled Lima and added to a tense political ambiance.

In trying to temper labor demands and assuage vested interests, it was abundantly clear that, above all else, APRA wanted to win the pending election. Despite the schisms, when Haya de la Torre landed at Limatambo airport in January 1962 (after another long sojourn in Western Europe), the largest political crowd in Peru's history greeted him—a throng estimated at 150,000. His appearances in major cities generated excitement, but also sporadic confrontations. Students and Aprista rebels tried to disrupt his rally in downtown Cusco, with a fight leaving dozens injured and one dead. Some of the boss's most vociferous critics were now from within his own party. This division was aggravated when the unpopular President Prado gave Haya de la Torre his endorsement.

Fernando Belaúnde, in contrast, appealed to the more idealistic. As he had done in 1956, he campaigned almost exclusively in the "other" Peru, the distant hinterlands away from the capital. Popular Action even convened its nominating convention in the remote Amazonian city of Iquitos. Backwater Peru endured two great tragedies in the electoral season. In January, the twenty-two-thousand-foot extinct volcano, Huascarán, unleashed a mammoth avalanche that obliterated a dozen villages in the Santa River valley, including the sizeable town of Ranrahirca. At least 2,900 perished, the vast majority indigenous poor—some bodies were washed down the entire length of the river to the coastal port of Chimbote. In March, indigenous groups carried out land seizures in the vicinity of the mining center of Cerro de Pasco. The army soon arrived to forcibly repossess the estates, leaving eighteen protestors dead. These incidents aroused national awareness of the rural backlands, and played into Belaúnde's electoral approach.

The third major player in the election was none other than General Odría. Having spent the Prado years in a comfortable self-exile in the friendly United States, Odría enjoyed some quasi-official American support for a return to power. Given the ultimately stagnant six years under Prado, his busy (if corrupt and chaotic) Ocenio did not seem, to some, so bad. Perhaps he could again generate big aid packages from Washington. The elite, tired of so much labor unrest, fondly recalled his strong-arm tactics that shut down the troublesome unions. And yet when Odría returned and launched his campaign in the highlands' city of Huancayo, protests left four dead and sixty injured, and prompted him to curtail further public appearances.

Peru was at a tense crossroads. The 1962 election was momentous. When the results came in, Haya de la Torre led with 557,000 votes, or 32.9 percent—just shy of the 33.3 percent needed to preemptively win; Belaúnde drew 543,000 votes, and Odría (perhaps artificially inflated) polled 481,000. APRA did well in congressional races, with 88 house and 26 senate seats to Popular Action's 62 and 16, respectively. Combined, the two grassroots parties swamped the electoral system, making it clear that aristocratic or military rule was broadly unpopular. In this context, the nation was stunned by the televised announcement, days later, that General Odría would oversee an interim government.

Behind the scenes, as in 1956, strange forces were at work. This time, the army informed Haya de la Torre that it would not accept him as the nation's chief executive. The context was a flurry of leaks relating to the Aprista leader's sexual orientation. A lifelong bachelor, Haya de la Torre was gay. Peru's conservative culture regarded homosexuality as scandalous. Long a topic of gossip and innuendo, threats to reveal this fact appear to have prompted the elderly man to willingly cede his bid for the presidency (he in fact probably won it—evidence suggests that his vote tally was manipulated downward).

The military imposition was deeply unpopular, but after a brief suppression of civil liberties, a special election was arranged for mid-1963. Rights restored, political life resumed. In what amounted to a second round, Belaúnde continued to relentlessly campaign, while Haya de la Torre made notably less effort. The genteel architect finally won the presidency, edging APRA's leader while burying Odría—who enjoyed considerable aristocratic support—by a more than three-to-two margin. Had change finally come? Many believed so, but time would tell a more nuanced, if not entirely different, story.

CHAPTER ELEVEN

The Left Transcendent

Since independence in 1821, Peruvian political life had been dominated by a powerful Limeño elite. The ascent of Fernando Belaúnde to the presidency in July 1963, while controversial—given the ostracizing of APRA's Haya de la Torre—was still widely heralded as the start of a new and more democratic chapter in the nation's history. Coinciding with a time of robust global economic growth, a general optimism pervaded Peruvian politics.

A man of courage and integrity, Belaúnde held convictions shaped by his personal experiences. Descended from a well-to-do (but not aristocratic) Arequipeño family, he received an excellent Catholic education at the insistence of parents who had earlier embraced political change in the form of Nicolás Piérola's turn-of-the-century Democratic Party. Driven into exile during the Leguía Oncenio, the family settled near Paris, where a thirteen-year-old Fernando beheld the euphoric arrival of the American aviator, Charles Lindbergh. He later went to the United States to study, first in Miami and then at the University of Texas. His sojourn in Austin coincided with the first term of Franklin D. Roosevelt, a politician of striking self-confidence and optimism, who employed practical policy prescriptions in the midst of the Great Depression. After working in Mexico City, Belaúnde returned to Peru, where he established the first architectural program in the country at the National School of Engineering.

Like Roosevelt, Belaúnde favored practicality over political doctrine. He also believed in utilizing the state to stimulate economic growth when the private sector was feeble. In sum, since independence, government expenditures in Peru had been modest, with only the military receiving significant support—though education had seen steady increases since the late nineteenth century. Belaúnde's government accelerated expenditures, and began to undertake larger-than-ever public works. Its most visible endeavor was a massive housing project in the Jesús María district of Lima. A horseracing track favored by the rich had relocated farther out of the city, leaving prime real estate available for development. The government acquired the land, and routed funds and resources into what was soon christened *Residencial San Felipe*.

Belaúnde, as an architect, took a keen personal interest in the project. He appointed one of his best former students, Enrique Ciriani, to draft the broad plan. Ciriani and many other architects engaged Residencial San Felipe with passion. Their concept was to create a "city within a city," a livable complex of high-rises around open communal green spaces. The project was a great success, easily attracting middle class tenants—the area remained a much-coveted enclave into the early eighties. The government recovered its expenditures and then some, and went on to build less ambitious housing projects, using San Felipe as a prototype.

The national government worked hand in hand with Lima's local authorities on other major infrastructure projects. Together, they opened a new international airport, named after famed Peruvian-born aviator Jorge Chávez—who had overflown the Alps in 1910. The biggest project, however, was the *Vía Expresa Paseo de la República*, a modern highway that cut from near the downtown of Lima southward. It was a massive undertaking. The freeway dropped eighteen feet below ground level, allowing for scores of bridges to cross it uninterrupted. Excess rock and dirt were hauled to the so-called *Costa Verde* (Green Coast). Here, the beachfront was extended under several miles of sheer cliffs, allowing for—what else?—another expressway.

The primary mover behind the Vía Expresa project was Lima's popular mid-sixties mayor, Luis Bedoya Reyes. A devout Catholic educated in religious schools and the University of San Marcos, Bedoya Reyes was a close friend of Belaúnde; like him, he was groomed for political life under José Bustamante, whom he had served as press secretary. In 1956 he joined the new Christian Democratic Party, and briefly served in Belaúnde's cabinet as Minister of Justice. As Lima's mayor, Bedoya Reyes staved off political challenges from the Left, ensuring—as in so much of Latin America—the dominance of pro-capitalist developmentalism in the 1960s. In 1966, he participated in Peru's first-ever televised debate, against Aprista Jorge Grieve. He fared well, and won reelection despite the horrific disruptions caused by the Vía Expresa's construction.

Figure 11.1. Several miles long, Lima's *Vía Expresa* was one of the defining public works projects of the 1960s. Sunken and visually arresting, it was costly and time-consuming to build. The dedicated bus lanes of the *Metropolitano* system (center), added later, made more practical sense than the highway's design. A subway, however, would have been even better.
Photo by the author

In the heady late sixties, with ample funds from a buoyant economy, Bedoya Reyes's municipal administration oversaw many additional projects: the widening of major thoroughfares, expanded bus services, and construction of a public library and an art museum among them. His was a model of government that favored the middle class, however; working-class areas gained little from these and other works. Building a subway would have helped underclass residents much more than the Vía Expresa, but middle-class citizenry demanded improved roadways for their beloved automobiles.

The working class found solace in distractions such as *fútbol*, but also suffered disproportionately in one of Peru's greatest civic tragedies—ironically right alongside the Vía Expresa. On May 25, 1964, a raucous crowd in the National Stadium watched an Olympics qualifying match against Argentina. When a Uruguayan judge refused to grant Peru a penalty kick at the end of the game, portions of the crowd began to storm the field. In response, police fired canisters of teargas (a relatively unknown means of crowd control in Peru at the time). Panic ensued. Thousands at the north end of the stadium fled the noxious gas by rushing down to the exits. But the metal shutters in this section of the stadium were closed. As fans pressed forward, scores were crushed to death, while many others died by asphyxiation. The official death count was 328, but evidence suggests that it was in fact much higher. In the wake of the tragedy, the Bedoya Reyes administration renovated the stadium, reducing its seating capacity.

Guerrillas and Economic Nationalism

Reflecting worldwide trends, leftist idealism flourished in 1960s Peru, especially among middle-class youth and college students. Simultaneously, the 1962–1963 year of political uncertainty and Haya de la Torre's conniving gave impetus to APRA's decline. As Apristas in congress pro-actively blocked the Belaúnde administration from implementing meaningful agrarian reform, hundreds left the once-idealistic party, among them some of its most active and impassioned members.

New leftist organizations multiplied, especially after the 1959 Cuban Revolution, which saw the island-nation seize and nationalize extensive U.S.-owned properties. University students met in coffee shops and argued over policy and ideology for hours—some declaring themselves Trotskyites, others Maoists, and still others Stalinists. New groups broke off from there. Stalwarts gave public speeches, and university classrooms saw vigorous and often highly polemical debate. Indeed, by the early sixties state universities began to become little more than political workshops; earnest, education-oriented professors were often removed by popular student demand.

The vast majority of these avowed leftists moved only from armchair to armchair. Very few even considered taking to the field. But a few did attempt to put their stated beliefs into practice. Among these was a bookish Luis de la Puente. Born to a wealthy provincial family, de la Puente was briefly exiled as a rebellious Aprista before earning a law degree in Trujillo. Enamored by events in Cuba, he decried APRA's caution. In an incident with party enforcers, he shot a fellow Aprista to death—probably the point where he felt there could be no turning back. After a stint in jail, he publicized the creation of the Revolutionary Leftist Movement (MIR), declaring his intent to lead a revolution as its supreme commander in Lima's Plaza San Martín. A few score joined him, including a charismatic Afro-Peruvian, born of poverty, named Guillermo Lobatón. MIR members received military training in Cuba, then attempted to launch a *foquismo*-inspired revolt near Amazonia.

These efforts did not go well. For many years before their arrival, select areas of the eastern Andean foothills had seen agrarian unrest. But when light-skinned urban "guerrillas" showed up and told indigenous locals that they should rise in revolt, most were reticent. Very few of the revolutionaries spoke native languages; the cultural gap between them and their hosts was great. Sustaining a revolt without an above-ground network of support is almost impossible. Ironically, the dark-skinned Lobatón created a sensation among the Ashaninka tribe, some of whom began to follow him as an almost messianic figure. But when the Peruvian Air Force unleashed napalm, courtesy of the United States, the Ashaninkas' world entered an apocalypse.

Guillermo Lobatón's classroom indoctrination about Marxism in East Germany, and limited guerrilla training in Cuba, provided thin odds against the U.S.-equipped and advised Peruvian Rangers and Marines. Helicopters allowed for rapid army movement, while guerrillas trudged slowly via trails, on foot. Lobatón did outlast the supreme commander—dying in combat in January 1966, three months after de la Puente was captured and shot. Though it has been estimated that the U.S. and Peruvian army spent $10 million to eliminate roughly one hundred MIR guerrillas in 1965–1966 (or U.S. $100,000 per kill), the extermination was complete. Peru's first modern guerrilla "war" affected about fifteen villages and had lasted only a few months.

The Belaúnde government collaborated closely with the United States to destroy the MIR and maintain order in the countryside. And yet one of the improbable features of the administration was its rocky relations with the United States—the nation where English-fluent Belaúnde had attended university. In the mid-sixties, the Democratic administration of Texan Lyndon B. Johnson played hardball with Peru over a small U.S. oil interest called the International Petroleum Company (IPC). The consequences of this confrontation were momentous.

Operating a small but lucrative field in northern Peru for decades, the IPC disputed the nature of Hispanic subsoil rights, was embroiled in endless legal proceedings, and owed Peru's government extensive back taxes. For several years under Belaúnde's watch the issue festered. In the mid-sixties, the United States demanded a resolution favorable to the company (which although modest, was a subsidiary of the powerful Standard Oil conglomerate). When Belaúnde balked, Washington curtailed economic aid and disrupted loan guarantees. It declined to allow the purchase of F-5 fighters, to the consternation of Peru's generals. When Belaúnde appeased the military by purchasing *Mirage* fighters from France, the United States in turn was miffed.

In mid-1968, the IPC issue came to a head. Belaúnde, facing pressure from aristocrats and the political right (which had been investigating alleged "communist influence" in his administration), signed an agreement that gave the American oil firm what it wanted. But what then unfolded was a sequence of spectacular errors befitting a dark comedy. The contract was leaked to the press, with a dissident Peruvian official revealing that its eleventh page was missing. In fact, Belaúnde and other authorities had inexplicably crammed all of their signatures onto the bottom of page ten, but an additional page specified a pay scheme in IPC's favor. When the press and public demanded the eleventh page be revealed, Belaúnde announced (with apparent sincerity) that the original had been lost. This incredible incompetence further fueled the scandal, with most Peruvians believing—not improbably—that their government had engaged in subterfuge. Belaúnde's government fell to a military coup just a few weeks later.

The Velasco Military Regime

It is often misstated that the IPC scandal toppled Belaúnde. In truth, his government was wedged between competing political forces, the dominant strain of which was that of a rising and potent political left. In the contentious tug-of-war at play in Peru, the center could not hold. The aristocrats and right disliked Belaúnde for his middle-class roots and "wasteful" public works; APRA viewed him as its preeminent rival; the grassroots left found his personal style and aloofness demeaning and his middle-of-the-road policies disappointing. It was only a matter of time before his government fell, and the preponderance of forces indicated that when it did so, Peru would lurch decidedly leftward.

The tensions and contractions in the body politic were reflected within the military. There had always been the possibility of a reform movement within the Armed Forces since the 1930s, but even in this context the triumph of a cadre of resolutely progressive officers is surprising. In explanation, the personage of Juan Velasco looms large. Born on the northern coast into relative poverty, Velasco and his ten siblings endured the stigma and low expectations of the underclass. Joining the army as an enlisted soldier, young Juan worked his way upward, obtaining a seat at the military academy, where his studiousness helped make him first in his class.

Velasco took the military's nationalist rhetoric to heart. As a young officer, he was truly affronted by the patronizing attitude of American officers, and the historical bullying of weak nations by major powers. He and other comrades-in-arms found the war against the MIR guerrillas distasteful—and alarming. They saw that, without meaningful reform, a revolutionary movement could take root in Peru. Answering this threat, they advocated what they termed Integrated Security, whereby a nation develops solid socioeconomic fundamentals in order to stand on its own militarily. To Velasco, a progressive administration was the best path to national security.

The military coup in October 1968 was greeted by large protests in Lima. But six days into power, Velasco nationalized IPC's controversial oil field, and the protest movement quickly subsided. It was soon apparent that this was a different kind of military *putsch*—one authentic in its nationalism. A few months later, the regime appropriated all of IPC's holdings, and folded them into a state oil company called Petroperú. Over the next two years, Velasco nationalized much of the essential features of the economy: water resources, telecommunications, and later, most of the long-prosperous but now declining fishmeal industry. The El Niño effect in 1972 did damage to the coastal fisheries, as its warm water flushed across the Humboldt Current. In order to revive the business, Velasco assertively enforced the 200-mile coastal seas claim, obligating Japanese and American tuna trawlers to leave.

Washington, of course, was displeased, but Velasco's timing was impeccable. America was absorbed in its own contentious politics, elections, the Vietnam War, and (within years) Watergate. Heightened Cold War tensions also played in Peru's favor. The United States was reluctant to press too hard, as Velasco indicated that he was willing to turn to the Russians for help—in fact, his government bought military hardware from the Soviet Union. Joining the Third World's non-alignment movement, the regime hosted high-profile diplomatic meetings, while opening several embassies in the Eastern Bloc. Typically, the United States has been able to use its Armed Forces and overwhelming presence to ensure ideological compliance in Latin America; Velasco's Peru was a stark exception.

In June 1969, General Velasco announced his hallmark program: agrarian reform. Over the next three years, much of Peru's traditional haciendas were broken up, with land given to the interior's widely impoverished, mostly dark-skinned peasants. Much has been written about this epic program, which was as visionary as the land reform in Fidel Castro's Cuba. But was it a success? Assessing its outcome is not easy. Though the rural poor were broadly grateful, agricultural productivity dropped in its wake. That a major operation such as this was needed is beyond dispute, yet the economic surgery was done with little finesse—prosperous, modernizing estates were cut up just like aged, traditional ones. Corruption dogged the entire process, which likely should have been carried out more slowly and with greater care. The government established collective farms, but these lacked administrative efficiency and critical access to technology and capital. All round, it was an audacious undertaking, sloppily executed.

The expropriation of foreign-owned estates, including lucrative sugar plantations along the coast, was broadly popular. So too was Juan Velasco, who was warmly cheered by crowds in public. While this affection was genuine, it also reflected the adept propaganda of the regime. From its inception, the military government shut down contrarian media outlets and seized others—firing critics while empowering those who praised it, often by creating media-owning collectives. The government also proactively employed artists, filmmakers, and musicians.

These and other propagandists created a pantheon of popular characters and images, using in particular the historical figure of Tupac Amaru II to represent the "revolutionary" regime. They worked in a bureaucracy called SINAMOS (*Sistema Nacional de Apoyo a la Movilización Social*, or National System for Social Mobilization)—a creative acronym, as it also spelled "without masters" (*sin amos*). And yet the Velasco project was very much top-down, like Argentina's Peronist movement that partly inspired it. It fostered a cult of personality around Juan Velasco himself.

This later dimension proved problematic, as the general's health was failing. In 1973, Velasco had his right leg amputated due to an aneurism. Convalescence took months. His strong personality had kept things moving. Now, his absence and rising disengagement sapped the energy from the top of the regime. So too, the worldwide economic slowdown that began in 1973 limited its options and undermined further possibilities. Inflation began to take hold. Raucous grassroots forces undertook their own initiatives, or challenged the government's policies directly—most notably the nationwide teachers' union, which resented new bureaucratic oversight of the still-dilapidated educational system.

Early on, Velasco's regime had grossly overacted to an incident of civil unrest—a misstep that would have grave national consequences. The problem surfaced in 1969 in Ayacucho, one of Peru's poorest highlands regions. When the regime's Ministry of Education decreed policy changes, including penalty fees for students who repeatedly failed classes, false rumors spread among the indigenous population that the government was ending free public schooling. These rumors were fanned by a small Maoist sect, called the Red Faction, which had come to dominate life at the Ayacucho's sole university, in its regional capital. When Red Faction–led protests erupted in the small city of thirty thousand, local police panicked and used brute force. As conditions deteriorated, the government in Lima dispatched military-trained anti-terrorism units, which again overreacted. A live-fire incident left at least twelve protesters dead, and wholly alienated the broader region. By the regime's mistake, the previously obscure Red Faction effectively gained tens of thousands of region-wide partisans. It later became known as *Sendero Luminoso*, or Shining Path (chapter 13).

It was the Velasco government's unfortunate task to deal with Peru's greatest natural disaster in recorded history. At 3:23 p.m. on Sunday, May 31, 1970, a devastating earthquake struck the north-central region of Áncash. With an epicenter under the ocean, 44 miles southeast of the industrial port of Chimbote, and a magnitude of 7.75 on the Richter scale, the tremor flattened entire buildings for one hundred miles. In the valley of the Santa River (where an avalanche had struck in 1962), mudslides killed thousands. A mix of glacial snow and earthen debris estimated at one hundred million cubic yards rolled down from Mount Huascarán, at a culminating speed of 180 miles per hour. It buried the entire city of Yungay—out of a population of eighteen thousand, only four hundred survived. Even the diversion dam at the Duck Canyon hydroelectric facility was lost, as was a key access bridge. Power outages lasted for months, and rescue crews struggled for days to even reach the remote, hardest hit villages.

Foreign response to the disaster was limited, and aid grossly insufficient. The United States gave Peru only ten million dollars, and that only as a loan—the money had to be repaid. Briefly visiting hospital ships and

Figure 11.2. In addition to very limited financial assistance, the U.S. government sent Patricia Nixon in a diplomatic gesture of concern after the Áncash earthquake. Arranging an itinerary and security for the visiting dignitary was hardly what government officials needed to be doing at such a difficult time. Here, the First Lady walks among rubble piles with Consuelo Gonzáles de Velasco, her Peruvian counterpart.
Source: Richard M. Nixon Presidential Library

dog-sniffing rescue crews favored the affluent neighborhoods in Chimbote and other coastal cities—indigenous peoples in the interior were largely left on their own. In time, though, the Velasco government set up the Reconstruction and Rehabilitation Commission (CRYRZA by acronym), which carried out years of rebuilding. The government did relocate Andean towns to safer areas, and work to build earthquake-proof clinics and emergency facilities. The collective loss was great, however, with the Áncash quake killing an estimated seventy thousand, ranking it as one of the worst natural disasters in world history.

Lima's Prodigious Growth

Post-earthquake poverty and despair prodded hundreds of thousands to migrate to Lima, the prosperous heart of the nation. With a population of 650,000 in 1940, the metropolis boomed to 1.8 million by 1961 and to over 2.5 million in 1967—when it ranked as the forty-sixth largest city in the world. By 1984, after a surge in the seventies, this figure doubled. Located just a dozen miles inland from the Pacific Ocean, the urban leviathan spread in all directions.

Miles of flat agricultural lands to the west of the city's center turned into urban sprawl over three decades. Much of this area, which today comprises primarily the middle-class district of San Miguel, had been acquired by an enterprising Italian immigrant, Fortunato Brescia Tassano. His haciendas here grazed cattle and produced milk for Limeños, while his Tasa Corporation on the nearby coast tapped into the emerging fishmeal and fish oil market. When Fortunato died in 1951, his two sons expanded the family's real estate interests via Grupo Breca, a conglomerate that moved into banking and insurance as well. Generous Velasco-era "expropriations" of haciendas in San Miguel augmented the clan's wealth; by the early twenty-first century it was far and away the richest Peruvian family, with assets worth billions of dollars.

While light industry and housing projects dotted the westward landscape, it was to the south of Lima's center that the moneyed classes primarily migrated. This process, begun with the construction of the Vía Expresa, eventually shifted the capital's material core into an area today known as Surco, to the south of San Isidro and Miraflores, two other bastions of mid-century middle-class life. Within Surco, and in isolated pockets in hills to the southeast, aging elite constructed posh mansions, abandoning their traditional enclave in Lima's center. Upscale service sector businesses and private schools and universities followed, while corporate offices also began to favor the southern suburbs. High-rise condominiums sprouted atop the dramatic cliffsides of the Costa Verde, as an adjoining area called Barranco became a favored residential enclave of the affluent in the eighties.

On the fringes of the metropolis—even on the south side—arose myriad poor barrios, many homes to highlands' migrants in search of work. Squatting on still-vacant land, migrants constructed ramshackle huts of cardboard and plywood. The capital's desert climate aggravated conditions for the poor, most of whom lacked access to potable water. Life for many in the late twentieth century became a struggle just to eat and survive.

The progressive Velasco regime tried to assist urban migrants and sometimes had notable success—as reflected in the case of Villa El Salvador. When hundreds of squatters appeared on the extreme southern outskirts of Lima in May 1971, the government relocated them into what it dubbed *Pueblo Joven Villa El Salvador*, or a "Young Town." From the start, the area saw land set aside for future broad streets and public buildings; zoning safely separated residential areas from an industrial park. Today Villa El Salvador has over four hundred thousand residents and is still notably poor. But the simple act of foresight also worked wonders: at little cost, by organizing the layout of the barrio, life was made better over the long run.

Figure 11.3. Rural migration has ringed much of Lima with slums, many positioned on hillsides. There is, however, an element of upward mobility at play. Over time, cardboard and plywood give way to concrete and cinderblock, while communities eventually acquired basic services such as trash removal, sewage, and electricity. Such is the case with the now well-established Leticia barrio, in Rimac District.
Photo by the author

A Shift to the Right

Lima's rich were uneasy with the direction and pace of change under Velasco, and watched with interest as rifts emerged within the military government during the course of 1975. A rebellion by the always conservative National Police in February, which left hundreds dead and injured, created a crisis atmosphere in the capital. The appointment of Francisco Morales Bermúdez as Minister of Defense, combined with a cabinet shuffle and command shake-up in the Navy, presaged removal of the ailing Velasco, in what amounted to a bloodless coup in August. With the support of a conservative clique of army officers, Morales Bermúdez became president, a post he held for the next five years.

Although he vowed to continue the policies of his predecessor, the new chief executive steadily moved Peru's body politic to the right. Grandson of a president, and son of an army colonel assassinated by Apristas in the 1930s, Morales Bermúdez represented the ideas of the still-influential elite. While technically continuing Velasco's diplomacy of nonalignment, Peru's military quietly began to collaborate with that of the United States. The government retroactively paid various U.S. corporations for select properties nationalized under Velasco. Economically, it welcomed oversight from the International Monetary Fund (IMF), a Washington-based financial institution closely tied to large U.S. and European banks.

Under Morales Bermúdez, Peru's economy notably deteriorated. The decline was not entirely his fault: the heyday of global growth passed in the mid-seventies, and an inflationary cycle ravaged most of the West's currencies. Still, citizens were anxious as real wages dropped sharply, unemployment rose, and even some basic goods became unobtainable. As always, the IMF's recipe for Third World recession was more belt-tightening. Austerity mandates triggered cuts in subsidies, while the prices of gasoline, cooking oil, and public transportation rose. Periodic protests and riots followed. When General Velasco died in 1977, some two hundred thousand turned out for his funeral—the largest in the nation's history, the event an obvious public repudiation of Morales Bermúdez's increasingly stern rule. In the same year a nationwide general strike unfolded, further pressuring the regime to either change course or cede power.

Politically, the president increasingly sought civilian allies. He reached out to APRA, which continued to shift to the right, even after the aged Haya de la Torre finally died in 1979. The party that had battled communists and taken control of much of Peru's organized labor in the 1940s now more than ever represented the middle class; many unions had in fact broken free of its grip and reengaged the politics of the left. The military government deported belligerent unionists by the hundreds. Morales Bermúdez linked his security forces to the CIA-orchestrated Operation Condor, which facilitated the abduction, disappearance, and murder of hundreds of political activists throughout Latin America in the seventies. In 2017, a court in Italy convicted a very elderly Morales Bermúdez for participating in these crimes against humanity, ensuring that in his twilight years the general could not leave his native country.

Trying to answer his multiplying critics, Morales Bermúdez announced the convocation of a constituent assembly, the drafting of a new constitution, and the return to civilian rule via elections in 1980. To his chagrin, the balloting brought back to power Fernando Belaúnde, who again appealed to rural Peru, through a media-savvy campaign, to mobilize support for his Popular Action Party—which nearly won control of the new bicameral congress. A public outpouring of electoral celebration suggests that the elderly architect enjoyed extensive goodwill, as he yet again vanquished APRA (albeit without Haya de la Torre) at the polls. Little did he and his supporters realize how difficult things could become, and that his second term in office would be far rockier than his first.

CHAPTER TWELVE

Life and Culture, 1948–1980

The postwar era saw great cultural productivity in Peru. The expansion of radio and the arrival of television transformed especially urban lives and reshaped popular culture. The country's most famous writer, Mario Vargas Llosa, began his rise to international acclaim. Women like Blanca Varela overcame difficult odds to reach audiences, while Afro-Peruvian women like Lucha Reyes overcame nearly insurmountable odds. Reflecting global trends, the sixties and seventies exuded much youthful idealism, irreverence, and passion on the forefront of artistry.

Postwar Literary Rebels

Peru's rich literary tradition flourished in the postwar decades as a generation of writers born in the 1920s and 1930s came of age. Many penned brilliant works even in relative youth. Such was the case with Oswaldo Reynoso. Born in 1931 in Arequipa, Reynoso developed an early love of books, while receiving a quality education in the city's best Catholic schools before matriculating into the National Normal School (known as *La Cantuta*). He developed a pronounced anti-clerical streak, with rebellion a hallmark of his lifelong literary corpus. In his youth he had also observed and participated in Arequipa's working-class unrest, which featured many general strikes.

Reynoso's empathy for the underclasses drove him to seek out street life among the working poor in Lima. This quest in turn produced his riveting and controversial collection of short stories published as *Los Inocentes*

(1961). Jarring tales of what is dubbed "urban realism," *Los Inocentes* introduces readers to the lives of restless adolescent males, while employing vernacular underclass speech known as *jeringa*. It presages later Latin American works, such as Brazilian Paulo Lins' *Cidade de Deus* (*City of God*). The book shocked the aristocracy, which it criticizes, and appalled many devout Catholics, some of whom decried its sexual revelations—including passages involving homosexuality—as pornographic. This kind of critique seemed to make Reynoso even more contrarian, and willing to challenge both political norms and social conventions in his later works.

Challenging artistic norms came naturally to young Jorge Eduardo Eielson, a poet born in Lima in 1942 to a North American father and Peruvian mother. After his father died prematurely, his mother saw to it that he received an excellent education—he mastered French, along with English and Spanish, by early adulthood. Eielson was enamored of the sea, with some of his first poetry celebrating its mystery and beauty. He was far less enamored of his birthplace; Lima was periodically mocked in his poems, though select passages suggest a love-hate relationship. Venturing off to France on a scholarship in 1948, he embraced Europe and lived most of his life there, primarily in Italy. Once well-known, he moved onto the visual arts. His rudimentary works, made of cloth and twine, fetched tens of thousands of dollars around the time of his death in Milan in 2006.

Peru's most renowned female poet of the late twentieth century is Blanca Varela. A *Limeña* born in 1926, she bonded in childhood closely with her talented mother, who was an accomplished musician and artist in her own right. A young Blanca enjoyed a secure and privileged life—she did some child acting on *Radio Nacional*. Swimming in artistic circles of the affluent, she married an architect-sculptor (see below), and the young couple headed off to Paris where they intermingled with prominent expatriates and French intellectuals. They socialized with France's famous philosophical couple, Jean-Paul Sartre and Simone Beauvoir. Future Nobel laureate Octavio Paz, then working in Mexico's Parisian embassy, encouraged Varela to publish her poetry, the first book of which appeared in Mexico City several years later. Though her corpus is not particularly large, it spans decades and demonstrates great linguistic care.

The mid-twentieth century produced Peru's most popular fiction writers. Julio Ramón Ribeyro penned a plethora of short stories, always drawing on his wit, humor, and use of irony, while frequently narrating the life of a hapless protagonist pressed by impossible circumstance. Novelist Alfredo Bryce Echenique's extensive writings in the 1980s and 1990s never matched the accomplishment of his first and most celebrated work, *Un Mundo para Julius*

(*A World for Julius*, 1970). Julius is the inquisitive child of a 1950s aristocratic Limeño family in economic decline; he bonds with the household's servants, and wrestles with his privileged place in an unjust world.

The most celebrated Peruvian writer of all is of course Mario Vargas Llosa, influenced especially by Ribeyro, with whom he also had a stormy relationship. Born in Arequipa in 1936 to middle class parents who soon separated, Mario was raised by his grandfather, who served in a diplomatic post in Bolivia. As a teen, with his parents reunited, he lived in the south Lima suburb of Magdalena del Mar. His father, who cared little about his literary aspirations and with whom he struggled to relate, sent him to a military academy. This experience ironically provided the fodder for his first novel, *La ciudad y los perros* (*The City and the Dogs*—but published in English as *The Time of the Hero*), a 1963 publication that won him acclaim, yet was also decried by

Figure 12.1. Not easily read, Blanca Varela's poetry evokes a certain existentialist despair coupled with nearly constant surrealist imagery. Stanzas are not rigid, and lines rarely rhyme. Before her death in 2009 Varela had won a small but impassioned following in the Hispanic world and beyond. Most of her books have been translated into multiple languages.
Source: Museo Metropolitano de Lima

conservatives as an affront to the Peruvian army. Having dropped out of the military school, Vargas Llosa completed his studies at San Marcos University and worked for a year as a journalist before turning his attention to full-time writing.

Early novels made him famous. *La ciudad y los perros* was followed by *La casa verde* (*The Green House*)—perhaps his best—about a brothel and one of its workers, with a touch of magical realism besides. His more famous 1969 book, *Conversación en la catedral* (*Conversation in the Cathedral*) is a bitter-spirited and darker work that addresses many political issues, including the Velasco military regime—which he repudiates. It reflects a thinker in transition. As a university student, Vargas Llosa was a self-professed Communist and admirer of Fidel Castro; by the early seventies he quarreled openly with his former literary icon, Colombian leftist Gabriel García Márquez, whom he notoriously assaulted at a conference in 1976. The mid-seventies onward saw Vargas Llosa write shorter and arguably inferior works, including mystery and crime novels. In 1981, he produced *La guerra del fin del mundo* (*The War of the End of the World*), a historical yarn about a messianic cult and war in nineteenth-century Brazil. History and crime were both prevalent in his *La fiesta del chivo* (*The Feast of the Goat*, 2000) about Dominican Republic strongman Rafael Trujillo and his assassination.

Though his family was not oligarchic it was well-connected, and early in his career Mario Vargas Llosa received significant press coverage. He became a cultural and political fixture of Peruvian life by the 1970s, long before he ran for president in 1990. Years earlier, though, he undertook a controversial investigation of the murder of journalists covering the Sendero war in the highlands. He evoked strong reactions from different sectors of society, some positive, others negative. His attention to detail, instilled by San Marcos mentor Raúl Porras Barrenechea, a historian (Vargas Llosa very nearly pursued a history PhD), speaks to the meticulous care evident in his writing. But the 1990 electoral defeat seemed to sour Vargas Llosa on his homeland. In old age he has lived primarily in Spain, even accepting the title of *marqués* from the Spanish monarch. It has been an unusual path for a onetime communist. He won the Nobel Prize for literature in 2010.

The Golden Age of Television

Television arrived in Peru in 1958. The first broadcast was made by the Ministry of Education's Channel 7, but within a very short time private commercial stations took to the air. Among these was *Panamericana Televisión*, owned by Genaro Delgado Brandt—a media mogul who had already developed Peru's first nationwide radio network. Lima's enthused middle class rushed to purchase televisions imported from the United States. This new technology, a product of quantum physics with its electron-beaming Cathode Ray Tube, was the marvel of a decade.

Content was of course the immediate challenge. Each TV station—all located in or around central Lima—constructed basic studios and created low-budget productions. While some educational and news-oriented shows soon appeared, the most appealing were those with entertainment value. Music predictably became a major feature. Comedy also rose quickly to the fore. Talent for the new medium was primarily drawn from radio, though some theater dramatists switched to the new medium as well.

National Radio of Peru (RNP), with its excellent studios and experienced staff, provided the most important personnel for the upstart television industry. Several writers and actors migrated from a popular radio show called *Loquibambia*. The most famous of these was Tulio Loza. Born and raised in the highlands, Loza was sent to Lima by his education-earnest parents for schooling, but although he studied at the University of San Marcos, he found his niche in mass media. Loza's comical skits in early broadcasts led to his own production, *El Show de Tulio Loza*, which became popular by the early 1960s. Loza's comic successor was Hugo Muñoz Barrata, who starred in a series called *El Tornillo* (*The Screw*) during the 1970s.

Loza's comic genius engaged a sociological dimension of society: drawing on his own experiences, he repeatedly caricatured a highlander lost in the urban jungle that is Lima. This clash of *cholo* (which in Peruvian Spanish denotes someone of rural or parochial origin) and the norms of a sophisticated and urbane middle class has many potentially humorous dimensions—both to the hundreds of thousands of migrants but also to their inadvertent city-dwelling hosts. Simply put, Loza portrayed an endearing "country bumpkin." The humor was similar to what Americans found in the Barney Fife character of the *Andy Griffith Show* and in the sitcom *The Beverly Hillbillies*.

Given its modest dimensions, the nascent television industry was predictably influenced by external forces. In its early years, Buenos Aires disproportionately shaped the medium. The Argentines had already produced a variety of shows, and some Peruvians visited their studios, while several Limeño producers adapted or replicated popular sets and scripts. The advantage of a common language fed this influence and collaboration. Chile, too, had a rapidly advancing television industry, but for reasons of national pride, predictably, fewer Peruvians looked to Santiago for inspiration. Dubbed TV shows from the United States were penetrating Latin markets by the mid-sixties, but were comparatively slow to make their way to Peru, a secondary and far less lucrative market.

As was common in nearly all of Latin America, both radio and television infrastructure and distribution consolidated over time. Delgado Brandt's sons inherited his business interests, and one, Manuel, worked to create *Radio Programas del Peru*, or RPP—which despite its name evolved into the nation's foremost TV network by the early 1980s. Manuel's brother Héctor was a friend and confidante to President Alan García, and saw to it that RPP gave the APRA administration favorable coverage, until things got so bad that nearly all of Peru had soured on the government. Media consolidation tended to reduce artistic access to the broader public, and create mega-stars in acting, music, and literature, as was the case of Mario Vargas Llosa.

Temporary change came to mass media with Juan Velasco's military government. Many radio and TV stations were compelled to work with

SINAMOS (see chapter 11), the bureaucracy designed to generate public support for the regime. SINAMOS enlisted the participation of artists, filmmakers, and intellectuals, especially those with left-leaning credentials. Héctor Béjar, a sociology professor at San Marcos University and longtime functionary of the Peruvian Communist Party, was one such person. He engaged in guerrilla activity in the early sixties, but received an amnesty from Velasco and worked for SINAMOS, along with Hugo Neira, a fellow academic who became its director. A young filmmaker named Federico García Hurtado also embraced SINAMOS, himself the son of a professor. His 1977 film *Kuntur Wachana* celebrated the regime's agrarian reform.

Post-Velasco film production was more uneven. García Hurtado continued to work with several former SINAMOS participants to produce a biopic, *Tupac Amaru* (1984) that celebrated the life of the revolutionary Tupac Amaru II in two and a half hours, complete with uniformly cruel Spanish antagonists. In the late seventies a promising young director-photographer duo emerged in Francisco Lombardi and José "Pili" Flores Lucera, childhood friends from the southern city of Tacna. Like their hometown, both were proudly Peruvian, and sought inspiration from the rich canopy of national literature. In 1978, they produced a film short titled *Cuentos inmorales (Immoral Tales)*, based on Reynoso's *Los Inocentes*. Three years later they shot the more ambitious *Muerte de un magnate (Death of a Tycoon)*, a whodunit about the strange death of Luis Banchero Rossi, the fishmeal entrepreneur who was found murdered in his east-Lima mansion on New Year's 1972 (the outspoken Banchero, who had political ambitions and many enemies, was also born in Tacna).

Television and film augmented radio in reaching the masses. As Peru's population surged to beyond fifteen million in the mid-1970s, these mediums defined popular culture, which swamped (by numbers) all other forms of creative expression. Still, the accomplishments of Peru's postwar artists remain impressive. The underrepresented medium of photography came to be defined by Martín Chambi, who had established a gallery in Cusco in 1938 and made his fellow indigenous highlanders the focus of his attention. By the time of his death in 1973, Chambi had thirty thousand negatives, his camera's eye consistently good. A retrospective at New York's Museum of Modern Art in 1979 effectively introduced a global audience to Chambi.

Though the *Indigenismo* represented by Chambi and José Sabogal (see chapter 9) endured, several other artists branched into Modernism. Much celebrated among these was Sérvulo Gutiérrez, who was keenly influenced by—and may have briefly studied with—the avant-garde Argentinian Emilio Pettoruti. By the early fifties Gutiérrez was fully engaging Abstraction, around the time of his famous and fiery tryst with Doris Gibson, founder of

Figure 12.2. Sérvulo Gutiérrez's Abstract work *Don Juan* (1952) features thick strokes of bold colors—a hallmark of his paintings in this period. Typically Gutiérrez opted for primary colors, while growing distinctively fond of oft-neglected black. A boxer in youth, largely self-taught as an artist, Gutiérrez lived a Bohemian's life, dying relatively young at age forty-seven.
Source: Museo del Banco Central de Reserva del Perú

Peru's foremost newsmagazine, *Caretas*. Fernando de Szyszlo matched Gutiérrez's Modernism in sculpture. Married to Blanca Varela, he often created works in plastic.

Popular Music

Mid-century Peruvian music included much in style indebted to both Europe and the passing aristocracy. Such was the genre of *Vals Criollo* (Peruvian waltz), and the career of Chabuca Granda (real name María Isabel Granda Larco). Born of a wealthy family in the elite Lima enclave of Barranco, Granda sang gentle songs of nostalgia, the most famous of which was her 1956 work *Fina Estampa* (Fine Appearance), about a stylish gentleman strolling in public—to the delight of swooning women. Seemingly incongruent for Granda were songs in the 1960s that she penned and performed in memory of Javier Heraud, a university student and budding poet who was gunned down as a guerrilla fighter at age twenty-one.

Bolero, the genre of mellow, romantic music arriving in Peru from Cuba and especially Mexico in the 1940s (see chapter 9), began to flourish in the late 1950s synchronous with the fast rise of television. In the mid-fifties an Ecuadoran named Julio Jaramillo was successfully imitating the style of Cuban Pedro Infante, while gaining radio airtime in Peru. He in turn encouraged the breakout career of Pedro Otiniano, arguably the true "father" of Peruvian bolero. Popularly known as Pedrito, *El Señor de Amor* (The Gentleman of Love), the Lima-born vocalist enjoyed early success on radio crooning out smooth love ballads.

Otiniano was soon eclipsed in popularity, however, by a Callao-born Lucho Barrios, who ultimately became the figure most associated with bolero. The squat and chesty Barrios, known as Señor Marabú (*Marabú* is both a percussion pattern and the title of his most popular album), first enjoyed commercial success in Ecuador, and somewhat to the chagrin of his compatriots—won more hearts south of the border in Chile, where he used state-of-the-art recording studios in Santiago. His appeal subsequently went transnational, and gained him a continent-wide following. As with most bolero, the lyrical theme of his songs was often the contended ecstasy of joyous love. Yet Lucho often wailed about treachery—predictably in a *machista* culture, always on the part of the woman; happy songs like *Nido de amor* (Love Nest) were counterbalanced by the likes of *Mala* (Evil Woman) and *Adultera* (Adulteress).

The number of well-known bolero performers multiplied in the heyday of television in the 1960s. Appearances on Lima's several commercial stations, or RPP's budding multi-station network, helped launch careers. Record sales in Peru rose sharply, with vinyl 45s (single-song records) pressed by the nation's sole manufacturer, Discos MAG. Musically, at a time when Mexican bolero was moving toward heavily endowed arrangements with strings, the Peruvian version tended to still favor the more stripped-down sound of just three or four overlaid guitars.

Ideal to this format was a trio called *Los Morunos*, who were promoted by Radio Sono and eventually accessed TV. The band's popularity in the 1960s allowed for nearly constant national touring. *Los Morunos* played regional festivals, small auditoriums and movie theaters, and occasionally upscale restaurants. The trio was inspired by a New York (Puerto Rican) band called *Los Panchos*, which had developed great appeal throughout much of Latin America over the previous decade. When *Los Panchos* finally came to Peru in 1976, they were enthusiastically received; original *Los Morunos* member Manuel Ortíz performed with them on several occasions.

Though bolero had arrived, Música Criolla continued to be favored by many. To the degree to which the term *Música Criolla* simply means Peru-originating music, of course, the two genres effectively overlap—*Los Morunos* were vintage Peruvian, singing mostly ballads written by compatriots. Even musically the line between the two genres is not sharp, with many songs recorded as both bolero and criolla. Such was the case of Peru's most famous popular song since *El Plebeyo*, Mario Cavaguaro's *Osito de felpa* (Teddy Bear). The tragedy communicated by its lyrics is obvious: *Teddy Bear, playmate of my child, My Beloved who one night was taken by the Lord; to see you so sad* . . .[1] Cavaguaro, a chemical engineer by training, wrote the song in 1951. Over several decades dozens of artists throughout Latin America performed or recorded versions of it, including *Los Morunos*.

Many Peruvian composers in the early postwar period were writing Criolla songs by the score. One of the most successful was Augusto Polo Campos. Born to a junior ranking army officer, Polo Campos grew up in the working class Rimac neighborhood of north Lima, and began writing even as he pursued a career as a policeman. His lyrics exuded local and national pride, with references to neighborhood landmarks, and titles such as *Esta es mi tierra* (This is My Land) and *Limeña* (Woman from Lima). He penned songs for many TV shows, including *El Show de Tulio Loza* in the 1960s. Surprisingly, Polo Campos himself did not play guitar, nor master any instrument.

---

1. The full, famous opening stanza in Spanish is: *Osito de felpa / Juguete de mi hijo / De mi chiquitito / Que una madrugada se llevo de Señor. / Al verte tan triste / creeras un sueño / que tu fiel amigo / se nos haya ido para no volver.*

Although never overtly political, Polo Campos held to generally conservative positions (and as a policeman in the 1950s, he helped repress the outlawed Apristas). Hence, it is of great irony that this middle-class male wrote the most significant song in the career of Lucha Reyes, the most remarkable and unlikely of Criolla stars. An Afro-Peruvian born to poverty in Rimac, Reyes's father died when she was six. She frequently went hungry as a child, while also suffering from diabetes. At age sixteen, she married a police sergeant who abused her. Abandoned, with two young sons, she worked menial jobs, often as a cook. She was bedridden and hospitalized for months, but recovered, and began to sing in a small Rimac club.

Radio Victoria discovered Lucha Reyes, and aired her repeatedly on its *El Sentir de los Barrios* (The Pulse of the Barrios) show. She thereafter participated at the Teatro Pizarro's Sunday Música Criolla revues. A subsequent RCA contract produced a flurry of hits in the early seventies, foremost of which was Polo Campos's composition *Regresa* (Come Back)—a song filled with lyrical irony, given her life story. Reyes briefly had her own show on Radio Victoria that gained a loyal following in Lima's slums. A true child of the underclass, whose joy of singing was transparent, Reyes died of tuberculosis at age thirty-seven in 1973, ironically on October 31, *El Día de Canción Criolla* (National Creole Song Day).

Reyes's authenticity is exceptional, especially given the time period. The power of mass media drove record sales to new heights in the 1970s and beyond, but it also removed the dynamic of public sentiment weeding out—or partially selecting—future stars. Fame and recording success were all but predetermined in corporate boardrooms, where big hand-in-hand record labels and distribution companies signed select artists and aggressively promoted them through advertising. Since these corporations transcended national borders, it is no surprise that Peruvians listened to and embraced bigger-than-ever musical acts from other nations. A few Peruvians themselves received contracts and promotion, as well.

The number of outsiders who received heavy radio and television exposure in Peru are too many to mention, but among them was Puerto Rican Hector Lavoe, whose salsa and occasional bolero numbers saturated the airwaves and won him the moniker "Singer of Singers." Lavoe's personal life was a mess; he descended into heavy substance abuse and performed erratically—until attempting to commit suicide by jumping out of a nine-story hotel room balcony in San Juan, Puerto Rico. He survived the fall in 1988, but his career did not—he was effectively finished as a recording artist thereafter.

Peruvians who obtained corporate marketing and great commercial success include Callao-born Iván Cruz, who transitioned from singing salsa in the 1970s into *Bolero Cantino*, or the genre of songs popular with drink. An artist with RCA Victor, his career has spanned decades and produced a dozen Gold Records (sales of over five hundred thousand). Critically, his best music was his earliest, including the popular yet starkly simple *Me dices que te vas* (You Tell Me You're Leaving). A reckless behind-the-scenes life of substance abuse wore on Cruz's body. He eventually embraced evangelical religion and occasionally began to preach, as well as sing, as he drifted into retirement. The corporate model that generated careers like that of Iván Cruz would grow stronger as the twentieth century wound down. In music, comic acting, and also in literature, a decades-long Golden Age in the mid-twentieth century was passing into memory.

CHAPTER THIRTEEN

The Tumult

In 1980 Peru returned to civilian rule after twelve years of military governance. Fernando Belaúnde won the election with 43 percent of the vote, staving off a threat from an Aprista candidate who positioned himself to the left of the former president. During and after the election, large strikes disrupted major economic sectors, as workers (some white-collar) demanded higher wages in a time of accelerating inflation. Many of these strikes were orchestrated by APRA, embittered in defeat and seeking to unsettle the new government. A now elderly Belaúnde was to find Peru much more difficult to govern during his second turn at the wheel.

Enter *Sendero Luminoso*

Just as Belaúnde returned to office, a pseudo-revolutionary movement emerged in the highlands. It was led by a charismatic egotist named Abimael Guzmán. Like so many communist leaders worldwide (Vladimir Lenin held a title of nobility), Guzmán was not from the working class; his father was an accountant on a hacienda. Born out of wedlock, Abimael was raised in the port city of Callao, primarily by an uncle who saw to it that he received a good education. Young Abimael matriculated into university in Arequipa, where he joined the Communist Party and developed a dogmatic faith in class struggle, even as he trekked along a singularly bourgeois course in life. He became a philosophy professor at a national university campus in Ayacucho in 1962, and eventually gained bureaucratic control of this peripheral institution. A trip to China introduced him to Mao's regime—despite the Cultural Revolution, in which students denounced their teachers—and he thereafter led a pro-Maoist splinter group away from Peru's conventional Communist Party.

Marrying the daughter of a prosperous local hacendado (estate owner), who also somewhat strangely professed communism, Guzmán seized the opportunity presented by the Velasco regime's ill-advised education policy, as much of Ayacucho Province embraced a raw anti-government fervor in the wake of its heavy-handed tactics. In the mid-seventies he quietly resigned his professorship and prepared, along with his wife and a few other followers, to foment revolution. Taking great lengths to evade government surveillance, he and his organization, which now claimed to be the *true* Communist Party of Peru, trained a few score fanatical cadre in the art of killing. In one of their first attacks, erstwhile comrades tortured to death an unarmed sugar mill owner in rural Ayacucho, as several of his newly "liberated" workers tried in vain to save him. The "People's War" had begun. Soon this organization was known as *Sendero Luminoso* (Shining Path), a term taken from the writings of Mariátegui.

Guzmán taught his followers to be ruthless and, in a spirit strikingly similar to that found in cultist sects and Islamic *jihad*, instilled in them the idea that any measure taken was justified by the final results. Senderistas were instructed to pose in the countryside as hitchhikers, lure policemen into picking them up, and then heartlessly slit their throats. That highly indoctrinated followers were willing to commit such acts is surely true; but compiling conclusive tallies of such crimes committed is difficult—very few human rights organizations were collecting field data at the time. Sendero did ultimately kill hundreds of policemen, mayors, and other local officials in and around Ayacucho in the early eighties.[1] These acts of calculated and cruel murder sent thousands of others throughout the highlands fleeing for fear of their lives.

One of the dastardliest features of Sendero violence was Guzmán's insistence that his followers eliminate "bourgeois elements" that—by any reasonable accounting—were in fact progressive. In one early gesture, Sendero blew up the tomb of General Velasco with dynamite. In the highlands, Peace Corps projects, mission charities, and health clinics were targeted. Assassins killed educators and volunteers in impoverished villages. These defenseless "soft targets" were easy to eliminate, and their murder instilled great fear in

---

1. The later Truth Commission report concluded that three thousand died in the incipient violence, though this estimate—like the report's final tallies—might be incorrect (see chapter 15).

the masses. But it also seeded resentment. Sendero Luminoso made little attempt to win hearts and minds—a strategy that would later fuel a fiery grassroots backlash against it.

The presence of the state was never strong in the highlands, and by 1982 Guzmán's Sendero held sway over much of the region, partly through terror but also by default (policing was long-abusive and incompetent, helping drive the rural hinterlands into Sendero's waiting arms). The insurgency took direct control of hundreds of villages, generally to the bewilderment of the inhabitants. Guzmán himself was disinterested in things native—he had rarely interacted with indigenous peoples, and made no attempt to learn Quechua. Yet his influence had slowly penetrated parts of the countryside through the presence of indoctrinated teachers trained at the regional university.

Embracing the Maoist model, Guzmán believed that Peru could be converted to a Marxist state through rural insurrection. His Sendero organization now appointed students to govern native towns. Flying red flags on main squares, these communities beheld the bizarre phenomenon of peasants marching around in practice military drills, while carrying sticks (as mock rifles) and singing songs about the joys of Marxism. It is hard to get into the minds of locals and gauge what they were thinking. Evidence suggests that many liked the elimination of thievery and petty crime through draconian punishments; various civic gestures also offered the allure of a more just society. But the Senderista disregard for age and the role of elders, among other dictates, must have surely troubled them.

Guzmán himself, meanwhile, morphed from an egotist into a megalomaniac, convinced that he was the "Fourth Sword" of worldwide Marxism, alongside Marx, Lenin, and Mao. Admiring students painted his picture on walls and proclaimed him *Presidente*, albeit with an exaggerated physique—the pudgy Guzmán appeared slim and fit. That a Peruvian could be so significant appealed to many (partly out of a nationalistic urge, ironically); hundreds of lower middle-class students in Ayacucho *wanted to believe* that they could be part of something breathtaking and great; their lives, trapped as they were in a backwater region with high unemployment, offered little hope of significance otherwise. Memories of the repression in 1969 permeated Ayacucho in particular with an acute resentment of the establishment in Lima, and a hatred of its invariably lighter-skinned soldiers and police.

Of course, the insurrection meant that those forces would return. It was easy for the army to occupy Ayacucho city proper. The intelligence services soon set up safe houses, and began to arrest and torture students by the hundreds. Scores disappeared. Taking towns in the countryside posed no real difficulty either, but Senderistas were able to kill isolated soldiers with small

Figure 13.1. Sendero propaganda endlessly glorified revolutionary struggle. This drawing from an organizational pamphlet represents the idyllic People's Classroom. At the heart of the rural insurgency was not the peasantry, but Peru's poorly funded, second-rate educational system. Sendero's most resolute cadre emerged from regional university campuses and secondary schools, where many were indoctrinated by radicalized teachers.
Source: Lugar de Memoria

arms fire and roadside ambushes. Soon the elusive enemy, evading pitch battle, turned frustrated soldiers against the local populace. Mestizos from the coast naturally distrusted the reticent, Quechua-speaking Natives, and as they saw comrades-in-arms die they began to hate them. Various army massacres unfolded, even as Guzmán instructed his own cadre to retaliate in kind. Villagers were soon caught between two forces, both of which demanded their absolute obedience. Few human rights organizations or independent sources documented what happened in Ayacucho during 1983–1985, but by any accounting it was horrific. Later studies (see Chapter 15) concluded that low tens of thousands of native peoples perished in the middle of an ideological firefight they had never invited and could never fully understand.

A Sputtering Political Establishment

As the Sendero insurrection took hold, Peru's political class delivered next to nothing. To the surprise of nearly all, reelected Fernando Belaúnde opted to pursue a neoliberal economic model in the early eighties that shunned statist intervention and favored foreign capital. Determined to win the favor of the United States from the start, he appointed aristocrat Manuel Ulloa Elías as both prime minister and Minister of Finance. Son of a diplomat and scion of a prestigious family, a young Ulloa had worked as an executive in New York for W.R. Grace, the very enterprise that arose out of the Grace Brothers' pact with the Cáceres government in the late nineteenth century. Close to New York bankers and IMF economists, he now pushed so-called free market economics that, in fact, catered to large foreign corporations at the expense of local entrepreneurs. A playboy who never established stable relationships with women (he was married four times), Ulloa himself lived a jet-setting life that provided much fodder for gossip columnists. He was more at home in Manhattan or Madrid than in Lima—and had little patience for Peruvian locals who dared to criticize him.

Ulloa slashed corporate taxes, further reduced state subsidies and social programs, and urged Belaúnde to curtail Peru's money supply in order to rein in inflation. Portions of Petroperú (the state oil company) were re-privatized, to the delight of Wall Street. Ulloa quickly lifted price controls on basic food staples and gasoline, triggering social unrest and general strikes. The government mandated "terrorism" penalties for anyone caught in resistant acts of violence. Belaúnde's second government was beginning to resemble that of General Odría, the man whose strong-armed mismanagement of Peru had first inspired his entry into politics.

The neoliberal recipe did not work. By 1982, inflation accelerated to nearly 100 percent, local banks began to fail, and Peru slid into a deep recession. Ulloa arranged for more IMF loans, and the nation's debt burden rose sharply. Disillusioned, the public increasingly turned to the political left. Intermittent general strikes rocked the capital, students created new revolutionary groups, and Belaúnde became even less popular than Morales Bermúdez had ever been. Ulloa was finally forced to resign, heading off to a comfortable life of *tertulías* and sexual escapades in Spain, where he would die in old age.

Dead-end economic policies and popular frustration empowered the political left as never before. An umbrella organization, called the *Izquierda Unida* (United Left or IU), formed to back various candidates. By 1983 and 1984 these were easily winning local races. In Lima, the IU successfully elected Alfonso "Frejolito" Barrantes as mayor—the first major office-holding by the left in Peru's history. Barrantes' administration launched a series of social programs, including one that provided free milk to poor families, and generated much enthusiasm in the capital. But several IU candidates were gunned down by Sendero before they could take office, adding to a rising sense of chaos.

Into this mess now stepped APRA. In 1984, facing unprecedented popular opposition, Belaúnde fired his second Minister of Finance, reversed austerity plans, and attempted to appease his critics. These moves came as he unleashed the full weight of the army on Sendero. He then shuffled and reshuffled his cabinet yet, despite everything, the center-right of body politic entered the 1985 elections discredited. Building upon the rhetoric of his 1980 predecessor, an Aprista named Alan García kept the historic party to the left and won the presidency. APRA, at last, had come to power.

Alan García looms large in modern Peruvian history, as one of the nation's most adept politicians. He had been raised by impassioned Apristas—his mother a schoolteacher, his father an accountant. By the time of his mid-century childhood, APRA had become something of a club-like social institution, evincing great familial loyalty. Sacrifice was expected and honored; Alan's own father had been briefly imprisoned under Odría. As a teenager, Alan joined the party and took political classes at its downtown Lima headquarters, the *Casa del Pueblo*. He soon stood out—literally. Growing to six feet, three inches in height, he towered over most of his fellow countrymen. He was also ambitious. After studying sociology and law in Paris, he returned to Peru and rose in the party, becoming its secretary. An elderly Haya de la Torre favored him. Quick to smile, and radiating an infusive optimism, he won the presidency in 1985 at age thirty-six.

His ascent to power was a time of hope for many in Peru who looked to their young president for leadership and a new direction. García seemed determined not to disappoint. Faithful to APRA's originally leftist tenets, he was quick to speak in populist terms. He vowed to fight corruption, criticized the United States, and cut Peru's debt payments. He also briefly reined in the military, and ordered its generals to prohibit the killing of civilians and regard basic human rights. All of this energy and vision unfolded within months of taking office, but García's fundamental premise was wrong: he assumed that by force of action he could set Peru's course.

Terrorist attacks continued, and García's commitment to a clean counterinsurgency war lasted less than a year. In June 1986 Sendero prisoners staged a coordinated uprising in three big prisons near Lima. The conditions of their confinement were inhumane, and many of the inmates had been denied due process—though most were probably guilty of violent crimes. The common Latin American practice of prisons effectively run by prisoners allowed them to organize and create Sendero communes. They built homemade weapons and took control on an appointed day, when García's government was prominently hosting diplomats of nations connected to the Socialist International. Outraged, the president authorized the security forces, with army support, to crush the uprisings. There was no mercy. At the island facility of El Frontón, evidence suggests that soldiers summarily shot scores of recaptured prisoners, slashing with knives any who still breathed afterward.

In economics, García encountered market conditions that stymied his every policy. His timing was spectacularly bad. He took office just as a wave of debt swamped the entire Third World. A global financial meltdown was averted by the transfer of bad debt into the Washington, D.C.–based IMF. The dollar strengthened as commodity prices plummeted. The only way to survive the storm was to cling to powerful financial anchors—American banks, lending agencies, and foreign capital.

The APRA government did just the opposite, cutting the moorings loose as the waves came crashing in. Foreign capital fled Peru, as the wealthy transferred their money into dollars (while many physically headed to Miami). García printed money, but then attempted to control inflation by freezing prices. He began to nationalize the banks, but then aborted the move—an erratic misstep that helped unleash hyperinflation. Peru's currency collapsed, its GDP sank by 25 percent in four years, and by 1989 much of the middle class had lost their lifelong savings. By early 1990 García's approval rating was at 6 percent. Instead of a messianic savior, he had become the most reviled president of the twentieth century.

Rebels Gain Ground

The economic collapse coincided with a sharp rise in terrorism. Unlike much of the nation, Sendero Luminoso was financially solvent. Some evidence suggests that years earlier it had moved into the Upper Huallaga River valley, in the remote Amazonian region of northeastern Peru, where it levied taxes on coca leaf producers tied to Pablo Escobar's Medellin Cartel. It also continued to skim money off the balance sheets of select educational institutions. The organization used these funds to better equip its guerrilla forces, though as a principle it continued to avoid open battle with the vastly superior army (which also appears to have had its hands in coca leaf production).[2]

In its Ayacucho and southern base, however, all was not well. Villagers began to collaborate with the army, setting up military-coordinated *rondas*, or local militias. On patrol, they reported the presence of any Senderistas

---

2. Sources of Sendero funding continue to be a matter of conjecture and debate. Even at its height the insurgency still woefully lacked funds, and was never even close to a match with the Armed Forces in either resources or numbers.

to authorities, while sometimes overreacting. In one famous incident, locals stoned eight journalists from Lima to death, perhaps thinking they were guerrillas. The failure of the Sendero movement to psychologically win over Natives was becoming very apparent. Once-fertile revolutionary ground was lost; Sendero moved its operations broadly northward, into the central valley closer to Lima.

As Sendero Luminoso shifted gears, a small Lima-based guerrilla organization prospered. The Revolutionary Movement Tupac Amaru (MRTA) began operations with a bank robbery, which in turn funded clandestine political schools and arms purchases. Its use of force was much more selective than that of Sendero, and often merely symbolic. It bombed several Kentucky Fried Chicken restaurants (after evacuating occupants), for example, as a protest against U.S. capitalism. By the late eighties the primarily urban-based MRTA likely had only a few hundred active participants, while Sendero had a few thousand.

Though the MRTA called for revolution on behalf of indigenous peoples—and was named after the native-leading eighteenth-century insurrectionist—none of its senior leadership was dark-skinned. When the MRTA attempted to establish operations in the countryside it failed miserably, with villagers singularly unenthused and the rival Sendero organization primed to kill its cadre. The MRTA *did* also take root in a segment of the Huallaga River valley, however, where among other activities it carried out social cleansing, executing drug addicts and gays.

MRTA leadership rested on Víctor Polay Campos, a personal friend of the president. Raised an Aprista, he and García attended graduate school and once even briefly roomed together in France. When he was captured at a hotel in the highland's city of Huancayo in 1989, it was purely by happenstance. García's Defense Minister was staying in the same hotel, and his security entourage literally stumbled, accidently, upon the sleeping guerrilla. Polay Campos' fall deflated the organization, though he had not cultivated the personality cult of Sendero's Abimael Guzmán. A planned MRTA attack in the highlands was easily thwarted by an army patrol weeks later, with scores of guerrillas killed and captured. In retaliation, the MRTA assassinated García's retired Defense Minister, in his car in Lima's upscale Surco District.

That Polay Campos was first arrested in Huancayo is telling. The city had become a revolutionary focal point in the late eighties. When Sendero arrived here, it murdered several local officials and NGO volunteers, and took control of the National University of Central Peru (UNCP). MRTA members on campus were assassinated, Sendero leaflets declaring the rival group counterrevolutionary. UNCP was then turned into a Sendero workshop, complete

Figure 13.2. After his 1989 arrest, the MRTA's Polay Campos was locked in a maximum-security prison. His followers methodically dug a tunnel and freed him in July 1990—a remarkable feat of persistence and primitive engineering. All, however, was for naught. When he attempted to meet contacts at a Lima restaurant, the famous guerrilla was easily recaptured.
Source: Lugar de Memoria

with red flags and banners, portraits of "President Gonzalo," and classrooms used for speeches by cadre instead of lectures by faculty. Its dining hall fed activists and their supporters, and—in an ideological gesture—local families of poor students. Typical of its knack for showmanship, Sendero announced its consolidation of power in Huancayo with a series of bonfires around the city that collectively took the shape of a hammer and sickle.

Using the Huancayo region as a base, Sendero soon announced its arrival in the capital itself. Its urban operatives hung dogs and cats from streetlights and lampposts, with ghoulish announcements that Sendero was coming. Graffiti to the same effect appeared throughout the mega-city. In November 1989, Sendero gunmen opened fire on a festival crowd in La Victoria District's Plaza Manco Cápac (undoubtedly chosen partly for its name). Other members dropped what appeared to be explosive devices, though when a bomb squad tended to these, every one turned out to be fake. The Sendero gunmen—there might well have only been two—escaped. The attack at Manco Cápac showed just how much fear and chaos a few fanatics could sow with relatively little risk or effort. But as with its approach in the countryside, Sendero was positioned only to alienate the urban population, rather than win residents over to its side.

The Senderistas were also starting to anger urbanites by repeatedly striking the electrical grid. Blowing up pylons connected to hydroelectric power in the mountains was easy, and cast coastal towns and cities into darkness. This bred fear, but also resentment. Increasingly even many once-sympathetic Peruvians viewed the guerrillas as a scourge upon the land. As the end of Alan García's term approached, many were ready to seek a new direction, one inimical to the ideas and aspirations of the political left.

The Rise of Alberto Fujimori

The 1990 election was a watershed in Peru, with new sociopolitical dynamics at play. Not only was the political left discredited—by both domestic considerations and the collapse of the Soviet bloc—but so too, political parties seemed to have moved beyond their heyday. Both García's APRA and Belaúnde's Popular Action held little appeal, while grassroots mobilizing through party structures was clearly in decline. Mass media was changing as well. Newspaper readership steadily fell, even as more Peruvians favored lurid tabloids and drew their political conclusions from the nation's six television stations, most owned by aristocratic families or corporations.

In this milieu, the politics of personalism ascended to new heights: political fortunes rose on the backs of charismatic figures with media savvy and appeal. Positioning himself for the presidency in 1990 was the much-celebrated novelist Mario Vargas Llosa, who had the support of most of the Limeño elite. But an obscure Japanese-Peruvian academic, Alberto Fujimori, tossed his hat into the ring after gaining a modest following by hosting a TV commentary-talk show (ironically on National Television at the behest of Alan García, who disliked Vargas Llosa and wanted to empower fresh alternatives).

Aided by public relations consultants, Fujimori ran a brilliant campaign. He mingled with common people, drove a tractor to his rallies, and used other imagery that exuded a work ethic and pragmatism that seemingly might extricate the nation from its momentous problems. He was the *anti-candidate*, the presumed clean outsider who could vanquish the corrupt powers-that-be. The stiff and conceited Vargas Llosa, in contrast, attended formal ceremonies and surrounded himself with the white-skinned well-to-do with whom he was most comfortable. He looked elitist; Fujimori appeared as a "man of the people." Though Vargas Llosa held the edge in the first round of voting, momentum shifted during the runoff, and Fujimori won the presidency. A minority of media outlets had given him favorable coverage opposite a tiresome barrage of Vargas Llosa advertisements everywhere.

The most immediate problem for the new administration was hyperinflation, Peru's currency having completely collapsed at an annualized rate that briefly exceeded seven thousand percent. The rare specter of hyperinflation obliterates savings in local currency—but of course much of the middle class had converted their savings into U.S. dollars, one of the core reasons for hyperinflation in the first place. The poor, without savings, endured on a barter economy. Implementing a strict fiscal regimen of austerity and sky-high interest rates, dubbed *Fujishock*, coupled with the recapitalization of banks (in part via infusions of foreign aid), inflation dropped to 140 percent in 1991 and down to just 10 percent four years later.

This fiscal restoration made Fujimori immensely popular, especially with the upper and middle classes. The president used this newfound political capital to execute a power play. In April 1992, his government orchestrated the *Fujigolpe*, a quasi-military coup that saw him disband congress and temporarily suspend civil liberties. Fujimori was not about to share credit for his economic success, and unfolding anti-terrorism accomplishments, with the rest of the political establishment. In the name of preserving democracy he temporarily abolished it. His move came at a time when the trend in Latin America was decidedly against military intervention, and it drew public condemnation from the United States and other powers, though behind the scenes their response was more nuanced.

Chapter Thirteen

The *Fujigolpe* was a bitter pill for APRA and Alan García. García had quietly supported Fujimori, and hoped to wield influence in his government. Instead, Fujimori was playing the "outsider card" to the hilt, portraying himself as the nation's redeemer against a decadent body politic. And it was obvious to all that it was working: there were no significant protests or public outcry against his power move, and polling data in fact soon showed substantial support for it. In time APRA created a fanciful narrative of how a persecuted Alan García resisted, shrewdly hid himself in a neighbor's rooftop water tank, and adeptly fled the country as so many of his party's senior members were placed under house arrest. In fact, the discredited former president drove to the Colombian embassy without incident and left Peru for a comfortable exile in France. He and the political parties of the past were now nearly irrelevant. Fujimori was the man of the hour, victorious over the *políticos*, and poised to vanquish the guerrillas.

CHAPTER FOURTEEN

The Dictatorship

In the summer of 1991, Alberto Fujimori ventured to Mexico, where a Catholic university gave him an award as a proponent of democracy. Nine months later he disbanded Peru's congress and suspended civil rights in his *Fujigolpe*. In fact, Fujimori had little regard for democratic practices, and instead appeared to crave raw power. Within a few short years, his presidency matured into an authoritarian dictatorship, its corruption as brazen as that of Manuel Odría's.

The Gangster

As Fujimori came into office in 1990, Peru's policing and intelligence services rapidly expanded, in large part because of financial and technical assistance from the United States. At the center of their reorganization was the *Servicio de Inteligencia Nacional* (National Intelligence Service, or SIN), a highly secretive espionage organization. Its head was one Vladimiro Lenin Montesinos, ironically the son of erstwhile Arequipeño communists who had named him after the Bolshevik founder of the Soviet Union.

Montesinos was anything but a communist. As a young man, he mastered English and received training from Americans at the School of the Americas in the Panama Canal Zone. He appears to have made connections with U.S. intelligence officials at that time. Under the Velasco regime, he leaked information to the United States and took an unauthorized trip to Washington, D.C., which resulted in his arrest, dishonorable discharge from military service, and brief imprisonment. Some circumstantial evidence suggests that he had links to the Central Intelligence Agency.[1]

Montesinos had friends in high places, both within and outside of Peru. He received a San Marcos law degree without the requisite course of study, and soon served as counsel to a shadowy network of apparent drug traffickers. In the late eighties, he defended a group of army officers charged with massacring twenty-eight civilians in Ayacucho. Improbably, stalwart witnesses in the case prematurely died, while others who recanted their testimonies became inexplicably wealthy. Montesinos had few moral qualms; his was a life of unabashed ambition in far rightist circles within the Peruvian military. But he and others of his ilk were outnumbered by conventional officers, and Montesinos was harried and driven into periodic exile—until Alberto Fujimori obtained the presidency.

Suddenly, the most corrupt and opportunistic of army officers began to ascend into positions of power. Montesinos networked with some of the richest of the rich, most notably Dionisio Romero, a banker who under Fujimori became one of Peru's first billionaires. If Fujimori was the face of the regime, Montesinos was soon its backstage manager. He created a security state within the state, a fraternity of brothers who disregarded laws and operated like a gang. Honest army and police officers were dismissed in 1990–1992 in the name of eliminating corruption. Others, including some who had previously crossed paths with Montesinos, were arrested and charged with treasonous activities—the spymaster himself on at least one occasion participating in a vindictive torture session. Ethical senior officers in both the Armed Forces and National Police were obliged to retire.

Though coercion and threats were common, the primary method of Montesinos's control was bribery. With a bottomless supply of funds from the super-rich, drug traffickers, and perhaps the CIA, Montesinos bribed at will. He bought off judges, and within a short time had effective control of the judiciary; he bankrolled lawyers and major law firms. He bribed key government bureaucrats, including auditors and tax department accountants. After international pressure compelled Fujimori to reconstitute the congress as a new constituent assembly, Montesinos bought off party leaders and politicians. By 1993 Peru was increasingly a nation with little functional regard for the rule of law; it was becoming a money-greased and power-based gangster state.

---

1. Montesinos's relationship with the CIA has long been a subject of speculation and dispute. The Center for Public Integrity charged in 2001, without revealing its confidential source, that the Agency directly gave him ten million dollars, while PBS's *Frontline* alleged that he had long-lasting CIA contacts. Heavily redacted documents obtained by the National Security Archive are highly suggestive but ultimately inclusive.

Montesinos's bribery network extended to the media. Several media moguls willingly collaborated with SIN's media-censoring staff, most notably José Enrique Crousillat, who oversaw *América Televisión*, a network partly owned by a rightwing Mexican billionaire. Dozens of newscasters, editors, and journalists were also on the SIN's extracurricular payroll. But conversely, the thorn in Montesinos's side was Latina / Channel 2, owned by businessman Baruch Ivcher, who sanctioned exposés on the Fujimori regime. Ivcher was eventually compelled to sell his station, when it inexplicably lost its broadcasting license.

Vladimir Montesinos exerted remarkable behind-the-scenes power by the mid-1990s, though Fujimori remained in the spotlight. In fact, the gangster astutely avoided exposure, even limiting the mention of his name in the press while rarely allowing himself to be photographed. This raises an interesting question: who was really in charge of the country? Was Montesinos a puppet master, even pulling the strings of the congenial Fujimori? The two men had an intimate relationship, yet it is difficult to dissect their social interaction. Montesinos had his hands in nearly everything, however, and surely was at least nearly an equal with the president, if not his Rasputin.

The War on Terror

The violent Sendero Luminoso movement enabled Montesinos and his SIN. Most of the exceptional measures taken by the spymaster and Fujimori were justified in the name of the preservation of order. The war against the guerrillas was the regime's *raison d'être*, and if Sendero had not existed, it is difficult to see how such an abusive police state could have taken root. As Sendero launched its arbitrary and heartless attacks, frightened Peruvians readily ceded their rights and democratic prerogatives to the opportunistic men who promised to save them.

In 1991–1992, after Fujimori came to power, Sendero Luminoso accelerated its terror campaign in the capital. Bombings became almost routine. Methods included rapid-strike dynamiting, with two or three guerrillas positioning and fusing a bomb, or sometimes simply lighting and launching an explosive device from a speeding automobile. These attacks hit soft targets: government buildings, banks, gas stations, and local police precincts. More serious was the detonation of powerful car bombs, a tactic that had gained favor years earlier in the Middle East. In June 1992, Senderistas blew a car bomb in the middle-class district of San Isidro, and in July they struck on Tarata Street in upscale Miraflores, killing 25 and injuring 155. But all of these attacks were merely quick-gratification fireworks. There was little meaningful strategy behind

Figure 14.1. The shell of one of the Tarata Street buildings after the July 1992 attack. The car bomb was likely comprised of over a thousand pounds of dynamite—the biggest Sendero blast ever. But the location was even more significant. Striking in an upscale neighborhood, the attack shocked the well-to-do, who increasingly supported the Fujimori regime's police-state measures without question.
Source: Lugar de Memoria

them, much less an attempt to woo public opinion. On the contrary, Sendero gave the Fujimori regime countless public relations gifts—as the bombs went off, the hardline president watched his approval ratings rise.

Meanwhile, a police task force independent of Montesinos's SIN, but extensively aided by a logistics team from the CIA, was on the trail of Guzmán. Concluding that the asthmatic guerrilla chieftain was in Lima itself rather than the air-thin highlands, detectives began a systematic investigation. Months of tedious surveillance, eavesdropping, tracing cars and movements, and scouring through garbage cans turned up rare but intriguing clues. Patience was essential: any rush toward action could prompt Senderista leaders to move further underground. In September 1992 all the hard work paid off. A carefully planned raid on a nondescript house nabbed "Fat Cheeks," as Guzmán had been code-named, in a bloodless raid. Predictably, Fujimori soon took the credit, and his political fortunes rose even further. He and Montesinos arranged to humiliate Guzmán, displaying him to the press donned in black-and-white prison stripes, in an oversized cage befitting an animal.

The capture of Abimael Guzmán was a great psychological blow to Sendero Luminoso. For years, his elusiveness had fed an aura of mystical power. Why could a modern state, with the wonders of technology and hefty policing apparatuses, not find him? If Guzmán could outsmart the powers-that-be, then maybe his prophecies of final victory were true. But with his capture, and footage of a clearly passive and befuddled "Leader" broadcast repeatedly on television, the magic was lost. The strict hierarchical nature of the guerrilla organization made it now subject to collapse. The Sendero's house of cards came crashing down.

Both before and after the capture of Guzmán, the SIN and overlapping units of Military Intelligence waged a shoot-'em-up dirty war, especially within the environs of Lima. The extent of this state terror will never be fully known. Neither human rights groups, journalists, nor academics have had meaningful access to the extensive undercover world of the intelligence services, which carried out hundreds of clandestine operations, most among the slum-dwelling poor. The mysteries of state terror are so complex that, some bombings attributed to Sendero might have in fact been carried out by the SIN. We know that some of the SIN's special anti-terrorism units were effectively waging war on still-functioning portions of civil society.

In this context it is important to nuance the nature of the Sendero insurrection, and not turn all Senderistas into caricatures of psychopathic killers. As the movement took wind, thousands of Peruvians of different views and stripes embraced it. Many secondary, and especially university, students considered themselves Senderistas, marched and sang, attended secret meetings, and killed no one. The movement was ill-defined from the start—but even more so after it migrated out of Ayacucho—and by the early nineties it was operating haltingly, in many different areas with very different local actors. Military Intelligence and the SIN painted all opponents of the state, however, with the same brush. There was little distinguishing between terrorists and posers or, for that matter, legitimate political dissenters.

Typical of the Fujimori regime's purge was what happened at UNCP, the branch university in Huancayo. Police and army troops first raided the Sendero-controlled institution, then later took physical possession of it—setting up a headquarters in its dining facility. Students, staff, and faculty were searched regularly, identified, and photographed. Select, known Senderista student leaders then disappeared. By 1992, the locked-down campus had checkpoints and periodic forced assemblies, where hooded informants fingered people. Many of those persons were subsequently abducted, their bodies turning up along roadsides in the nearby valley, typically bearing the marks of torture. In mid-1992, at the height of the repression, dozens of students and even some professors were selectively murdered by state agents. UNCP took on an aura of subdued indifference, as the broader university community reengaged its conventional work and turned away from the traumatic happenings.

Two sample and highly informative cases of state terror did see daylight. Both involved a shadowy SIN-linked death squad called *Grupo Colina*, and both occurred early in the dictatorship. In November 1991, a six-man task force arrived at a nondescript building in Lima's working-class *Barrios Altos* district. Rushing onto the second floor, it ordered two dozen supposed guerrillas to lie down, then opened a withering fire with silencer-equipped submachine guns. Within a couple of minutes, fifteen persons were dead, including an eight-year old boy.

A second incident occurred at the teachers' university, known as *La Cantuta*, just two days after the Tarata bombing. With much media fanfare, Fujimori had ordered the army to occupy and eradicate subversion on university campuses (though when he arrived at San Marcos University for a photo-op, students pelted the presidential entourage with rocks and bottles, forcing him to flee). In the middle of the night at La Cantuta, *Grupo Colina* whisked away nine students and a professor, executing them on the outskirts of Lima hours later. Concerned that the hastily buried bodies might be found, they retrieved and reburied them. But there were leaks. Congresspersons opened an investigation, and the second burial site was found and excavated, with just enough press coverage to trigger a public reaction.

So too, the Barrio Altos incident lingered. The newspaper *La República*, a faithful critic of Fujimori, would in particular not let go of the story. A courageous prosecutor, Ana Cecilia Magallanes, relentlessly pursued leads while a female judge, Antonia Saquicuray, supported her. Select congressional deputies also launched an inquiry, touring the massacre site and helping to identify the army officers involved. The April 1992 *fujigolpe* was inspired in part by this investigation—the cessation of legislative power effectively shutting it down. But it and the La Cantuta case hung in the public conscience for years, and were eventually used to prosecute Fujimori after his government collapsed in 2000.

The dictatorship committed other distinctive crimes. It appealed to the latent racism embedded in the coastal urban middle class. Fujimori spoke of an "Indian problem," in a nation where the native half of the population was growing at a rate much faster than that of whites. In the mid-nineties the government launched a birth control program in the highlands that ultimately sterilized over three hundred thousand indigenous women. Tens of thousands were forced to undergo the procedure against their will,

Figure 14.2. A member of congress examines the bagged corpse of one of the Cantuta massacre victims, a reporter at her side. Cantuta was one of the very few cases of state terrorism to receive media coverage—television in particular emphasized only Sendero atrocities. Yet probably a majority of the war's victims died at the hands of state security operatives.
Source: Lugar de Memoria

threatened with fines and intimidated, or in some cases forcibly herded onto trucks and driven off to state-run clinics.

The Regime Persists

In June 1995, the war against Sendero substantially over, the Fujimori regime reconvened a highly compliant congress and passed Amnesty Law Number 26479, with neither public discussion nor debate. The measure freed all army soldiers and police officers from any liability for human rights violations committed since 1980. The few enlistees held in custody for the La Cantuta executions were released. Realizing how dangerous the law was to democracy itself, Judge Saquicuray ruled its key provisions unconstitutional. The Fujimorista congress then passed a second measure, holding that no court could override any part of the previously passed amnesty bill; it also forbade any further investigation into the Barrios Altos "matter." Public approval of Fujimori was sky-high and, as these laws passed, he easily won reelection to a second term. The vast majority of Peruvians, too, had no patience for disrespectful, trouble-making women like Magallenes and Saquicuray.

The unicameral legislature operated under a new constitution, which gave disproportionate power to the executive. The 1993 charter stipulated a range of economic parameters that emphasized private property rights, while limiting the capacity of the state to intervene in the economy. This facilitated a massive land-grab by corporate investors, who created new mega-farms, often tied to export crops, along the coast and in portions of the highlands. Wealthy Peruvians also reacquired vast tracts of land, reversing the effects of Velasco's vaunted agrarian reform. *Latifundio* (land concentration) had returned to Peru.

This process was in keeping with the broader neoliberal prescriptions of the regime. In a time when the International Monetary Fund wielded great power, Peru sold off government-owned entities to private investors, often at cut-rate prices. It promoted an economic model that favored foreign corporations, while interfacing much of the elite-owned banking sector with international capital. A core of super-rich businessmen amassed even greater fortunes, several poised—even in such a poor country—to become twenty-first-century billionaires. The wheeling and dealing, with privatizations yielding nearly U.S. $4.4 billion by the year 2000, facilitated more graft. Fujimori, his family members, and close associates all became very rich; his aide Víctor Joy Way skimmed tens of millions of dollars off imported goods contracts. Wall Street investment banks and ratings agencies praised Fujimori's government as business-friendly. Corporations gave him personal gifts—American Airlines, for example, sent him a helicopter as an expression of its high esteem. But the regime's sell-out economic policies were antinationalistic, clearly done to the great detriment of Peru.

Neoliberalism became a negative word for segments of the public, especially the lower classes. After the 1995 election, support for the government waned. Fortunately for the regime, the still-fighting MRTA guerrillas played into its hands. For most Peruvians, the personification of the MRTA in the mid-nineties was an American. Lori Berenson, famously shown wild-eyed and shouting after her 1996 capture, was an idealistic and naïve New York college student. She was a gift to Fujimori propagandists, in that it allowed them to portray the MRTA as a project of foreign interlopers.

In December 1996, twenty-one MRTA guerrillas seized the residence of the Japanese ambassador during a high-brow party. The brilliantly planned attack nabbed several hundred elite. Releasing the majority, while appealing for negotiations, the guerrillas demanded freedom for their jailed comrades (including Berenson), changes in governance, and an end to neoliberal policies. A four-month hostage crisis ensued, generating worldwide media coverage. Feigning interest in talks, from the start Fujimori and Montesinos prepared a military solution. Building a replica of the house on a nearby army base, military personnel meticulously planned an assault, tracing the daily patterns and movements of the hostage-takers. At the real residence, while blaring loud music, they dug tunnels. On April 22, 1997, they carried out a lightning strike, freeing the hostages and killing the guerrillas (though at least one appears to have been taken alive and then executed).

Fujimori's approval ratings soared again, as citizens of all stripes celebrated the accomplishment of the Armed Forces. The role of U.S. military advisors in planning the operation was kept from the public. The image of the president, standing over dead guerrillas while singing the national anthem with Special Forces commandos, appeared on newscasts for several weeks. Coating the triumph with nationalist propaganda, the incident helped sustain Fujimorism, even as it reduced social programs and cut corporate and elite taxes even further. For the MRTA, the defeat was a blow from which the organization never recovered.

As the MRTA faced its demise, the Sendero movement also largely continued to flounder, though with some unusual dimensions that raise intriguing questions. Different subgroups of the insurgency survived the capture of Guzmán. Eventually, many of these coalesced around the leadership of Óscar Ramirez, son of an army colonel and—remarkably—a cousin of Vladimiro Montesinos. Some Senderistas became little more than drug cartel enforcers, but these may have also been heavily infiltrated by the SIN or Military Intelligence. A modest revival of Sendero fortunes late in the decade suggests a thick web of intrigue, with perhaps select officers in the security services recognizing the usefulness of terror cells for the perpetuation of their own importance—and the flow of U.S. military aid.

For his part, Montesinos was in communication with the FARC guerrillas in nearby Colombia, and helped arrange the selling of arms to them—to the chagrin of at least a few U.S. intelligence agencies. There is so much that academics do not know about the inner workings of state security apparatuses, but tantalizing information suggests that all is often not as it appears. Conversely, other players seem earnest in their tasks. The U.S. Drug Enforcement Agency assisted in an operation that seized 174 kilograms of cocaine on a Peruvian Air Force DC-8 that had taken Fujimori on a diplomatic tour of Europe.

Fujimori Falls

The complexities of the dictatorship were great. The seedy underbelly of government operations was massive, with many participants. Bribery was the dominant weapon, with terror options limited by a scrutinizing web of exterior actors, including the Organization of American States (OAS) and the United Nations. There was very much a populist edge to the regime, too. Fujimori's birthday often inspired public rallies, most notably in 1999, when ten thousand gathered in Lima's upscale Miraflores District and the festivities received live TV coverage. By defeating the hated guerrillas, the government generated much genuine good will. The president's appointment of several women to cabinet positions—a first in Peruvian history—also pleased many. But there were lots of small leaks in the giant ship: Fujimori's ugly divorce from Susana Higuchi saw his ex make revealing statements about corruption before she migrated to Japan.

The missteps made Fujimorism's voyage more difficult as the millennium ended. Few were surprised when the president announced that the constitution would be changed, and that he would run for yet another five-year term. A divided pro-democracy opposition saw this as an opportunity. It still had some resources, including segments of the print media and select journalists who had refused to be bought off. A new phenomenon in Peru, that of cable television, also complicated things. *Canal N* began as the country's first twenty-four-hour news channel.

Though he had to work overtime, Montesinos appeared to have everything under control. With tightly staged rallies for "El Chino," as the president was known, and a danceable campaign song, all was set for an easy victory in the first round (the constitution stipulating two rounds of presidential voting, unless the leading candidate surpassed 50 percent).[2] SIN-managed tabloids smeared political opponents, while the opposition was all but ignored on television. Rival campaigns endured relentless police harassment and intimidating personal surveillance. Meanwhile, the U.S. Clinton administration was on board, signaling its acceptance of a third term. But then, with just weeks left to go, the frayed opposition unexpectedly coalesced around one surging counter-candidate.

Alejandro Toledo was an improbable challenger, but he had taken a play out of Fujimori's own book: He reached out to native highlanders, who under the new constitution were compelled (via fines) to vote. Even more, Toledo was indigenous himself, born into poverty before obtaining a college

---

2. Fujimori was of Japanese-Peruvian descent, but in Peruvian popular culture all Asiatic peoples are commonly referred to as "Chinese," a term without derogatory intent.

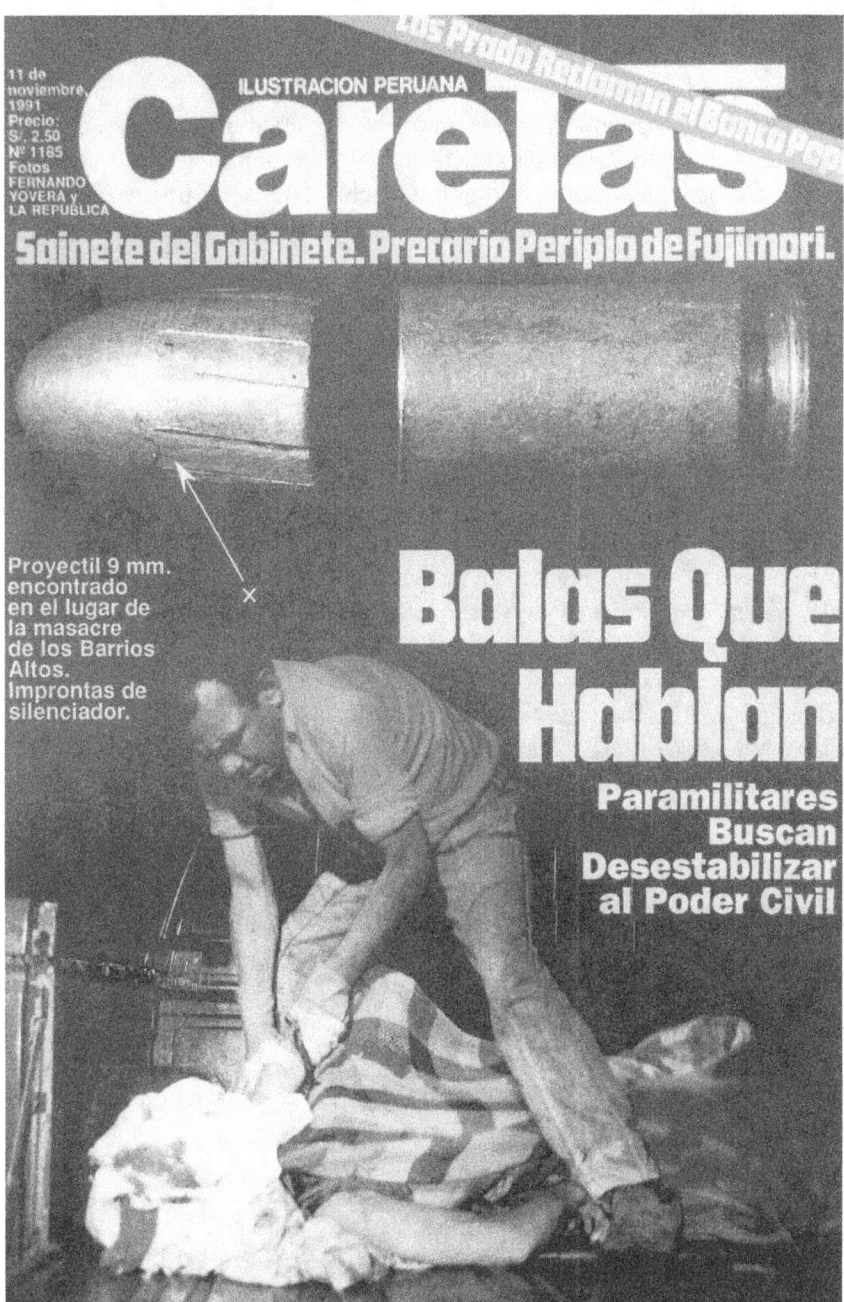

Figure 14.3. Constantly nipping at the Fujimorist regime were two important print-media outlets—the newspaper *La República*, and the newsmagazine *Caretas*. SIN's Montesinos was unable to bribe his way to control of these two venerable press organs. Fortunately for the government, a small minority of Peruvians read their news—the vast majority listened to radio and watched television.
Source: Lugar de Memoria

education and an eventual Stanford economics PhD, through the assistance of foreign aid programs. While Fujimori helicoptered into villages, donned local dress, and gave away gifts (with money from graft), Toledo celebrated his ethnic heritage, often speaking in Quechua. As Peru's first major indigenous candidate since Sánchez Cerro, he generated authentic enthusiasm in the highlands.

Peru's largely anti-Fujimorist intelligentsia had doubts about Toledo. His opposition to the dictatorship was late in coming. He also had many proverbial skeletons in his closet, though his wife preempted the regime's possible release of lewd sex tapes by warning the public in advance that they might appear. Reservations notwithstanding, Toledo was the man of the hour, and in the first round of multiple candidates he ran strong enough to prevent an outright Fujimori win.

As evidence of electoral fraud mounted, Toledo refused to participate in the second round. He personally led massive protests on Inauguration Day. Aggressive police repression on the streets of downtown Lima drew some international press coverage, while stiffening the opposition's resolve. Outside forces, including the United States, waivered in their commitment to Fujimori. And then, just weeks later, the dam broke. On September 14, *Canal N* broadcast leaked videos of Montesinos buying off politicians, as he stuffed wads of cash into satchels in a hotel room. The tapes mesmerized the nation, and triggered the spymaster's flight to Panama ten days later.

With Montesinos gone, Fujimori appeared adrift. He ensconced himself in the National Palace, making contradictory public statements. He suddenly flew on short notice to the United States, where Secretary of State Madeleine Albright received him and signaled continued U.S. support. But then, Montesinos suddenly returned to Peru; rumors of a pending military coup flourished. In one bizarre episode, Fujimori led a caravan of National Police on an ostensible hunt for the fugitive around suburban Lima, TV crews in tow. Donning a black leather jacket and shouting out orders, his stunt conveyed an almost clownish quality.

Montesinos's control within the military was tenuous, most generals were reluctant to execute a coup at a time when military takeovers were deemed no longer acceptable. He again left the country. A middle segment of public opinion turned against the government, as *Canal N* continued to air new "Vladivideos." Pressed by the OAS, Fujimori addressed the nation, announcing that he would step down and call new elections. When this ploy backfired, he flew off to a diplomatic meeting in Asia but then did not return. Instead, he landed in Japan, where he resigned en absentia, revealing that he secretly held Japanese citizenship.

Special elections in 2001 saw Alejandro Toledo as the frontrunner, though he faced a surprisingly strong challenge from APRA's Alan García, who returned with much fanfare from his exile in France. With Toledo's ascent into the presidency, Peru's most grim and arguably strangest political chapter came to an end. The Fujimori dictatorship had exercised arbitrary rule, but had also tapped into some of the worst undercurrents of society, thriving in a culture of brazen misogynistic power, avarice, and racism. Its shadow would continue to loom over the nation in the early twenty-first century.

CHAPTER FIFTEEN

The Neoliberal Republic

The legacies of Alberto Fujimori's 1990–2000 dictatorship have influenced Peruvian politics in the early twenty-first century. Fujimori's dramatic fall in 2000 did not eradicate the seminal features of his authoritarian regime. Though its powerful security apparatuses diminished (and SIN was formally abolished), its ideological presumptions—such as the unabashed glorification of the Armed Forces—continued. Portions of the bribed and coerced media, too, remained faithful to the Fujimorist vision. More importantly, its neoliberal economic model persisted, to the disappointment of much of the populace. Quinquennial elections have provided opportunities for citizens to seek an alternative, but the quest has thus far been largely in vain.

The Wrong Man

A political vacuum is nearly inevitable when a dictatorial regime crumbles. Unfortunately for Peru, Alejandro Toledo was poorly equipped to fill it. An insecure man who badgered subordinates while unable to assume personal responsibility, he appears to have had a long history of substance abuse—reputedly sporting a cocaine habit through much of the nineties. His unlikely political success in 2000–2001 raised popular hopes, but these were soon dashed.

Toledo's administration faltered from the start, reeling from scandal to scandal. The most noteworthy was a paternity lawsuit involving the president himself. It turned out that Toledo, married to a French-born anthropologist, fulfilled a voracious sexual appetite with mistresses on the side. Early in his presidency revelations of a child out of wedlock riveted the press—and public—as he refused to acknowledge a teenaged daughter or take a DNA test, until compelled to do so by a court order. In conservative Peru, his obvious moral lapses helped drive his approval rating down to just 10 percent by 2003. Portions of the holdover Fujimorist press admittedly had it out for him, but Toledo was a spectacularly easy target.

So too, his continuance of neoliberal policies doomed his government. Throughout his rise to power Toledo boasted of his academic credentials, promising to create millions of good-paying jobs. In fact, on his watch the economy slowed, as a 2001–2003 global downturn undercut commodity prices, even as a third of the population still lived off diminishing international food assistance programs. U.S. attention, diverted by the 9/11 attack, shifted to the Middle East, and its aid packages (and military assistance) also greatly shrank with the wind-down of the Sendero rebellion. A former World Bank economist, Toledo refused to entertain the levying of new taxes on either the rich or foreign mining corporations, even though their operations and profits (especially in gold and copper) soared.

To deal with the legacy of the internal war, the president did authorize the creation of a Truth and Reconciliation Commission (CVR by Spanish acronym), reflecting a common practice in human rights work—as advocated by NGOs connected to the Inter-American Court of Human Rights and the United Nations. In mid-2001 the twelve-member commission began to oversee a massive compiling of information. Led by academics, it managed a staff of five hundred that set up documentation centers throughout Peru, ultimately gathering some seventeen thousand individual statements. Funded primarily by foreign donors, the CVR was seen by many as an example of outside interference. Its hearings received limited media attention, and public interest in its activities was subdued.

In mid-2003, the CVR stunned most Peruvians by releasing its conclusion that nearly seventy thousand had died in 1980–2000 violence. It found that Sendero was responsible for 54 percent of the deaths, the MRTA 1.5 percent, and state actors the remaining 44.5 percent—three-quarters of these committed by the Armed Forces. Conservatives and Fujimorists were outraged. In November, President Toledo apologized on behalf of the state for these crimes. The CVR advanced forty-five cases to the judiciary for criminal prosecution, but very few gained legal traction. No significant military or security personnel were prosecuted for the disappearance of many thousands, the vast majority of the victims being darker-skinned and poor. The Commission made an array of recommendations as well, including constitutional

Figure 15.1. A CVR forensics team uncovers a mass grave in the highlands. The 2008 exhumations in the village of Putis confirmed a December 1984 massacre by the Peruvian army that left 123 peasants dead. No one has ever been prosecuted for the crime—the Armed Forces reporting that all documents relating to the incident have unfortunately been lost.
Source: Lugar de Memoria

protections against the future use of military courts and arbitrary arrest and detention. Most of its recommendations were ignored.

The Truth Commission findings have been much debated, with initial critique coming from the right in defense of the military. In fact, more recent evidence suggests that the number of deaths is inflated—perhaps no more than fifty thousand died in the violence, though better evidence also indicates that the state and its security forces proportionately killed significantly more (perhaps as much as 60 percent).[1] But the propaganda machine of the dictatorship had performed its work. Even in 2003, over 40 percent of Peruvians viewed Fujimori and his government positively; the army has remained one of the nation's most trusted institutions.

As the nation downplayed the Truth Commission's findings, political momentum still rested with the political right. From Japan, Fujimori signaled

---

1. For an analysis of how the CVR may have inadvertently distorted its statistical projections, see Silvio Rendon, "Capturing correctly: A reanalysis of the indirect capture-recapture methods in the Peruvian Truth and Reconciliation Commission," *Research and Politics* (January–March 2019): 1–8. Rendon's computations project forty-eight thousand total deaths, with 58.3 percent accredited to state agents and 38.3 percent to Shining Path (and 3.4 percent to other parties).

his intention to compete in the upcoming 2006 election. In order to fan the flames, he flew into Chile. Within hours of his arrival, however, he was arrested. The tug-of-war between powerful demagogues and law-honoring human rights crusaders played out in the land of Augusto Pinochet. The Chilean left, fighting for years to hold an arrested Pinochet accountable for his long dictatorship, came to the aid of Peruvian activists. A drawn-out legal battle saw the Chilean Supreme Court order Fujimori's extradition and, after more judicial maneuverings, he was flown into Lima in 2007. His conviction for rights abuses upheld, he received a twenty-five-year prison sentence. By this time, too, his shadow Vladimiro Montesinos had also returned, faced trial and conviction, and began a long stint in jail.

The Unlikely Return of Alan García

Alejandro Toledo's presidency was effectively irrelevant by mid-term. He had no answers for the nation's problems, and his administration floundered in incompetence. In 2005, amazingly, the president appointed a new foreign minister without fully consulting his cabinet. His prime minister resigned in protest, then the new minister quit a day later. The subsequent appointment of Pablo Kuczynski, another U.S.-trained World Bank economist, did bring some stability to the executive branch, though no change of direction. Toledo's approval ratings were in single digits for most of the remainder of his time in office.

As the 2006 elections approached, many Peruvians were looking for change. Although the insurgencies of the late twentieth century had discredited armed rebellion, the high-profile and apparently promising rule of Venezuela's Hugo Chávez raised hopes for transformation via the ballot box. On the cusp of the electoral season, in December 2005, nearby Bolivia elected an indigenous president, Evo Morales, who ideologically described himself as Chávez's "younger brother." It seemed that a wave of left-leaning change was sweeping across the Andes.

Making an appeal along these lines was a new political player named Ollanta Humala. At first glance, Humala had convincing leftist credentials. His lawyer-father defended labor unions and was once a member of the Communist Party. Born in the province of Ayacucho, Ollanta himself was familiar with rural Peru's economic plight. But the middle-classer had chosen a military career for himself, enrolling as a teenager in Chorrillos Military Academy outside of Lima. He was sent into Amazonia to fight the Sendero Luminoso insurgency; years later, evidence emerged that he used extrajudicial killings in his quest to exterminate the rebels. In the midst of the

Fujimori regime's disintegration, he launched a small and easily suppressed military coup, for which congress subsequently pardoned him. Alejandro Toledo appears to have been leery of Humala's ambition, and sent him off to France as a military attaché during his term. He retired from service as a lieutenant colonel in 2004 and soon launched his campaign for the presidency.

As Humala drew (sometimes questionable) comparisons between himself and Hugo Chávez, whom he professed to admire, the middle ground of the electoral field was claimed by a tirelessly plotting Alan García. García ran strong in 2001, while the passage of time helped even more forget the APRA leader's abysmal first term in office. García toned down his rhetoric, spoke in terms of having matured, and moved decidedly to the right. The political right itself, however—after Fujimori's arrest—was staked out by Lourdes Flores Nano under a so-called National Unity coalition, which appealed to an Humala-fearing and García-tepid Limeño middle class. She was helped along by running mate Arturo Woodman, a popular sports promoter. García's centrist position paid off, though, as he reached the second round and then drew from Flores Nano's bypassed ranks. The media and conservative establishment were clearly uneasy with Humala, and favored the magnetic former president.

García's second term (2006–2011) was a stark contrast to his first. He governed from the right, receiving the accolades of bankers and businessmen. He enjoyed cordial relations with the United States, worked with international financial institutions, and signed free trade agreements. Corporate taxes remained nearly nonexistent, government spending was steadily paced, and any hint of inflation quickly checked. The neoliberalism of Fujimori and Toledo continued. Commodity prices rose—especially that of copper—and, coupled with favorable capital reserves, allowed for a few new public works. García favored high-profile projects, such as the renovation of the national *fútbol* stadium and the sprucing up of secondary schools and university campuses. The construction of a stylish national theater received much media acclaim in the capital. Yet budgetary outlays for social programs, education, and healthcare largely stagnated.

Prospering companies and healthy bank accounts made for sloshing money. Generous kickbacks were made to politicians, many of whom held office only briefly (García's cabinet was a revolving door—he changed his Interior Minister alone seven times). Short-term officeholders had little reason to be ethical; graft was even wider and deeper than in his notoriously corrupt first administration. Teams of government lawyers suppressed investigations and badgered an inquisitive judiciary into submission. Many journalists, some apparently bought off, pandered to the government and ignored evidence of dirty laundry. Instead of focusing on admittedly sometimes

Figure 15.2. During his second presidency the divorced Alan García was involved in a relationship with Roxanne Cheesman, an economist from Minnesota who worked for a U.S. mining corporation. They had a son, Federico, born out of wedlock. Despite the controversy, the couple often made public appearances together.
Source: Museo de Minerales Andrés Del Castillo

complex investigative tales, TV cameras highlighted the "human side" of the seemingly benign administration. García's young son Federico, whom the president often doted over in public, became something of a celebrity.

The biggest scandal involved under-the-table payments for oil exploration and drilling rights in the Amazon. In October 2008, *América Televisión's* investigative newscast *Cuarto Poder* (Fourth Power) aired telephone calls that revealed the arrangement of bribes by senior officials in Petroperú. These in turn led to Jorge del Castillo, García's prime minister, "fixer," and right-hand man. But to the disgust of many Peruvians, subsequent queries went nowhere. In January 2009 the entire matter was dismissed by a critical vote in congress.

Meanwhile, in the Amazon, a network of indigenous groups and NGOs were opposing oil drilling by staging rallies and blockading highways. A June 2009 confrontation with National Police resulted in roughly three dozen deaths and scores of injuries. García, the once-articulate leftist, blamed the indigenous villagers, calling them "terrorists," while backing the oil industry. In the months that followed, many media outlets critical of the president were harassed and a few lost their broadcast licenses. The corruption of

García's government was increasingly matched by its audacity. Its tactics were not that far removed from those of Fujimori.

The worldwide financial crisis of 2007–2008, however, gave the administration pause, and economic growth (top-down as it already was) stalled in the second half of the president's term. Civil society was recovering from the difficult Fujimori years, and several independent NGOs and organizations proved determined anti-corruption foes, most notably one called *IDL Reporteros*. Brazil's judiciary was investigating a giant construction firm named Odebrecht, and questions were being asked and names were cropping up—but this would all take time. In the short term, Alan García had to deal with some very disillusioned ideologues from within his own party. How could an *Aprista* promote neoliberalism, condemn native protests, and praise corporate free trade agreements, given the party's long history of struggle? What did APRA even stand for, in the context of this kind of governance?

Lima—Megapolis

Both Toledo's and García's (second) government did very little to develop the interior of Peru, continuing a decades-long neglect especially of the highlands. Acute poverty continued to define large swaths of the native-dominated region. Low-protein diets stunted physical growth, the stature of the rural poor in the twenty-first century was on average nearly three inches less than that of coastal residents. Lack of economic opportunity has spawned despair and fed an array of social problems, including alcoholism and spousal abuse.

Under the neoliberal model, the only substantial development came in the form of roads and rails for the benefit of mining interests. A nearly complete lack of regulations allowed for epic pollution; Peruvian smelting towns like Cerro de Pasco are among the most polluted in the world. Arsenic and mercury lace the soil, while locals drink a water supply contaminated with lead—when introduced into the bloodstream, lead triggers a host of mental and physical illnesses. Children born near major mines and smelters often suffer lifelong disabilities or partial incapacitation. Toxins fill the air, as smokestacks lack the scrubbers and filters that are mandatory in the First World.

One developmental exception, however, was the highlands tourism mecca of Cusco and the great Inca ruins at Machu Picchu. The so-called Inca Trail was first conceived by the progressive Velasco government, in the wake of Cusco's international-grade airport opening in the mid-1960s. Backpackers at first favored the venture, but posh advertising campaigns began to draw hundreds of thousands of annual visitors by the mid-1990s, when Fujimori's regime granted monopolies to private investors who upgraded hotels and transportation links. Successor administrations have allowed these monopolies to continue, ensuring that tourists typically pay over U.S. $100 for a train ride of less than twenty miles. Taking a cut, Inca Trail tourism has proven lucrative to the government. By the end of García's second term, seven hundred thousand were annually visiting Machu Picchu and Cuzco, allowing Peru to vie with Brazil as the Number One South American tourism destination.

First World tourists among these visitors did not, by and large, visit Lima, but the megapolis continued to draw rural poor like a giant magnet. Immigrants piled into its massive slums, while seeking jobs and access to healthcare and education. The metropolitan population rose from 7.3 million in 2000 to nearly nine million just a decade later—over 30 percent of Peru's population lived in and around Lima by 2010. The city had become Latin America's fifth largest, behind Mexico City, São Paulo, Buenos Aires, and Rio de Janeiro. No other city in Peru compares; Arequipa reached only one million inhabitants in 2017. As always, Lima has received a disproportionate amount of governmental attention and spending.

Under García, the flagship public works project was the Metro, or what Limeños refer to as the *Tren Eléctrico*. One of Lima's great shortcomings is the lack of a subway, though a dedicated-lane bus system had been developed in the late twentieth century. In poor nations, where a majority of the population does not own cars, complex mass transit systems are essential. A subway was conceived and begun in García's first term, but aborted as the currency collapsed. In 2010, construction began at a rapid pace on Line 1 of the Metro, elevated on an enormous concrete viaduct that eventually ran thirteen miles in length (making it the longest "bridge" in the world). Service began with much fanfare in 2012.

The capital's affluent population had migrated in an extension roughly parallel to the Metro's course, though the car-owning middle-class residents rarely use the train. Long-favored districts like San Isidro and Miraflores were increasingly surpassed in comfort by the spacious ambiance of (Santiago de) Surco and its environs, with a particularly wealthy enclave in Casuarinas. Here, the well-to-do inhabit an American-style suburbia, with landscaped private yards and swimming pools. Though the richest Peruvians continued to send their children (especially sons) to U.S. universities, a host of private preparatory schools and new universities sprouted up in and around Surco, along with scores of shopping centers, strip malls, and chic restaurants and nightclubs.

Disappointment and Dead Ends

As Alan García governed from the right in 2006–2011, Ollanta Humala stood to his political left, relentless in his criticism. He participated in and supported anti-government rallies and strikes, and joined in condemnation of incidents of police repression. To many, he appeared to in fact represent a Peruvian Hugo Chávez, a leftist-populist who would rectify social imbalances and check the upward concentration of wealth.

But Humala's political prominence was matched by a new voice on the far right. A movement intricately tied to the vaunted family's name, Fujimorism had been waiting for Alberto's eldest child to come of age. His daughter Keiko was already familiar to Peruvians: in her mid-twenties, after her parents' divorce, she had played the role of First Lady. In 2010, her backers launched a political party called *Fuerza Popular* (Popular Force) to catapult her into office. As with her father's campaigns, the party soon introduced snappy dance songs, scantily clad women, and bright colors (mostly orange) at its well-orchestrated rallies, along with free drinks and candies. It was generously funded, reputedly receiving under-the-table contributions from *Banco de Crédito*, a major bank connected to the billionaire-friend of Vladimiro Montesinos, Dionisio Romero.

García left office in 2011 with respectable approval ratings, but under the 1993 constitution could not run for reelection. Disillusioned and principled Apristas were trying to take control of the famous party, effectively splitting it into irrelevance. Augmented by new cable channels, the more-powerful-than-ever mass media turned its spotlight on the colorful Keiko, though it could hardly deny coverage to Humala—the presumed frontrunner. Alejandro Toledo ran for an improbable second term, while his associate Pedro Kuczynski also threw his hat into the ring.

As Humala campaigned, he shifted his rhetoric to the right, distancing himself from Venezuela's Chávez and instead praising Brazil's more moderate Lula da Silva. In the first round, Humala garnered 31.7 percent of the vote to Keiko's 23.6 percent, with Kyczynski in third place with 18.5 percent. In the second round, Humala moved even farther to the right, and by doing so cut into Fujimori's appeal to Lima's large and influential middle class—even the political guru and conservative author Marío Vargas Llosa endorsed him. He narrowly won the presidency with 51.4 percent of the vote.

What everyone was asking, of course, was if Humala had changed his tune for political reasons. Was he, in fact, a system-challenging Chávez-in-waiting? The answer quickly became apparent. Though he did convince congress to modestly nudge up taxes on the big mining corporations, he decidedly pursued neoliberal policies, while unleashing the police on protesting native peoples even faster and with more brutality than had been done by García. His government passed an amnesty law that preemptively absolved any police officer who killed someone in the line of duty. It cut environmental regulations on mining companies and further gutted their enforcement.

Humala also upped García on corruption—a difficult task, given the frantic illicit activity of his predecessor. First Lady Nadine Heredia and Martín Belaúnde, his campaign manager, oversaw money laundering operations, primarily tied to public works contracts. A Spanish construction company that had made generous contributions to Humala's campaign subsequently received U.S. $50 million in government deals. These were arranged by Belaúnde, who received kickbacks and in turn shifted money into private bank accounts held by the First Couple (the First Lady was also generously "hired" as a business consultant). When the scandal broke in 2014, and Belaúnde fled to Bolivia, the Humalas pled innocence and expressed shock at how dishonest their aide had been. Few believed them.

By early 2015, Ollanta Humala's approval rating was at 16 percent. Mired in scandals like his predecessor Alejandro Toledo, his presidency was for all practical purposes over. His conservative governance triggered massive defections from his clearly misnamed Nationalist Party. The organization was so weak as the 2016 elections approached that it was unable to even field a presidential candidate.

By the middle of the 2010s Peru's trio of successive neoliberal administrations had effectively delegitimized the political system. As Humala's government faltered, what had become the mainstream center—based on media-promoted political campaigns and the preferred economic model of international capital—was no longer viable. The entire foundation of the political system was increasingly at risk. Much of the populace was now alienated from the actual *process* of elections, voting, parties, and candidates.

Ironically, macro-economic indicators, as touted by big U.S. investment banks and the financial press, heralded Peru as the shining star of Latin America. GDP growth rates were solidly above 5 percent year after year, significantly outpacing the entire region. But the way in which such numbers are tallied is highly problematic. When Peru exports a product, its value is registered as equal to a portion of the Gross Domestic Product (GDP). But when foreigners own the means of production, oversee exportation, and then sell the commodity solely for their own (or stockholders') benefit, it clearly does not help Peruvian nationals much. GDP thus badly misrepresents what is (or is not) happening on the ground.

Figure 15.3. Even by First World standards Lima's elevated *Tren Eléctrico* (Metro) is quite a sight. Its massive aqueduct is designed to survive an earthquake of 9.0 on the Richter scale. By 2019 *Linea 1*, with its twenty-six stations, was moving nearly one million passengers on weekdays. The system's sleek green-and-white trains are made in Italy.
Photo by the author

Long-established mining operations grew bigger in the early twentieth century, aided by advances in geological technology that allowed for easier detection of mineral deposits and more efficient extraction. Several former and older mines were revived, with new deposits exploited. Peru, so very poor, is one of the richest nations in the world in terms of metallurgy. Silver, lead, copper, zinc, and gold abound, as do a host of lesser minerals few of us readily know, such as tellurium, rhenium, and bismuth. Copper production doubled in the mid-2010s alone, making the nation the second largest producer worldwide.

Mining corporations, like enormous Volcan Mining, are mostly registered as domestic enterprises and run by wealthy Peruvian professionals, but they financially interface with investment capital (often via "parent" companies) abroad—especially from the United States, Spain, and increasingly, China. Peru's wealthiest man by the mid-2010s was its most successful financier and banker, Carlos Rodríguez Pastor, who not only linked segments of the mining sector to foreign capital, but also underwrote enormous swaths of the retail sector, much of it through his Panama City–based holding company *InRetail*.

A major hallmark of neoliberalism has been the concentration of wealth upward. Peru had six billionaires by the mid-2010s, and several dozen super-elite worth hundreds of millions of dollars. The top 20 percent of the population has consistently possessed about half of the nation's wealth since the turn of the millennium. In multiple rural provinces, including some that are home to big mining operations, per capita income levels have actually declined when adjusted for inflation, though population growth also factors into this statistic. Though wealth *has* trickled downward, alleviating some of the worst poverty, ample evidence still contradicts the glowing annual reports of the World Bank and other investor-connected institutions. Despite the mining boom, Peru remains terribly poor.

It does not follow, however, that its disillusioned citizens will necessarily turn to the political left. Three unwavering neoliberal administrations had bankrupted the nation's political system, but as relentless corporate bribery set off corruption-scandal fireworks, the far right positioned itself to benefit. One of the most important conduits of its ascent came in 2015, with the expansion of Willax Television. Previously a cable station, Willax was purchased and renovated by Erasmo Wong Lu, a Chinese-Peruvian businessman who made money in a chain of upscale grocery stores in suburban Lima. Worth roughly U.S. $350 million, Wong poured about $25 million in Willax, moving it to free digital transmission, while dramatically upgrading studios, personnel, and the quality of its programing. Willax is ideological, brazen in its promotion of Keiko Fujimori's *Fuerza Popular* (which Wong has also directly financed), and favors a far rightist ideology.

As the 2010s wound down, the discredited neoliberal establishment would be pressed, first by the Fujimorist far right, and eventually by the left. Contemporary Peru has been marked by political crisis and a new tension that has yet to resolve itself. The breadth of the nation's remarkable political history suggests that no easy answers are forthcoming, and that the future will behold much drama and more than a few surprises.

CHAPTER SIXTEEN

Life and Culture since 1980

As in all the world, Peruvian contemporary culture has been defined by the power of mass media and the rise of the internet in the digital age. Yet in 2020, 60 percent of Peruvian households still lacked internet access, while a majority of the population (in 2023) lives without cellphones. This technology gap has deprived millions of knowledge about global trends, yet has also allowed for the persistence of unique and localized expressions of creativity.

Artists and Ethnic Identities

The late twentieth century witnessed the extension of Peru's marvelously rich traditions in poetry and popular music. Many erstwhile poets who had emerged in the sixties and seventies reinvented themselves over subsequent decades. One of the most significant of these was José Watanabe, a Japanese-Peruvian born among the sugar plantations of the northern coast.

Watanabe had a contented childhood with his many siblings in a small town, where he developed an introspective spirit. As a boy, he spent long hours on the banks of a small nearby river, observing birds and developing an acute appreciation of the physical world around him. His Japanese father read him many *haiku*—short, nature-celebrating poems in the Eastern meditative tradition. This legacy is transparent in his always concise and evocative, often free-verse poetry:

> *The injured pelican left the sea,*
> *and came to die on a small rock in the desert.*

> *He searched, for a few days,*
> *for a dignified place for his final rest,*
> *and there struck a beautiful dance-like frozen pose.*[1]

Another sensitive poem, titled "*Acerca de la Libertad*" ("About Freedom"), recounts the tale of a young boy who purchases a caged bird, then wrestles with whether or not to free it—was this story autobiographical?

Watanabe's career spanned nearly four decades, though he was inactive through much of the seventies and early eighties. He undertook screenwriting later in his career, among other works adopting Vargas Llosa's *La ciudad y los perros* (see chapter 12) for production under Francisco Lombardi in 1985. Prolific in the 1990s, he made his greatest popular appeal via an anthology, published in Spain and Venezuela (2004–2005) shortly before his death in 2007.

Delicately crafted and refined poetry reaches thousands; the easy-rhyming poetics of popular music reach millions—through radio, television, and more recently the internet. But while *boleros* (ballads) and imported musical variations like *salsa* have filled the corporate-managed airwaves, *Música Criolla*—homegrown Peruvian music, especially of ethnic origin—has endured. Of particular note on this count is the work of Tania Libertad.

Born on the north coast, where Música Criolla originated, Libertad (her full name Tania Libertad de Souza Zúñiga) suffered early in life due to an overbearing and abusive policeman father. A supportive (though musically disinclined) mother often came to her aid, while an early contract with RCA-Victor provided an avenue of escape. Coming into adulthood in the 1970s, Velasco's military regime exposed Tania to nationalistic yet progressive ideas. It was migration to Mexico, however, that launched her international career. With excellent recording facilities and technicians, and a subsequent contract with PolyGram, she obtained stardom. In 2009 she received a Lifelong Achievement Grammy, having sold over twelve million records worldwide.

Thus one of the twenty-first century's better-known Peruvians, Libertad is striking in her authenticity and devotion to her musical roots. Even in the 1980s she often opened her shows with Afro-Peruvian songs. In the early 2000s she recorded two Música Criolla albums. Despite all of the commercial machinery behind her, she has marked her career with refreshing innovation. She has long used Afro-Peruvian rhythms and instrumentation—sometimes explaining to audiences the history of songs, or the techniques employed in

---

1 José Watanabe, *La piedra alada* (Lima: PEISA, 2005). The Spanish reads: *El pelícano, herido, se alejó del mar / y vino a morir sobre esta breve piedra del desierto / Buscó durante algunos días, una dignidad para su postura final / acabó como el bello movimiento congelado de una danza.*

percussion. She befriended Chavela Vargas (Isabel Vargas Lizano), a Costa Rica–born *ranchera* singer in Mexico, and encouraged her career. Politically, she has expressed displeasure with various United States–backed regional wars and interventions—seeing in these a spirit of strong-armed dominance not unlike that of her abusive father.

With far less commercial success than Libertad's, but with an astounding commitment to both quality and cultural depth, has been the career of Susana Baca. A native of the seaside town of Chorrillos, Baca has spent her life celebrating Afro-Peruvian music and culture. She has written books, studied in detail instrumentation and techniques, and has recovered aspects of coastal Afro-Peruvian history otherwise lost to time. Her CDs on David Byrne's eclectic Luaka Bop label include her earliest and pioneering *The Soul of Black Peru* (1995), and have won her two Grammy Awards. In 2011, Ollanta Humala designated her Peru's Minister of Culture, but she quietly left the post months later, as Humala's anti-reform politics became evident.

In the 1980s, another Afro-Peruvian finally began to receive long-deserved recognition. Victoria Santa Cruz worked to reclaim Afro-Peruvian folkloric dance over several decades. In the face of relentless discrimination

Figure 16.1. Street art in Barranco, Lima's Bohemian coastal enclave. Relative poverty and a still-limited interface with the digital age has helped Peru retain a natural authenticity in art and even in popular culture. The homogenizing influence of corporate-sponsored mass media has been slowed, at least somewhat—though trends are predictably still favoring business-driven media.
Photo by the author

because of her gender, and especially her race, she made steady inroads in theatric circles. Her 1978 poem *"Me gritaron negra"* ("They Screamed 'Black!' at Me") has become an anthem for Black feminism in Latin America. Santa Cruz taught at Pittsburgh's Carnegie Mellon University in the last two decades of the twentieth century, and conducted folkloric dance seminars in Latin America and Europe. In 2022, on the centennial of her birth (she died in 2014), Peru's Ministry of Culture undertook a national commemoration of her varied accomplishments.

While the globalizing contemporary art scene has witnessed undue hype around select artists and their eccentric personalities—clearly a commercial angle, often fostered by public relations firms with the aim of inflating the value of their works—several accomplished Peruvians have continued to produce gripping art relatively under the radar. Such is Víctor Delfín. Born of modest means in 1927, also along the northern coast, he nevertheless graduated from the National Art School in 1958. For decades, at his studio in the Barranco District of Lima, Delfín has sculpted magnificent pieces. He frequently represents animals, and seems to prefer the medium of metal. His efforts to mobilize artists in opposition to the Fujimori dictatorship prompted police to visit his studio and attempt to intimidate him. By the early twenty-first century, Delfín had become one of the nation's most highly regarded living artists.

Fútbol, Food, and Faith

Peruvians love their music, but no introduction to Peruvian popular culture would be complete without addressing the three obvious national obsessions—*fútbol* (soccer), food, and faith. Peru's passion for fútbol has risen steadily over 150 years. The first single-sport clubs formed in the late nineteenth century, though the British-influenced Lima Cricket Club had introduced fútbol a couple of decades earlier. Destined for fame was *Club Alianza*, which began in the coastal town of Chacaritas, near Lima. Here immigrants, including many Italians and Chinese, promoted the early association with its jersey color of green—later changed to blue, then to its now distinctive black and white stripes.

Club Alianza is one of Latin America's most famous franchises. The team plays in a stadium in Lima's working-class district of La Victoria, popularly called "Matute" (after the specific barrio in which it is located). Opened in 1974, with a relatively modest seating capacity of thirty-four thousand, Matute is formally named after Alejandro Villanueva, Alianza's most famous historical player. An Afro-Peruvian, Villanueva was an exceptional striker, scoring multiple goals in games at the 1936 Berlin Olympics—to the chagrin of Aryan Supremacists. He died at age thirty-five in a typhoid epidemic only a few years later.

In the 1920s the *Federación Peruana de Fútbol* (Peruvian Football Federation or FPF) formed, bringing organization to league and international play. The FPF fielded teams in the *Copa América* (America Cup) competition among South American nations, which Peru hosted and won in 1939. In the World Cup, Peru has generally not fared well, though in 1970 it reached the quarter-finals before losing to perennial powerhouse Brazil. In 1978 the national team played the Netherlands to a draw, but was then mauled by an Argentinian team that went on to win the tournament. Hopes were high for the 2022 squad, but it fell in a last qualifier to Australia—a team it had beaten four years earlier at the World Cup in Russia. Thousands of wealthy Peruvians flew into Qatar and witnessed the agonizing 4–5 defeat, which came on penalty kicks.

Peruvians are immensely and rightfully proud of their distinctive cuisine. In globalized, corporate-led popular culture, the center of attention has been Gastón Acurio. Trained as a chef at Paris's prestigious Le Cordon Bleu, he and his German-born wife have internationally franchised their restaurant *Astrid & Gastón*, with the first of the chain located in Lima's upscale San Isidro District. Acurio has been the focus of documentaries, culinary magazines, and even a film (*Finding Gastón*, 2014). By 2022 he had two million followers on his Twitter account. But the marvels of Peruvian cuisine are hardly limited to five-star restaurants for the rich. In the highlands, the nuanced taste of the nation's hundreds of varieties of potatoes can easily be discovered, while myriad variations of seafood remain readily accessible to any casual traveler along the coast. A reputation for unique and exceptional food and drink has fed the tourist industry, with tens of thousands by the mid-2010s motivated to visit at least partly because of gastronomy.

Polling data in the 2010s showed Peru still deeply religious, with 86 percent of its citizens describing themselves as devout. Today, Protestants constitute about 15 percent of the population but, unlike many other regions in Latin America, Peru remains imminently Catholic. Like elsewhere, however, most Protestants are Pentecostal, with 75 percent believing in speaking in tongues and miraculous healings. They are also more inclined than Catholics to discuss religion with others and to evangelize, or attempt to win others to their faith.

Catholicism is practiced with great variance in devotion and orthodoxy. Papal visits have generated public excitement. In 1985 John Paul II became the first pontiff to visit Peru, with the left-of-center President Alan García memorably kneeling to kiss his hand. Endlessly fond of travel and enthusiastic crowds, the same pope returned just three years later—the public outpouring notably less animated the second time around. A more subdued style of touring came with Argentine-born Pope Francis in 2018. Content differed, too. John Paul II held visible court, giving a fiery address to clergy in the Plaza de Armas in which he demanded that they regard his authority; Francis, in contrast, ventured into Amazonia, where he criticized environmentally destructive mining practices and met with local indigenous leaders.

Popular expressions of faith continue in religious festivals and the veneration of saints. Two hundred years after its independence, Peru still witnesses fervency among the faithful, not unlike that practiced in colonial times long ago. New saints and cults periodically emerge. In the last thirty years, the most significant has been that of Ricardito—child-saint of the unemployed. Little Ricardo was born to a well-placed father, who served as personal secretary to President Manuel Pardo before dying of pneumonia in 1887 at age forty-four. Eight months old when his father perished, he succumbed to malaria at age six. Friends interred the boy beside his father, who was buried in the prestigious Presbítero Matías Maestro; in 1899, these wealthy associates erected a natural-sized marble statue of the child.

In the early 1990s, as the economy was ravaged by the Sendero War and the Fujimori government's austerity measures, poor from the barrios of northeast Lima began to seek succor in front of Ricardito's statue. Rumors spread of the improbable—that homage brought opportunities for work and good-paying jobs. This superstition spread through word of mouth, and visits to the gravesite rose exponentially. The devotion testifies to the strong desire of people to believe in an intimate and compassionate divine. Within the Catholic hierarchy some educated clerics have tried to temper such irrational, emotion-based belief; many others condone it with silence, while some proactively encourage it. Whether Catholic or Protestant, the vast majority of religious Peruvians believe in the inexplicable: supernatural blessings that unexpectedly make life better at critical junctures.

Contemporary Television and Film

Peru's small film industry struggled in the 1980s, after subsidies dried up with the end of the military government, and the economy began to falter in mid-decade. In an increasingly tense political atmosphere, it was also difficult to broach the sensitive topic of the unfolding Sendero war. But Francisco Lombardi did so in his 1988 work *La boca del lobo* (*The Wolf's Mouth*). While produced, as always, on a shoestring budget, the work communicates well by way of its evocative screenplay, making it one of Peru's better films. The tale is told from the perspective of Toño (Vitin Luna), a soldier in an army unit sent to occupy a highlands village in the early eighties. The seemingly invisible presence of Sendero Luminoso shows itself, first with the appearance of a red flag, and second, with an ambush that leaves one of Toño's closest friends dead. This attack prompts the arrival of a gung-ho lieutenant, Iván Roca (Gustavo Burro), who has no qualms with abusing the local population in order to find answers. Toño's perceptions change, as the film rolls toward its climactic and disturbing end.

Such thoughtful works, which critically examined the army's role in the violence, became impossible during the Fujimori years. Filmmakers and the broader media largely fell silent during the dictatorship. In the realm of news coverage, *Latina* was the only major TV outlet that challenged the regime and its police-state tactics. Its news diary, *Contrapunto*, airing on its flagship Lima station Channel 2, exposed government connections to drug-running and death squads in the late nineties. Latina's owner, Baruch Ivcher, refused bribes from spymaster Vladimir Montesinos and soon lost his Peruvian citizenship (though later he was able to file a successful lawsuit through the Inter-American Court of Human Rights).

Television and film changed with the times. Less overtly political material appeared in the 1990s. In 1992, TV screenwriter Eduardo Adrianzén generated excitement with a popular mini-series called *La Perricholi* (it aired again in 2011). The telenovela chronicled the colorful life of Micaela Villegas, an actress in the late eighteenth century who was also the mistress of a powerful Spanish viceroy. It followed many of the romantic formulas of Latin telenovelas everywhere, but it had spirit—if not always production polish. *La Perricholi* drew good ratings and launched the career of Mónica Sánchez.

The end of the Fujimori dictatorship allowed for greater creative freedom. In cinema, many finally engaged the traumatic topic of the war. Febrizio Águilar directed *Paloma de papel* (*Paper Dove*), a 2003 yarn that examines the disturbing role of child-soldiers. Juan (Antonio Callirgos) is a Senderista released from prison, who recalls the horrible events of his childhood, when the mayor and other leaders in his village were assassinated. He is ushered off to a Sendero training camp and indoctrinated, only to later return to his own village with the prospect of carrying out a massacre. He faces a life-decision not unlike that of Toño in Lombardi's *La boca del lobo*. Josué Méndez's gritty *Días de Santiago* (*Days of Santiago*, 2004) traces the daily life of a fictionalized ex-Marine. The former soldier resembles a hunted animal, unemployed and lost in the postwar urban jungle that is Lima. Dealing directly at times with discrimination by economic class, it is a disturbing film.

For his part, Lombardi used his independent Inca Films to produce *Mariposa negra* (*Black Butterfly*, 2006), a well-paced and skillfully shot thriller—the director yet again working with his childhood friend José "Pili" Flores Lucera as photographer. The protagonist, Gabriela (played by Melania Urbina), is a history teacher engaged to a judge who is mysteriously murdered. She and a journalist-friend are soon on the trail of the assassins, and in the process find corruption in high places as they seek revenge. Based on Alonso Cueto's novel *Grandes miradas* (*Great Looks*), the film won critical and popular acclaim, and speaks to the broad distrust of politicians in contemporary Peruvian society.

That distrust was arguably increased by changes in media ownership. Lima's Channel 2 / *Televisión Latina* was sold in 2012 by the principled Baruch Ivcher to a large investment group. Enfoca Andean Investments, headed by Jesús Zamora, had deep pockets and handled hundreds of millions of dollars in equity funds at the time, with shareholding in significant retail sectors throughout the Andean region. Predictably, the outlet's political proclivities soon turned conservative—Channel 2 reporters seemed to have little luck sniffing out the massive corruption greasing Alan García's second, pro-business administration. In more recent times its broadcasts have sank even lower, descending periodically into extreme right-wing hysterics (see chapter 17).

As the media broadly failed to deal with the complexities and dirty underside of the Fujimori years, filmmakers continued to break the silence. The mid-2010s saw a flurry of reflective films, two more based on novels by Alonso Cueto, one of Peru's most prolific twenty-first-century writers. *La hora azul* (*The Blue Hour*, 2015) tells the tale of a high-powered lawyer, who decides against his wife's advice to seek out the guerrilla-woman whom his recently deceased army officer father had held captive during the war. Cueto's novel *La pasajera* (*The Passenger*) inspired Salvador del Solar's 2015 *Magallanes* (Magellan) with a similar plot: a veteran who drives a taxi in Lima tracks down the native woman who, as a girl, was enslaved and raped by his military unit. *Magallanes* enjoyed success on the international film festival circuit, as did *La última tarde* (*The Last Afternoon*, 2016), in which two former guerrillas await the finalization of their divorce while reflecting on their youthful idealism, love, and postwar scars. The pensive depth of Peru's screenwriters has been impressive.

In contrast, television has predictably been of much lighter fare but has continued to entertain the public, with cable channels establishing an overwhelmingly foreign presence in the homes of the twenty-first-century's Limeño middle class. Still, there have been uniquely Peruvian contributions.

Eduardo Adrianzén built upon his success with *La Perricholi* via another miniseries, again starring Mónica Sánchez and titled *Eva del Edén* (*Eve of Eden*, 2004–2005).

The government-funded Radio and Television Institute of Peru (IRTP), part of the Ministry of Culture, has sought to highlight things Peruvian. For the last two decades it has produced a travelogue show, *Reportaje al Perú* (*Report to Peru*), with a mobile production crew that tracks down local culture and cuisine, especially in the highlands. Its primarily Lima-based show, *Sucedió en el Perú* (It Happened In Peru), has produced dozens of historical biographies. IRTP created and aired a successful historical telenovela, *El último bastión* (*The Last Fortress*), in 2018–2019. The thirty-five-episode series, featuring prominent actors and actresses, traced the Independence-era happenings in Peru by dramatizing the lives of a hacienda-owning family in a coastal town—with sufficient romantic adventure besides. Eduardo Adrianzén was the lead writer, with his wife María Luisa serving as producer. The series has some historical merit and, despite a modest budget and limited stage sets (though among the best ever produced by IRTP), drew a core of enthusiastic viewers.

Reasonably accurate historical drama was also an objective of Juan Carlos Oganes' film *Gloria del Pacífico* (2014), which recounts the early stages of the war with Chile and recreates the battle of Arica. Doing so on a total production budget of US $200,000, with a cast of thirty-five and just six hundred extras, is needless to say a daunting task. Less ambitious, but far more poignant, is *Canción sin nombre* (*Song without a Name*, 2019), by Columbia University MFA graduate Melina León. Written by León and Michael J. White, and shot in black and white by cinematographer Inti Briones, the film is based on the investigations into child trafficking by a journalist during Alan García's first presidency. Georgina, a native woman (played by Pamela Mendoza), has her baby abducted at a fake maternity clinic. It is a dark yet stirring work.

Though many films such as *Canción sin nombre* have portrayed Andean peoples, historically nearly the entire Peruvian film industry has predictably been based in Lima. In the twenty-first century, however, this is finally changing. The affordability of digital technology has allowed for production by additional filmmakers, many of whom are in the highlands. The landmark regional work was *El Huerfanito* (*The Little Orphan*), directed by Flaviano Quispe. Shot in Juliaca in 2004, it was a relative commercial success, with tens of thousands of eventual viewers.

Ever since *El Huerfanito*, film production has persisted in the southeastern cities abutting Lake Titicaca. Puno is the setting for the 2020 film *Manco*

Figure 16.2. A fundamental social and cultural tension in present-day Peru is local versus global. Whether in film or food, the authenticity and creativity of things Peruvian is slowly being usurped by brand-name corporate culture. On the south side of Lima, U.S. and European franchises increasingly own the marketplace as they cater to an Americanized middle class.
Photo by the author

Cápac (distributed in English under the name *Powerful Chief*). Similar in message and tone to *Días de Santiago*, it narrates urban migrant Elisbán, who wanders from job to job amidst grinding poverty. Director Henry Vallejo, who co-authored the script, faced multiple production challenges including a requisite change in actors (a debuting Jesús Luque Colque portrays Elisbán). Presented partly in Quechua, this minimalist film provides a damning indictment of the indifference of humanity to suffering, even as it moves unevenly to its jarring conclusion.

Like long-marginalized highlanders, more women are now directing and producing films. In recent accomplishments two Limeñas stand out: Claudia Llosa has migrated from a career in advertising to movie-making. Her *La teta asustada* (*Breastmilk of Sorrow*, 2009), shot over several weeks in villages just outside of Lima, dealt with the legacy of the Sendero war on indigenous communities. It was nominated for the "Best Foreign Film" Academy Award. Rossana Díaz Costa is a fast-rising director and screenwriter, who most recently adapted Bryce Echenique's novel *Un Mundo Para Julius* (2021) to the silver screen.

That Peru's modest film industry has survived into the twenty-first century is something of a miracle in itself. The difficulties of competing in a business swamped by the enormous budgets and polished mega-works of Hollywood are nearly insurmountable. Brazilian, Mexican, and Argentine films also penetrate the local market. Finances are a great challenge, as is marketing and distribution, with most transnational corporate powerbrokers unwilling to sponsor small, independent production companies like those of Peru. By sheer verve, Peru's cinematographers continue to repeatedly exceed all reasonable expectations—much like their nation itself. In film, culture, and history, Peru will undoubtedly engage and pleasantly surprise informed observers for decades to come.

CHAPTER SEVENTEEN

Crises, Covid, and Castillo

Contemporary Peru has lurched from crisis to crisis. The weight of a relentlessly growing population (though the *rate* of growth has slowed) continues to strain under an economic model in which money gravitates upward. The political system, subservient to neoliberal dictates in the early twenty-first century, has struggled to answer popular demands. In the midst of multiplying problems, the Covid epidemic hit, Peru suffering the world's highest mortality rates. Though in many ways at low ebb, the wearied nation continues its quest for political and economic answers.

The Politics of Corruption

The presidency of Ollanta Humala having faltered, the 2016 presidential race nevertheless unfolded with the influential television media still focusing on major political figures, thus ensuring that the "brand names" of Peruvian politics would most effectively compete. Keiko Fujimori launched her second campaign, with an expanding and better organized *Fuerza Popular* behind her. Alan García also ran again, but Alejandro Toledo, under scrutiny for corruption in his administration, prudently decided to leave the country for a teaching position at his U.S. alma mater of Stanford University. Pedro Kuczynski—another former World Bank economist and long-standing political player—declared for the presidency and received consistently favorable press coverage.

Increasingly fatigued by the same political package, public engagement waned in 2016. Particularly surprising was the disinterest in the efforts of García. His campaign drew paltry crowds, while in televised debates he was unusually taciturn. In the first round he captured just 6 percent of the vote, ensuring there would be no third term for one of the most significant politicians of the postwar era. For his part, Kuczynski harped endlessly on the need to combat corruption. This theme resonated with voters, though the rather bland presentations by "PPK," as he was commonly known, inspired little emotional response.

In the first round, Kuczynski garnered 21 percent of the vote, while Keiko Fujimori captured nearly 40 percent. The polarizing Keiko's strong performance roused the electorate, and the run-off campaign elicited far more popular energy. Fujimori had solid support in much of the highlands, and especially in areas where the Sendero war had been fought (here, even her imprisoned father was still widely popular). Other large swaths of Peru, along with the Limeño middle class, were divided. Two large rallies against Keiko's candidacy filled Plaza San Martín in the center of the capital, while a damning press report—by the América Televisión investigative newscast *Cuarto Poder*—revealed presumed links between one of her closest advisors and drug cartels. Investigations into her campaign's finances followed, and the shadow of drug-linked corruption began to sink her in the polls.

In the June 5 runoff, Kuczynski eked out a victory, though Fuerza Popular took 73 of 130 seats in the unicameral legislature. The embittering campaign left Fuerza Popular's cadre disinclined to cooperate with the new administration, and a dysfunctional government sputtered forward. Kuczynski's approval rating slowly sagged, then plummeted when revelations surfaced of his own improprieties with the Brazilian construction firm Odebrecht.

In December 2017, Kuczynski stunned the country by pardoning Alberto Fujimori. That pardon came just days after dodging a congressional motion of impeachment—during which many Fuerza Popular congresspersons improbably switched sides and supported the beleaguered president. Strange happenings continued into early 2018, when another impeachment vote was scheduled. At the center of these was Kenji Fujimori, Keiko's brother. Soon the obvious was revealed: back room deals had been cut, whereby Fuerza Popular was keeping Kuczynski in office in exchange for various counterincentives. Public outrage followed, and in March Kuczynski resigned. A relative unknown, Vice President Martín Vizcarra, now assumed office.

In the midst of the disintegrating Kuczynski presidency, corruption investigations finally ensnared Ollanta Humala. He and his wife, Nadine Herrera, were arrested for accepting bribes, and went in and out of jail during the course of subsequent legal battles. Simultaneous investigations turned up the evidence that Humala had ordered extrajudicial executions, as an army officer, while stationed in the Amazon in the early 1990s. Others showed that he had tampered with evidence and bought off witnesses in a separate case. As these and still other dirty dealings surfaced, Peruvians grew even more disenchanted with the entire political establishment.

The next to fall was Alan García. In some ways it is remarkable, given the brazen corruption of his second term, that it took so long to close in on the renowned politician. García lived mostly in Madrid after 2011, but periodically returned to his homeland. In late 2018, a court ordered his passport withheld while he was in Lima; he took refuge in the Paraguayan embassy and sought political asylum. After his request was denied, he was stuck in his posh house in south Lima, with little to do except wait for the trap to spring.

When police arrived to detain him, shortly after dawn on an April 2019 morning, García met them briefly on a staircase then hastily retreated into his bedroom. As the officers followed, he closed the door, put a .38 caliber revolver to his head, and pulled the trigger. He lived for nearly three more hours, finally dying on the operating table at a nearby hospital. Mercurial and temperamental through the breadth of his career, García's suicide came nevertheless as a great shock to all. A man whose healthy ego was inflated by the personality cultdom of APRA, he might well have *believed* that he did nothing wrong, but judicial evidence indicates that he and his cronies took millions of dollars from Odebrecht, and that both of his presidential terms could have served as textbook lessons in graft. Many Apristas, however, memorialized their leader as a political "martyr" as they gathered over his casket at the party's Casa del Pueblo headquarters.

Alan García's dramatic exit came shortly before a year many Peruvians would rather forget. In 2020 Peruvians saw the arrival of Covid, which rippled across the nation and claimed tens of thousands of lives, especially in the highlands. A poor country, Peru was among the last in the western hemisphere to receive sufficient doses of the vaccine. Halting attempts to restrict movement devastated an already fragile economy. By the end of the year nearly nine million Peruvians were living in abject poverty on a monthly income of less than one hundred U.S. dollars. Many struggled to feed themselves. The economy as a whole shrank by 13 percent in 2020.

At the helm in this difficult time was Vizcarra, whose lack of polish and pretense made him appear as an honest broker. Despite having been vice president, he was something of an outsider to the political establishment, and his appeals for caution as Covid spread convinced many citizens that he had their best interests in mind. He soon pushed forward several anti-corruption measures, too, and even voiced support for the heavyweight idea of eliminating legislative immunity (which forbids legal proceedings against a sitting congressperson). Public support for Vizcarra was comparatively strong and stable.

Soon, however, congress prepared to impeach him. Using the same constitutional concept with which it had targeted Kuczynski—a strangely worded qualification that allows an executive to be removed for lapses in "moral capacity," in November the legislature voted out Vizcarra. It then installed its speaker, Manuel Merino, an Acción Popular leader who faced ongoing corruption charges. To many citizens, it appeared that one of the nation's few honest politicians was being persecuted—that the foxes were taking control of the metaphorical chicken coup.

Merino's installation triggered a rarity in Peru: successful, largely spontaneous popular revolt. Protests rapidly erupted in Lima and several secondary cities, and when the National Police used excessive force in response, agitation on the streets only accelerated. Digital technology and the internet assisted in both spawning the protests and undercutting the established media's narrative about them. Educated youth were central to the remarkable movement. Perhaps, too, fatigue and frustration with Covid played a hand in this unusually strong public reaction. Merino's government lasted only six days.

The Politics of Fear

The coalition that brought Merino's government down was diverse, but certainly fueled in part by widespread disillusionment with the political class. Having said that, it was also something of anomaly. The most obvious trend in the last two decades of Peruvian political life has been the emergence of a very powerful far right. This phenomenon has been most clearly at play within the already-influential Limeño middle class.[1]

The rise of the far right has been tied to a collective culture of fear. Certainly middle-class angst was understandable with the urban bombings of Sendero Luminoso, culminating in 1991–1993. But incessant news reports on crime, especially in the television media, have aggravated the anxiety. Wealth concentration above the middle class, and economic desperation below it, have fed rising societal tensions. Ironically the first two decades of the twenty-first century were comparatively good for Peru (and the entire

---

1. A timely reminder that "middle class" refers to those who live a comfortable lifestyle roughly analogous to that of the U.S. middle class—not those with the median household income. In Peru, the middle class is an economic upper 15–20 percent of the population.

Figure 17.1. Willax Televisión's studios are located in south Lima. The preeminent media outlet of the far right, its political commentators are flashy and high-energy. Ironically, some of them once opposed the Fujimori dictatorship, most notably Beto Ortiz. Willax is quick to use law suits to threaten and silence its critics. Popular social media blogger Marco Sifuentes has been targeted regarding Ortiz's *Beto a Saber* show.
Photo by the author

Third World), as an economic expansion in the 2000s was followed by easy money in the mid-2010s. Major central banks printed trillions of fresh U.S. dollars after the 2007–2008 financial panic, and the global financial system flooded Third World countries with ample new loans.

There are many practical expressions of middle-class fear—an exponential increase in security-related businesses and services, the popularity of home alarm systems, increased gun sales, and the like. But the most overt physical expression in metropolitan Lima is a wall. A ten-foot high, razor-wire topped barrier weaves its way along hillsides beside the capital's sprawling southern suburbs. It is designed to keep the poor out; select entry-points exist for contracted workers, such as domestic servants and gardeners. The wall began improbably with Jesuits, who sealed off their rich-serving *Colegio de La Inmaculada*, a secondary school, from nearby squatters in 1985. An adjoining neighborhood association, in Surco's Casuarinas subdivision, extended it. Other groups followed, and today it runs through eastern Lima for over six miles.

But although the wall provides spatial control, it has psychological consequences. It humiliates the poor, who continually sense their unworthiness.

It reinforces the precepts of fear within the middle class—which subliminally regards those on the "other side" as different and somehow dangerous. Related to the wall is another stark physical contrast: in Lima's coastal desert climate, one side is well-watered and green, the other, bleak and brown. The poor pay several times their proportionate share of Lima's water bills, as they must hire tanker trucks to deliver potable water. A December 2022 court order that the wall be dismantled in 2023 may not be obeyed.

The palpable fear in Peruvian life has also translated into intolerance of diverse political views—the bedrock of functional democracy. In the post-Fujimori era, certain premises of the police-like state have endured, including the unquestioned sanctity of the Armed Forces. A hyper-conservative media establishment continues to dominate the airwaves. Lawsuits and other legal ploys are increasingly used to silence critics. Fueled by segments of the media, the general public has internalized a nearly proto-fascist abhorrence of the political left, to the degree that the long-term survival of the nation's democracy must be called into question.

Of course, anyone who even hints at Sendero sympathies has been open game. When ex-Senderistas attempted to register as a political party in 2011, they were barred. A subsequent amnesty movement for long-imprisoned Senderos (led mostly by family members) faced rabid media and public condemnation. When it held marches in Lima in 2017, the Minister of Interior, Carlos Basombrío, summarily denounced *all* participants as Senderistas—even though some accomplices were motivated by libertarian sentiments. Dozens of marchers were taken into custody and held for months incommunicado. Congress changed the law to make similar pro-amnesty marches criminal acts, with penalties of up to fifteen years in prison. In 2018, after Senderos held a public ceremony at a mausoleum for their dead, a sensationalist *Latina Noticias* TV broadcast on its *Puntofinal* show "investigated" what it termed the "Mausoleum of Terror." Authorities subsequently brought in bulldozers, surrounded by a phalanx of National Police, and demolished the burial site. Even *dead* Senderistas are somehow a threat to national security.

In the shadow of this Red Scare, fueled in part by proliferating conspiracy theories and hysterics on social media, came the remarkable 2021 presidential election. After Merino's government fell in November 2020, congress quickly appointed a stand-in executive from one of the few political party's that had opposed Vizcarra's removal. Francisco Sagasti of the small *Partido Morado* (Purple Party) was tasked with overseeing the forthcoming regularly scheduled elections. Erudite and genteel, an engineer by training, he began his interim by apologizing on behalf of the state for the shooting deaths of two anti-Merino protesters.

Sagasti's instincts were democratic and high-minded, but alas, Covid wreaked havoc on his short presidential term. An economic shutdown to control the virus was badly timed, and cases skyrocketed thereafter. Officially, by March 2021, the Covid death count was 45,000. Other data, such as that of cemetery interments, suggested the real count was in the range of 170,000. The mortality numbers rose into mid-2021, when Peru reached the highest death rate in the entire world. Its primitive healthcare system swamped, clinics and hospitals turned away the poor in droves. Those who could afford it bought oxygen for home use, often at inflated prices. By mid-2022, an estimated 214,000 citizens had died from Covid.

From the start of the campaign cycle, major media outlets hyped the candidacies of several far rightists. Among these was Rafael López Aliaga, a devout Catholic, Opus Dei member and life-long bachelor, who condemned homosexuality and abortion while professing to be in spiritual love with the Virgin Mary. Though a verbal champion of free market capitalism, López Aliaga had become rich through a monopoly granted him by Alberto Fujimori's government—he owns the short railroad to Machu Picchu that charges tourists an exorbitant sum for its services.

Also favored in the media was the candidacy of Hernando de Soto, an economist tied to international lending agencies who had penned a popular book espousing a supposed "Third Way" to economic prosperity. If De Soto had such miracle answers, one would have thought he might have already shared them. He had, after all, served as an economic advisor to the likes of Alejandro Toledo and (second-term) Alan García. Finally, the media gave robust attention to Keiko Fujimori, who was making her third bid for the presidency.

First round results in April came as a shock to all: In an overcrowded field splintered by the participation of seven major candidates, a political novice named Pedro Castillo led the pack with nearly 19 percent of the vote. In second place, with 13.4 percent, was Fujimori. In aggregate, however, the far right had captured roughly 40 percent of the vote, demonstrating that it was the dominant ideological force. The presidential runoff in the nation's bicentennial year would pit the far right against the far left, and a Japanese-Peruvian urbanite against a native-descended highlander.

The Rise and Fall of Pedro Castillo

Pedro Castillo's sudden appearance on the national stage was unprecedented. Though he had led a teachers' strike in 2017 that gained concessions from the short-lived Kuczynski government, he was a true outsider, largely unknown in Lima. His affiliation was with a regional highlands' party called *Perú Libre* (Free Peru) that had only a few thousand members. His first-round triumph took pollsters by surprise—though polls are disproportionately conducted by telephone, in a nation where a majority of the population does not have them. Castillo had trekked back and forth across rural Peru staging low-budget rallies on countless town squares, often speaking merely through a hand-held megaphone. His campaign slogan, "No More Poverty in a Rich Country," clearly struck a chord. It is a testimony to Peru's notably clean electoral system (in contrast to its political office-holding) that an authentic outsider could fare so well.

Within days of the first-round results, however, a new fear swept the Limeño middle class: that Castillo was a communist. López Aliaga was quick to claim that he was a Hugo Chávez in the making, and on the steps of the National Palace led his religious followers in a chant of "Death to Pedro Castillo!" Keiko Fujimori soon joined the hysterics, suggesting that her opponent was planning to subvert Peruvian democracy and install a Bolshevik-style dictatorship. The most fringe-of-the-fringe rightists, ex-army officer Daniel Urresti, contended that Castillo was guided by "Gonzalo Thought" (a reference to the imprisoned Senderista chieftain). In fact, Castillo had served as a young man in an *anti*-Sendero civil patrol, and was a practicing evangelical adhering to conservative social positions, including opposition to gay marriage.

The second round of voting saw Castillo win the presidency by the narrowest of margins. Yet after initially indicating that the balloting was fair, Fujimori held a press conference—just after the premiere polling analysis firm projected her to lose—announcing that systematic fraud had been perpetrated. She offered no substantive evidence. Weeks of legal wrangling and demonstrations began, bringing a palpable tension to especially downtown Lima even as thousands of indigenous citizens arrived in support of the president-elect. The far right's accusation was clearly an echo of the post-election fraud charges of Donald Trump, cable television heavy in its coverage of recent affairs in the United States. A "Stop the Steal" movement received extensive media hype—Willax even aired an incredibly dull car caravan protest for several hours. Thus propagandized, over time even many well-educated Peruvians convinced themselves that the election was rigged.

The jurists in charge of the long-reputable electoral commission found no significant fraud. In fact, perpetration of fraud by a small, outsider-party would have been exceedingly improbable. Rather telling, too, was the lack of middle-class interest in the commission's proceedings. These live-aired hearings, available on Facebook and other platforms, received almost no

Figure 17.2. Protesters square off in downtown Lima. In the foreground are rightists, flags and national colors on display, along with an occasional Israeli flag (Zionism has become a secondary cause for the far right). In the distance are Castillo supporters. Violence between the two groups has been common, though on this occasion—in December 2021—police successfully kept the peace.
Photo by the author

attention. Would not citizens want to know how "communists" had pulled off the scam of the century? On July 28, two hundred years after José de San Martín had declared Peruvian independence, a rather subdued ceremony saw the installation of Castillo. The nation was divided.

Within weeks of taking office, it was apparent that Castillo was in over his head. Wearing a wide-brimmed hat representative of his highlands' region, he was from the start stiff and awkward in ceremonies; when first arriving at the National Palace on inauguration day, he inappropriately greeted the doorman. Most of his appointees were political novices, unqualified for their jobs. His first chief-of-staff was apparently corrupt, caught stashing twenty thousand dollars in a hideaway in the men's restroom at the palace. Castillo himself rarely interacted with the press, instead sequestering himself with a clique of highly questionable "advisors." As things went sour, he changed his prime minister and shuffled his cabinet repeatedly. Ministries became rotating doors, the government nearly dysfunctional. In summer 2022, as Castillo increasingly acquiesced to neoliberal economic policies, Perú Libre asked for him to resign from the party; he complied.

Predictably, as Castillo struggled to govern, the far right pounced. Even before he took office, a rightist-dominated congress modified the constitution, effectively making the presidency more of a symbolic office, while empowering the Minister of State (now functioning like a prime minister). In late 2021 and early 2022, using the moral incapacity clause, congress twice tried to remove Castillo from office. As the economy slowed in late 2022, protests against him again mounted. A series of investigations indicated that the president and some in his inner circle, including intimate family members, were inappropriately accepting money under the table. But it was also true that Peru's political establishment held Castillo to a standard not seen before; had Alan García faced similar scrutiny, for example, he would have been hounded from office within weeks.

In December 2022 congress mounted yet another impeachment bid. It appeared that the vote would again fall short. Rumors circulated of congresspersons switching sides, however, and in a fluid situation Castillo panicked. In a strange midnight ramble he reminisced about his parents, and on the following morning (December 7) he took to the airwaves to announce the dissolution of congress and rule by decree. His attempt to duplicate the *Fujigolpe* was foolhardy: unlike Fujimori in 1992, he lacked popular support. More critically, the Armed Forces and National Police quickly pronounced against him. Within hours he was arrested by his own security detail. It was the height of folly for a man with a singular lack of political acumen. Conversely, questions will likely forever remain unanswered about the information given him by senior police and military personnel. Did army generals assure Castillo of their backing, so as to bait him to pull this stunt—and thus ensure his spectacular downfall?

With the military's blessing, Dina Boluarte assumed the presidency. Even within Peru's longstanding tradition of drawing vice presidents from obscurity, Boluarte was beyond the pale. The nation's new magistrate had garnered a mere two thousand votes in her only run for office— in a district mayoral contest in Lima in which she finished ninth. No one knew who she was. Though international press played up the story that Peru had its first female president, far more damning was the fact that the nation had its fifth president in just twenty-six months. The integrity of the entire political system was increasingly at peril.

At the behest of the Armed Forces, Boluarte quickly authorized a State of Emergency, which among other features allowed the army to suppress protests with excessive force. The document justifying the move charged that protesters were terrorists linked to the defunct Sendero Luminoso—a completely unrealistic assessment. At several locations troops simply gunned down Peruvians in cold blood. On a single January 2023 day in Juliaca at least seventeen people died—shot by the army with combat-grade weapons and ammunition provided by the United States. Nearly all of the dozens of deaths were in the highlands. Indigenous Peruvians bore the worst of the abuses, in shootings, beatings, arrests, and arbitrary detentions.

In February, the human rights organization Amnesty International observed what any clear-minded observer could see: that there was a racial dimension in the repression. Simply put—and there is no denying it—Peru remains a profoundly racist society. The nation's hyper-conservative media ignored the AI report, while the government prepared laws to protect police officers and soldiers from possible criminal prosecution. The United States' Biden administration continued to provide extensive military and police funding, despite the egregious human rights violations. By mid-2023 the Boluarte government had all of the markings of a soft military dictatorship. Five centuries after the cruelties of the Spanish conquest, how very little in Peru has really changed!

The Other Peru

The response to Castillo's election and subsequent fall reflects the critical reality of a divided Peru. The rift is not solely along ideological lines—the nation is profoundly fragmented by race, class, geography, and culture. In many ways, voting for Castillo was an appeal for integration by impoverished rural highlanders. The appeal was forcefully rebuffed by monied Limeños.

The "other" Peru, largely devoid of access to political power, is in the highlands. The need for brevity in this study, with its natural focus on Lima's national politics, has prevented nuancing this term. The vast region astride the great Andes Mountains is geographically complex, with significant population centers to the south and southeast (Arequipa, Cuzco, and cities near Lake Titicaca), and the predominantly rural Central Highlands. Stretching several hundred miles, the Central Highlands is typically just fifty or so miles wide, sandwiched between the Cordilleras Occidental and Central (Western and Central Ranges), until its valleys and plateaus broaden out to the south, beyond the notable colonial provinces of Huancavelica and Ayacucho (see map, figure 0.1).

It is in the heart of the Central Highlands that much of Peru's mineral wealth rests—rich veins of copper, lead, zinc, gold, and silver, though other pockets of valuable ores are scattered around the country, including iron deposits along the southern coast. Indigenous communities continue to bear

206 Chapter Seventeen

Figure 17.3. The spectacular highlands is a world apart. Here indigenous women in traditional clothing spin wool, as the longstanding practice of handwoven textiles continues. Villagers remain highly communal, too, though this inhibits individuality and freedom of expression. Local rondas, or civil patrols, enforce societal norms—meting out floggings for criminal activity but also frequently punishing nonconformists, as well.
Source: Museo del Banco Central de Reserva del Perú

the severe consequences of mine-related pollutants, including exposure to toxins, arsenic, and cancer-causing cadmium. Though some mining firms have periodically appeased locals by rolling in free beer-laden trucks, the business's motto could rightly be "profits before people." Mining executives have shown little concern for the well-being of locals.

The highlands have produced distinctive regional politics, and have periodically projected political figures onto the national stage before Castillo. Some of these have been strange. The *Frente Popular Agrícola del Perú* (Agrarian People's Front or FREPAP) is the political organ of Ezequiel Ataucusi, known as "Brother Ezequiel." A self-styled Biblical prophet, Ataucusi established a messianic religious cult that blends his Seventh-Day Adventist background with Incan mysticism. His followers have set up socialistic agrarian communes. In the 1990s he ran for president, though polling only about 1 percent, before his death at age eighty-two in year 2000. His corpse was placed in a glass coffin, followers keeping vigil in the belief that this "Jesus of the West" would arise on the third day. His remains instead began to putrefy, and were quietly buried. His son has inherited leadership of the organization, which secured an astounding fifteen seats in the national legislature via January 2020 special elections.[2]

While the highlands, with their mining communities, have a significant population, much of Peru's economic future likely rests in the sparsely settled Amazonian basin. Comprising nearly half of the nation's territory, it is a massive area the size of the nation of Ukraine. Peruvian Amazonia almost certainly includes the largest primary (never cleared) forest in the world. Great possibilities for long-term resource development, however, are being lost for short-term gain. Logging, mining, and agriculture are doing irreparable damage, while drug cartels also contribute to the destruction by carving out coca leaf farms in the deepest recesses of the jungle.

Legally, the government owns the vast majority of the undeveloped land in Amazonia, even as it grants concessions for various economic enterprises. Corruption mars the process from start to finish. Palm oil plantations abound, though they practice unsavory environmental and labor practices (palm oil is widely used in a range of products, from shampoos to potato chips). Meanwhile, illegal activities go unchecked. Loggers deforest well over one thousand square miles of rainforest each year, and the process is accelerating. A significant portion of the rare woods end up in U.S. residential construction. Deforestation is even more carelessly applied in agriculture. Much of the jungle is burned away for cattle-grazing. In this, rich topsoil is obliterated within a few years—it is a thoughtless waste of natural resources. Deforestation destabilizes riverbanks, triggering sedimentation and later flooding. Illegal mining fills the environment with mercury, a bonding agent used in leaching gold. Water pollution is extensive, destroying the livelihood of indigenous tribes who reside nearby. Scores of indigenous and human rights activists have paid with their lives for denouncing the environmental destruction and other abuses taking place in Amazonia.

In both highlands and Amazonian resource management, the recent Castillo government proved itself as complicit and inept as its predecessors—in fact, in some ways, even more so. The man who promised to set Peru on a new course, and deliver improvements to the hinterlands, did just the opposite. Though it took him awhile longer than Humala and García, he relied on police muscle to check anti-mining protest movements, most notably at the Chinese-owned copper pit at Las Bambas. The national government continues to allow foreign corporations to easily and cheaply exploit Peru's amazing resources. Mining firms evade taxes through the overly generous

---

2. During the upheaval of the Vizcarra presidency, congress was disbanded and special elections held. These saw a low turnout and eclectic mix of victors. There is no reason to believe that FREPAP has long-term staying power.

Obras por Impuestos (Works for Taxes) program, which enables them to write off as a "tax" activity such as road-building, which they would do anyway. Environmental regulations, to the degree that they even exist, are almost never enforced.

Until Peruvians collectively figure out that it is not in their interest to give foreigners a free hand to exploit their country, little can be done to reverse any of these trends. In fall 2022, Fuerza Popular and the political right—in control of congress—blocked a feeble attempt by Castillo's administration to increase taxes on mining corporations. Peru collects only about U.S. $1.5 billion annually from mining, or just 2.9 percent of its total revenue.[3] Ultimately this lack of authentic nationalism feeds the prosperity of the United States and other rich countries at the expense of Peru. Of course, U.S. policymakers are aware of this; Washington's support for Castillo was explicit as neoliberal economic policies continue unabated.

But the study of political history is exciting because of the element of surprise. No one could have anticipated the myriad twists of Peru's odyssey since independence. The future is not readily predictable, much less predetermined. A groundswell of real nationalism is possible—one that would produce a unity that transcends class and race, and opens up a collective strength heretofore largely denied. It would come with affluent Limeños viewing indigenous highlanders as their Peruvian sisters and brothers, with meaningful economic reform that routs money downward instead of upward, and inward instead of outward. It would come with a fresh dedication to pluralistic democracy and honest governance. While external forces playing upon Peru are great, the nation's destiny is still within the grasp of its citizens. At present such a sweeping transformation seems beyond improbable. Certainly, no current major political players—much less any senior military officers—will be the agents of change. But other, more truly patriotic and visionary Peruvians might, at some point in the future, step forward with the vision and determination necessary to guide their country to a better place.

---

3. And this is a percentage of a comparatively small budget. Peru's government currently spends about U.S. $56 billion each year, or roughly twice that of the state of Nevada. Government in Peru is less than one-tenth the size of the U.S. federal government *after* proportionate adjustment for population.

Suggested Readings

The historiography (writings of history) on Peru is rich, and has flowered especially in recent decades. The following abbreviated bibliography is limited to books, divided into English and Spanish, and lightly annotated in select cases where the title does not fully communicate content. Books that transcend the chronological (by chapters) breakdown are presented only once, in the first subsection in which they are relevant. English-language books that have been translated into Spanish appear only in the English-language listings, but with notation and the first portion of their Spanish-language title (all of the publishers are located in Lima). Predictably, for English-language scholarship, recent decades have generated disproportionate attention. The predominant listing of books on the twentieth century also reflects the primary focus of this text.

Chapters 1–3 (c. 1780–1867)

Espinoza, G. Antonio. *Education and the State in Modern Peru: Primary Education in Lima, 1821–c. 1921*. New York: Palgrave Macmillan, 2013.

García-Bryce, Iñigo. *Crafting the Republic: Lima's Artisans and Nation-Building in Peru, 1821–1879*. Albuquerque: University of New Mexico Press, 2009.

Klarén, Peter Flindell. *Peru: Society and Nationhood in the Andes*. New York: Oxford University Press, 2000. A weighty text that covers economic and social as well as political history. Published in Spanish as *Nación y sociedad en la historia del Perú*, Instituto de Estudios Peruanos, 2004.

Méndez, Cecilia. *The Plebeian Republic: The Huanta Rebellion and the Making of the Peruvian State, 1820–1850*. Durham: Duke University Press, 2005. Published in Spanish as *La república plebeya*, Instituto de Estudios Peruanos, 2014.

Love, Thomas F. *The Independent Republic of Arequipa: Making Regional Culture in the Andes*. Austin: University of Texas Press, 2017. Published in Spanish as *República Independiente de Arequipa*, Pontificia Universidad Católica del Perú, 2020.

Thurner, Mark. *From Two Republics to One Divided: Contradictions of Post-Colonial Nationmaking in Andean Peru*. Durham: Duke University Press, 1997.

Walker, Charles F. *The Tupac Amaru Rebellion*. Cambridge: Harvard University Press, 2014. Published in Spanish as *La rebelión de Túpac Amaru*, Instituto de Estudios Peruanos, 2015.

Walker, Charles F. *Smoldering Ashes: Cuzco and the Creation of Republican Peru, 1780–1840*. Durham: Duke University Press, 1999.

Chapters 4–6 (1867–1908)

Farcau, Bruce W. *The Ten Cents War: Chile, Peru, and Bolivia in the War of the Pacific, 1879–1884*. Westport: Praeger, 2000.

Klarén, Peter F. *Modernization, Dislocation, and Aprismo: Origins of the Peruvian Aprista Party, 1870–1932*. Austin: University of Texas Press, 1973.

Heilman, Jaymie Patricia. *Before the Shining Path: Politics in Rural Ayacucho, 1895–1980*. Stanford: Stanford University Press, 2010.

Mallon, Florencia E. *The Defense of Community in Peru's Central Highlands: Peasant Struggle and Capitalist Transition, 1860–1940*. Princeton: Princeton University Press, 1983.

Muecke, Ulrich. *Political Culture in Nineteenth-Century Peru: The Rise of the Partido Civil*. Pittsburgh: University of Pittsburgh Press, 2004.

Wilson, Fiona. *Citizenship and Political Violence in Peru: An Andean Town, 1870s–1970s*. Basingstoke, UK: Palgrave Macmillan, 2013.

Chapters 7–9 (1908–1948)

Coronado, Jorge. *The Andes Imagined: Indigenismo, Society, and Modernity*. Pittsburgh: University of Pittsburgh Press, 2009. Topical studies of *Indigenismo*, including a chapter on Martín Chambi.

de la Cadena, Marisol. *Indigenous Mestizoes: The Politics of Race and Culture in Cuzco, Peru, 1919–1991*. Durham: Duke University Press, 2000.

Drinot, Paulo. *The Allure of Labor: Workers, Race, and the Making of the Peruvian State*. Durham: Duke University Press, 2011. Published in Spanish as *La seducción de la clase obrera*, Instituto de Estudios Peruanos, 2016.

García-Bryce, Iñigo. *Haya de la Torre and the Pursuit of Power in Twentieth-Century Peru and Latin America*. Chapel Hill: University of North Carolina Press, 2018.

Hart, Stephen M. *César Vallejo: A Literary Biography*. Rochester: Boydell and Brewer, 2013.

Jansen, Robert S. *Revolutionizing Repertoires: The Rise of Populist Mobilization in Peru*. Chicago: The University of Chicago Press, 2017.

Masterson, Daniel M. *Militarism and Politics in Latin America: Peru from Sánchez Cerro to Sendero Luminoso*. Westport: Greenwood Press, 1991.

Mariátegui, José Carlos. *Seven Interpretive Essays on Peruvian Reality*. Trans. Marjory Urquidi. Austin: University of Texas Press, 1971. Published in Spanish as *Siete ensayos de interpretación de la realidad Peruana*, Amauta, 1928.

Quiroz, Alfonso W. *Corrupt Circles: A History of Unbound Graft in Peru*. Baltimore: Johns Hopkins University Press, 2008. Published in Spanish as *Historia de la corrupción en el Perú*, Instituto de Estudios Peruanos, 2013.

Parker, David. *The Idea of the Middle Class: White-Collar Workers and Peruvian Society, 1900–1950*. University Park: Pennsylvania State University Press, 1998.

Stein, Steve. *Populism in Peru: The Emergence of the Masses and the Politics of Social Control*. Madison: University of Wisconsin Press, 1980.

Wallace Fuentes, Myrna Ivonne. *Most Scandalous Woman: Magda Portal and the Dream of Revolution in Peru*. Oklahoma City: University of Oklahoma Press, 2017.

Chapters 10–12 (1948–1980)

Aguirre, Carlos, and Paulo Drinot, eds. *The Peculiar Revolution: Rethinking the Peruvian Experiment under Military Rule*. Austin: University of Texas Press, 2017. Published in Spanish as *La revolución peculiar*, Instituto de Estudios Peruanos, 2018.

Brown, Michael F., and Eduardo Fernández. *War of Shadows: The Struggle for Utopia in the Peruvian Amazon*. Berkeley: University of California Press, 1993. Two anthropologists study the MIR guerrillas and their indigenous Asháninka allies.

Lowenthal, Abraham F., and Cynthia McClintock, eds. *The Peruvian Experiment Reconsidered*. Princeton: Princeton University Press, 1976. An early collection of essays examining the Velasco regime. Updated and published in Spanish as *El gobierno militar*, Instituto de Estudios Peruanos, 1985.

La Serna, Miguel. *The Corner of the Living: Ayacucho on the Eve of the Shining Path Insurgency*. Chapel Hill: University of North Carolina Press, 1999.

Seligman, Linda J. *Between Reform and Revolution: Political Struggles in the Peruvian Andes, 1969–1991*. Stanford: Stanford University Press, 1995.

Chapters 13–14 (1980–2001)

Alcalde, M. Cristina. *The Woman in the Violence: Gender, Poverty, and Resistance in Peru*. Nashville: Vanderbilt University Press, 2010.

Cameron, Maxwell A. *Democracy and Authoritarianism in Peru: Political Coalitions and Social Change*. New York: Palgrave Macmillan, 1994.

Carrion, Julio F. *The Fujimori Legacy: The Rise of Electoral Authoritarianism in Peru*. University Park: Pennsylvania State University Press, 2006.

Conaghan, Catherine M. *Fujimori's Peru: Deception in the Public Sphere*. Pittsburgh: University of Pittsburgh Press, 2005.

Crabtree, John. *Peru under García: An Opportunity Lost*. Pittsburgh: University of Pittsburgh Press, 1992. Revised and published in Spanish as *Alan García en el poder: Perú 1985–1990*, Peisa, 2005.

Gorriti, Gustavo. *The Shining Path: A History of the Millenarian War in Peru*. Chapel Hill: University of North Carolina Press, 1999.

La Serna, Miguel. *With Masses and Arms: Peru's Tupac Amaru Revolutionary Movement*. Chapel Hill: University of North Carolina Press, 2020.

McClintock, Cynthia, and Fabián Vallas. *The United States and Peru: Cooperation—at a Cost*. New York: Routledge Press, 2003.

Starn, Orin, and Miguel La Serna. *The Shining Path: Love, Madness, and Revolution in the Andes*. New York: W.W. Norton, 2019.

Taylor, Lewis. *Shining Path: Guerrilla War in Peru's Northern Highlands, 1980–1997*. Liverpool: Liverpool University Press, 2006.

Chapters 15–17 (2001–Present)

Agüero, José Carlos. *The Surrendered: Reflections by a Son of Shining Path*. Durham: Duke University Press, 2021. Published in Spanish as *Los Rendidos*, Instituto de Estudios Peruanos, 2015.

Arce, Moisés. *Resource Extraction and Protest in Peru*. Pittsburgh: University of Pittsburgh Press, 2008.

Barrow, Sarah. *Contemporary Peruvian Cinema: History, Identity, and Violence on Screen*. London: I.B. Tauris, 2018.

García, María Elena. *Gastropolitics and the Specter of Race: Stories of Capital, Culture, and Coloniality in Peru*. Oakland: University of California Press, 2021.

McNulty, Stephanie L. *Voice and Vote: Decentralization and Participation in Post-Fujimori Peru*. Stanford: Stanford University Press, 2011.

Milton, Cynthia E. *Conflicted Memory: Military Cultural Interventions and the Human Rights Era in Peru*. Madison: University of Wisconsin Press, 2018.

Theidon, Kimberly Susan. *Intimate Enemies: Violence and Reconciliation in Peru*. State College: University of Pennsylvania Press, 2014.

Paredes, Maritza, and Rosemary Thorp. *Ethnicity and the Persistence of Inequality: The Case of Peru*. Basingstoke, UK: Palgrave Macmillian, 2010.

Schiwy, Freya. *Indianizing Film: Decolonization, the Andes, and the Question of Technology*. New Brunswick: Rutgers University Press, 2009.

For Those Who Read Spanish

Jorge Basadre is the celebrated master of Peruvian historiography, with his exhaustive multi-volume history—introduced in 1939 and updated over several decades—offering a most thorough treatment of the breadth of post-independence history. It is still an authoritative source on a few select chronological pockets, especially in the nineteenth century.

Basadre, Jorge. *Historia de la República del Perú*. Fourteen vols., twelfth ed. Lima: El Comercio, 2005.

Chapters 1–3 (c. 1780–1867)

Aguirre, Carlos. *Agentes de su propia libertad: Los esclavos de Lima y la desintegración de la esclavitud, 1821–1854*. Lima: Pontificia Universidad Católica del Perú, 1993.

Aljovín de Losada, Cristóbal. *Caudillos y constituciones: Perú, 1821–1845*. Lima: Pontificia Universidad Católica del Perú, 2000.

Anna, Timothy. *La caída del gobierno español en el Perú: El dilema de la independencia*. Lima: Instituto de Estudios Peruanos, 2003.

Bonilla, Heraclio. *Guano y burguesía en el Perú*. Lima: Instituto de Estudios Peruanos, 1984.

Chambers, Sarah C. *De súbditos a ciudadanos: honor, género y política en Arequipa, 1780–1854*. Lima: Red para el Desarrollo de las Ciencias Sociales, 2003.
Contreras, Carlos. *La independencia del Perú: ¿concedida, conseguida, concebida?* Lima: Instituto de Estudios Peruanos, 2020.
Flores Galindo, Alberto. *Aristocracia y Plebe: Lima, 1760–1830*. San Isidro: Mosca Azul Editores, 1984.
Gootenberg, Paul. *Caudillos y comerciantes: La formación económica del estado peruano, 1820–1860*. Cusco: Centro Bartolomé de Las Casas, 1997.
Miller, Rory. *Empresas británicas, economía y política en el Perú, 1850–1934*. Lima: Instituto de Estudios peruanos, 2011.
Walker, Charles. *De Túpac Amaru a Agustín Gamarra: Cusco y la formación del Perú republicano, 1780–1840*. Lima: Fondo Editorial PUCP, 2021.

Chapters 4–6 (1867–1908)

Chang-Rodríguez, Eugenio. *Pensamiento y acción en González Prada, Mariátegui y Haya de la Torre*. Lima: Fondo Editorial PUCP, 2012.
Contreras, Carlos. *La economía peruana frente al crecimiento del comerico mundial entre 1870 y 1913*. Lima: Instituto de Estudios Peruanos, 2019.
Denegri, Francesca. *Damas escritoras: Las ilustradas del diecinueve*. Lima: Editorial San Marcos / Recreo, 2007.
Gilbert, Dennis L. *La oligarquía peruana: historia de tres familias*. Lima: Editorial Horizonte, 1982. A reissued comparative study appears in English as *The Oligarchy and the Old Regime in Latin America*. Lanham: Rowman & Littlefield, 2017.
Gonzales, Michael J. *Azúcar y trabajo: La transformación de las haciendas en el norte del Perú, 1860–1933*. Lima: Banco Central de Reserva / Instituto de Estudios Peruanos, 2016.
Lossio, Jorge, and Emilio Candela. *Prensa, conspiraciones y elecciones: el Perú en el ocaso del régimen oligárquico*. Lima: Pontificia Universidad Católica del Perú / Instituto Riva-Agüero, 2015.

Chapters 7–9 (1908–1948)

Bonfiglio, Giovanni. *La presencia europea en el Perú*. Lima: Fondo Editorial del Congreso del Perú, 2001.
Burga, Manuel, and Alberto Flores Galindo. *Apogeo y crisis de la República Aristocrática*. Lima: Ediciones Rikchay, 1980.

Giesecke, Margarita. *La insurrección de Trujillo: Jueves 7 de julio del 1932.* Lima: Fondo Editorial del Congreso del Peru, 2010.
Gonzáles, Osmar. *El gobierno de Guillermo E. Billinghurst: Los orígenes del populismo en el Perú, 1912–1914.* Lima: Mundo Nuevo, 2005.
Luna Segura, Germán. *Magda en el Portal de los sueños. De su lucha por la mujer y su militancia en el APRA.* Lima: Ediciones Populares La Tribuna, 2017.
Molinari, Tirso. *El fascismo en el Perú: La Unión Revolucionaria, 1931–1936.* Lima: Universidad Nacional Mayor de San Marcos, 2006.
Pareja Pflucker, Piedad. *Aprismo y sindicalismo en el Perú.* Lima: Editorial Rikchay, 1980.
Peloso, Vincent. *Campesinos en haciendas: Coacción y consentimiento entre los productores de algodón en el valle de Pisco.* Lima: Banco Central de Reserva / Instituto de Estudios Peruanos, 2013.
Reedy, Daniel R. *Magda Portal, la pasionaria peruana: Biografía intelectual.* Lima: Ediciones Flora Tristán, 2000.
Tauro, Alberto. *Amauta y su influencia.* Lima: Editorial Minerva, 1986.
Wiesse, Maria. *José Carolos Mariátegui: Etapas de su vida.* Lima: Editora Amauta, 1985.

Chapters 10–12 (1948–1980)

Bedoya, Ricardo. *Cien años de cine en el Perú: una historia crítica.* Lima: Universidad de Lima, Fondo de Desarrollo Editorial, 1995.
Collier, David. *Barriadas y élites: de Odría a Velasco.* Lima: Instituto de Estudios Peruanos, 1978.
Manrique, Nelson. *¡Usted fue aprista! Bases para una historia crítica del APRA.* Lima: Fondo Editorial de la PUCP, 2009.
Matos Mar, José, and José Manuel Mejía. *La reforma agraria en el Perú.* Lima: Instituto de Estudios Peruanos, 1980.
Parodi Trece, Carlos. *Perú 1960–2000: políticas económicas y sociales en entornos cambiantes.* Lima: Universidad del Pacífico, 2001.
Peirano, Luis, and Abelardo Sánchez León. *Risa y cultura en la televisión Peruana.* Lima: YUNTA-Asociación Civil de Estudios y Publicaciones Urbanas, 1984.
Portocarrero, Gonzalo. *De Bustamante a Odría: El fracaso del Frente Democrático Nacional, 1945–1950.* Lima: Mosca Azul Editores, 1983.
Roca-Rey, Christabelle. *La propaganda visual durante el gobierno de Juan Velasco Alvarado, 1968–1975.* Lima: Instituto de Estudios Peruanos, 2016.
Sheahan, John. *La economía peruana desde 1950: Buscando una sociedad mejor.* Lima: Instituto de Estudios Peruanos, 2001.

Chapters 13–14 (1980–2001)

Comisión de la Verdad y Reconciliación. *Informe final*. Lima: Comisión de la Verdad y Reconciliación, 2005. El informe de la comisión que investiga la guerra interna desde 1980 a 2000.

Degregori, Carlos Iván. *La década de la antipolítica: Auge y huida de Alberto Fujimori y Vladimiro Montesinos*. Lima: Instituto de Estudios Peruanos, 2001.

Degregori, Carlos Iván. *Qué difícil es ser Dios: el Partido Comunista del Perú-Sendero Luminoso y el conflicto armado interno en el Perú, 1980–1999*. Lima: Instituto de Estudios Peruanos, 2010.

Gonzales de Olarte, Efraín. *El neoliberalismo a la peruana: Economía política del ajuste estructural, 1990–1997*. Lima: Instituto de Estudios Peruanos, 1998.

Gootenberg, Paul. *Cocaína andina: El proceso de una droga global*. Lima: La Siniestra y Universidad Nacional de Juliaca, 2016.

Gorriti, Gustavo. *Sendero: historia de la guerra milenaria en el Perú*. Lima: Editorial Planeta Perú, 1990.

Paredes, Carlos. *La hora final: La verdad sobre la capture de Abimael Guzmán*. Lima: Planeta, 2017.

Parodi Trece, Carlos. *Perú 1995–2012: Cambios y continuidades*. Lima: Universidad del Pacífico, 2019. El foco está en la economía neoliberal.

Vargas Haya, Héctor. *Frustración democrática y corrupción en el Perú*. Lima: Editorial Carlos Milla Batres, 1994. La énfasis está en el primer gobierno de Alan García.

Chapters 15–17 (2001–Present)

Caballero, Víctor. *Mototaxi: Auge y caída de Fuerza Popular*. Lima: Penguin Random House Grupo Editorial, 2019. Sobre los procesos políticos entre 2016–2019.

Manrique, Nelson. *Rumbo incierto, destino desconocido: El Perú bajo el segundo alanismo*. Lima: Sur Casa de Estudios del Socialismo, 2015.

Olivares, Daniel. *Joder para transformar: Mi última rendición de cuentas*. Lima: Penguin Random House Grupo Editorial, 2021. Experiencias de un congresista reciente.

Sifuentes, Marco. *K.O. P.P.K.: Caída pública y vida secreta de Pedro Pablo Kuczynski*. Lima: Planeta, 2019.

de la Torre López, Arturo. *La asociación evangélica de la misión israelita del nuevo pacto universal*. Madrid: Editorial Trotta, 2012. Un estudio del movimiento de Ezequiel Ataucusi.

Index

Abascal, José Fernando de, 4, 27, 31
Acción (publication), 90
Acción Popular (political party), See Popular Action
Acurio, Gastón, 187
Adrianzén, Eduardo, 189, 191
Afro-Peruvians, 5, 33, 106, 122, 133, 142, 184, 185, 186. See also specific persons
agriculture, 57, 128
agrarian reform, 113, 122, 125–126, 138, 164
Águilar, Febrizio, 189
Air Force (of Peru), 89, 91, 123, 165. See also military and militarism
airports and aviation, 91, 116, 119, 120, 164, 177
Alameda de Acho (Lima), 25, 35, 61
Alcedo, José Bernardo, 34
Alegría, Ciro, 88
alpacas, 57, 109
Amauta (journal), 81, 82, 84, 98, 101
Amazonia, 16, 56, 65, 79, 91, 92, 114, 122–123, 151, 174, 176, 188, 197, 207

American Airlines, 164
América Televisión, 159, 176, 196
anarchism and anarchists, 59, 78
Áncash (region), 127
Ancón, Treaty of, 53, 79
Andes mountains, 205. See also highlands
Amnesty International, 205
Amnesty Law (of 1995), 163
animals, 33, 35, 57, 154, 183, 186. See also horseracing, and specific animals
anticlericalism, 58
anti-Semitism, 90
APRA [American Popular Revolutionary Alliance], 82, 84, 85, 89, 90, 93, 94, 104, 110, 111, 112, 113, 115, 116–117, 122, 130, 131, 137, 145, 150, 154, 156, 177, 179, 197; repression of, 86–89, 94–95, 107–108, 114, 142. See also Haya de la Torre, and Alan García
Arana, Julio César, 56
architects and architecture, 26, 61, 97, 111, 120–121. See also balconies, Residencial San Felipe

Arequipa, 11, 19, 33, 63–64, 85, 94, 105, 133, 135, 145, 178
Argentina, 1, 4, 59, 94, 108, 121, 126, 137
Arica, 18, 53, 75, 79–80
aristocracy. *See* Limeño upper class
Aristocratic Republic (term), 53–54
Armed Forces. *See* army and army officers, military and militarism
army and army officers, 79, 85, 88, 91, 110, 123, 124, 135, 149, 151, 158, 162, 163, 165, 204–205; repression of APRA and, 95, 107, 108. *See also* Chorillos (military academy), military and militarism, War of the Pacific, and specific names of officers and battles
art (and art schools), 27, 31–32, *32*, 33–34, 65–66, 97–99, 134, 138, *139*, 140, *185*, 186. *See also* specific names of artists
Ashaninka (people), 123
Asia and Asian. *See* specific nationalities
Atacama Desert, 39, 41
Ataucusi, Ezequiel, 206–207
austerity programs, 150, 155, 188. *See also* International Monetary Fund
Avenida de los Descalzos, 61
Ayacucho, 47, 101, 126, 145, 151, 158, 174; Sendero Luminoso and, 146, 147–148

Baca, Susana, 185
balconies (in Lima), 26, *27*, 99
Balcázar, Francisco Rosas, 51
Balta, José, 38, 41
Las Bambas (mine), 207
Banchero Rossi, Luis, 108–109, 138
banks and banking, 15, 17, 38, 50, 79, 108, 110, 113, 114, 128, 130, 149, 151, 164, 172, 175, 179, 180, 182, 199. *See also* debt and finances, International Monetary Fund
Bard, Harry E., 74
Barbados, 56
Barranco (district), 62, 84, 129, 140, *185*, 186
Barrantes, Alfonso "Frejolito," 149
Barrios, Lucho, 140
Barrios Altos (district), 66, 103, 162
Basadre, Jorge, 53–54
Basombrío, Carlos, 200
Bedoya Reyes, Luis, 120–121
Béjar, Héctor, 138
Belaúnde, Fernando, 111–112, 115, 116–118, 131; presidencies of, 119, 123–124, 145, 148–150
Belaúnde, Martín, 180
Bellido, María Parado de, *32*
Beltrán, Pedro, 111, 113–114
Benavides, Óscar, 88–90, 94, 99, 104
Berenson, Lori, 164, 165
Billinghurst, Guillermo, 75, 80, 85, 100
billionaires (Peruvian), 128, 158, 164, 181, 182
Bingham, Hiram, 64
La boca del lobo (film), 188–189
Bogotá, 4
bolero (music), 106, 140, 141, 143, 184
Bolivia (Upper Peru), 8, 9, 14, 40, 41, 43, 76, 135, 174, 180
Bolívar, Simón, 4, 6–7, 17, 31, 34, 35, 66
Bolognesi, Francisco, 43–44, 59, 69
Boluarte, Dina, 204
Borgoño, Justiniano, 51
Bourbon Reforms, 1, 25
Brazil, 16, 136, 177, 178
Brescia Tassano, Fortunato, 128
Britain and British, 15, 22, 41, 50, 56, 57, 62, 82, 98, 111
Bryce Echenique, Alfredo, 134–135, 192
Buenos Aires, 1, 4, 14, 41, 104, 105, 137, 178

business and businesses, 55–57, 74, 108, 109, 110, 111, 122–123, 130, 142, 149, 152, 164, 175, 180, 181, 184, 187, 190, 201, 207–208. *See also* banking, debt and finances, mines and mining, United States of America: business interests and, and specific names of companies or products
Bustamante, José Luis, 94, 110, 120

Cabella de Carbonera, Mercedes, 69
Cáceres, Andrés Avelino, 45–47, 52, 70, 77, 77; government of, 49–53, 69
cajón (musical instrument), 103
Callao, 15, 22, 43, 51, 63, 78, 79, 95, 140, 142, 145
Canada, 94
Canal N (newschannel), 166, 168
Canción sin nombre (film), 191
Candamo, Manuel, 55
La Cantuta. *See* National Normal School
La Cantuta massacre, 162, 163, 163
Caretas (newsmagazine), 140, 167
Casimiro Ulloa, José, 65
Castilla, Ramón, 13, 14–18, 20, 22, 38, 39, 41, 58, 64
Castillo, Pedro, 201–204, 205, 207
Castillo, Teófilo, 66
del Castillo, Jorge, 176
caudillismo, 9, 20. *See also* specific names of caudillos
Cavaguaro, Mario, 141
cemeteries, 3, 66, 201. *See also* Presbítero Maestro Matías
Central Intelligence Agency (U.S.), 158, 158fn, 160, 165
Cerro de Pasco, 56, 117, 177
CGT. *See* General Confederation of Peruvian Workers
Chan Chan, 88
charities, 29, 63, 70, 109, 113, 146

Chávez, Hugo, 174, 175, 179, 202
Chávez, Jorge, 120
Chambi, Martín, 138
Cheesman, Roxanne, 176
Chile, 11, 14, 18, 22, 33, 57, 67, 71, 88, 140, 174; and war with Peru, 41–47, 53, 67–68; dispute over southern provinces, 79–80. *See also* Santiago de Chile, Valparaíso
Chimbote, 109, 110, 114, 117, 127, 128
China and Chinese, 20–21, 26, 29, 38, 75, 146, 186, 207. *See also* Maoism
Chincha Islands, 22
Chocano, José Santos, 68–69, 99–100
cholera, 5
cholo (term), 137
Chorillos (town), 15, 18, 35, 46, 62, 185
Chorillos Military Academy, 54, 110, 124, 174
Christian Democratic Party, 112, 120
Church (Roman Catholic) and Catholics, 2, 19, 25, 26, 30, 40, 70, 76, 89, 134, 187–188; orders, 26, 34; rituals and devotions, 29, 67; saints 35, 188; services and ceremonies, 28, 88, 188. *See also* anticlericalism, charities, Vatican, and specific names of clerics and popes
Ciriani, Enrique, 120
Cisneros, Consuelo, 32
La ciudad y los perros (novel), 135, 184
Civilians' Party [Partido Civilista], 38, 49, 51, 55, 76, 80
El clima de Lima (book), 3
Claridad (journal), 81
Club Alianza, 186–187
clubs – political and social, 7, 29, 37, 59, 64, 69, 77, 91, 186
coca (leaf) and cocaine, 57, 151, 171, 207
Codesido, Julia, 98, 98–99
cofradías, 28

Colombia, 8, 16, 79, 88, 108, 156, 165
Columbus, Christopher, 35, 68
El Comercio (newspaper), 63, 67, 88, 89, 100, 116
Comte, Auguste, 53
communism and Communist Party of Peru, 82, 88, 93, 112, 130, 135, 138, 145, 146, 157, 202. *See also* Martiátegui, José Carlos, Sendero Luminoso
Condorcanqui, José Gabriel. *See* Tupac Amarú II
Confederación General de Trabajadores Peruanos. *See* General Confederation of Peruvian Workers
congress, 8, 17, 37–38, 50, 67, 74, 87, 112, 131, 157, 158, 162, *163*, 175, 176, 200, 204, 208
conservatives and conservatism, 5, 19, 76, 81, 86, 94. *See also* Limeño upper class, and specific names of political figures and parties
constitutions, 8, 9, 13, 19, 20, 38, 78, 88, 131, 164, 166, 179
Contrapunto (TV show), 189
Convención (valley), 113
Conversación en la catedral (novel), 135
convivencia (cohabitation of government), 112
Copa América, 187
copper, 56, 175, 181, 205
corruption, 17, 110, 112, 125, 150, 157, 158, 164, 166, 168, 176, 177, 180, 190, 196, 197, 198, 203–204
Costa Verde, 120, 129
costumbrismo, 31
cotton, 21, 75, 111
covid (pandemic), 68, 195, 197, 198, 201
creoles, 1, 4, 7
Crousillat, José Enrique, 159
Cruz, Iván, 142–143
Cuba and Cuban Revolution, 88, 105, 106, 113, 116, 122, 123, 125, 140

Cueto, Alonso, 190
cuentos criollos, 100
Cuarto Poder (TV show), 176, 196
Cusco (Cuzco), 2, 64, 67, 110, 116, 138, 177–178

dance, 185–186
Darwin, Charles, 53, 65
debt and finances, 38–40, 50–51, 54, 55, 65, 79, 90, 90–91, 109, 112, 113, 127, 149, 150, 151, 175, 199. *See also* banks and banking
deforestation, 207
Delfín, Víctor, 186
Delgado Brandt, Genaro, 136, 137
Democratic Party [Partido Democrático], 49, 74, 75, 119
Denegri, Aurelio, 49
Díaz Costa, Rossana, 192
diplomacy, 16, 53, 79, 80, 91–92, 99, 108, 111, 113, 114, 130, 135, 151, 168
Discos MAG (company), 141
diseases, 5, 32
Dos de Mayo. *See* May 2
drug trafficking, 158, 165, 189, 196. *See also* coca (leaf) and cocaine
Duck Canyon, 109, 127

earthquakes, 26, 28, 110, *127*, 127–128
Echenique, José Rufino, 17–18, 41, 58
Ecuador, 11, 51, 140; war with, 91–92
education. *See* schools and schooling, universities
Eguiguren, Luis, 90
Eielson, Jorge Eduardo, 134
elections and voting, 34, 38, 54, 55, 76–77, 78, 79, 86–87, 90, 94, 108, 111, 114, 117, 131, 136, 145, 150, 154–155, 164, 166, 168, 169, 171, 174, 179, 180, 195–196, 201–203, 203, 204, 207. *See also* specific names of political parties

electricity and electrical grid, 63, 109, 114, 127, 129, 154
Elguera, Federico, 57
Elías, Domingo, 18, 51, 55
Enfoca Andean Investments, 190
engineering, 64–65
Enlightenment, 2–3, 7, 26
Enriquez, Trinidad, 71
environment and environmental issues, 79, 176, 177, 180, 188, 207, 208
Europe. *See* specific nations
exile and exiles, 9, 14, 77, 78, 81, 84, 117
exports. *See* trade and specific commodities

fascism, 84, 86, 89, 90. *See also* Revolutionary Union
Federación Peruana de Fútbol. *See* Peruvian Football Federation
Fierro, Pancho, 32
film and films, 56, 104–105, 138, 184, 188–193
Fina Estampa (song), 140
finances. *See* debt and finances, banks and banking
fishing and fisheries, 108, 113, 125, 128
fishmeal. *See* fishing and fisheries
Flores, Luis, 90
Flores Lucera, José "Pili," 138, 190
Flores Nano, Lourdes, 175
football, 62–63, 121–122, 186–187. *See also* National Stadium and names of clubs, players
foreign relations. *See* diplomacy
El Frontón (prison), 111, 151
France and French, 3, 15, 39, 44, 46, 51, 59, 62, 65, 66, 78, 81, 82, 97, 99, 101, 102, 119, 123, 134, 150, 152, 156, 175, 187
Francis (pope), 188
Free Peru (party), 202, 203
FREPAP [*Frente Popular Agrícola del Perú*], 206

Fuerza Popular. *See* Popular Force
fujigolpe (partial coup), 155–156, 157, 162
Fujimori, Alberto, 155–156, 157, 158–162, 163, 164, 165, 174, 177, 179
Fujimori, Keiko, 179, 195, 196, 201, 202
Fujimori, Kenji, 196
Fujimori dictatorship, 169, 171, 173, 175, 186, 189, 201
fútbol. *See* football

Gallo de mi galpón (film), 104–105
Gálvez, José (and Pedro), 18, 22, 55
Gamarra, Agustín, 9, 13, 14, 19
García, Alan, 137, 152, 156, 169, 175, 176, 180, 187–188, 195–196, 197; presidencies of, 150–151, 152, 154, 175–177, 178, 179
García Hurtado, Federico, 138
García Márquez, Gabriel, 135–136
General Confederation of Peruvian Workers [*Confederación General de Trabajadores Peruanos*], 87, 112, 116. *See also* APRA, labor and labor rights, communism and Communist Party of Peru
Germany and Germans, 65, 66, 78, 84, 91, 187
geography, 64, 65
Gibson, Doris, 138
Gil de Castro, José, 33–34
González de Fanning, Teresa, 70, 71
González Prada, Manuel, 58–59, 73, 80, 81–82, 83, 100
Gonzáles de Velasco, Consuelo, 127
González Vigil, Francisco de Paula, 20
Gorriti, Juan and Manuela, 69, 70
Grace contract, 50, 58, 75, 149
Graña Garland, Francisco, 94
Granda, Chabuca, 140
Grau, Miguel, 39, 42–43, 59
Great Britain. *See* Britain

Gregory XVI (pope), 35
Grieve, Jorge, 120
Grupo Breca, 128
Grupo Colina, 162
guano, 15
Guatemala, 99
guerrillas. *See* Revolutionary Leftist Movement, Tupac Amaru Revolutionary Movement, and Sendero Luminoso
Gutiérrez, Sérvulo, 138, *139*
Gutiérrez, Tomás, 39
Guzmán, Abimael, 145–148, 160–161, 165

hacienda and haciendas, 3, 60, 101, 128, 146
Haya de la Torre, Victor Raúl, 81, 82, 84, 85, 86–87, 89, 93, 94–95, 101, 108, 113, 115, *115*, 118, 122, 130, 150; political manueverings in 1956–63 period, 111–112, 114, 115–117, 119. *See also* APRA
health and healthcare, 57, 65, 81, 90. *See also* sanitation, medicine and medical, hospitals
Heraud, Javier, 140
Heredia, Nadine, 180, 196
Hernández Morillo, Daniel, 66, 97–98
Herrera, Bartolomé, 19–20
Herzog, Werner, 56
highlands, 5, 30, 44, 46–47, 55, 60, 64, 65, 74, 92–93, 99, 103, 109, 110, 114, 116–117, 126, 127–128, 137, 152, 160, 162, 164, 177, 187, 191, 197, 205–207; Sendero war in, 146, 147
highways. *See* roads and road construction
Higuchi, Susana, 166
homosexuality, 134, 152
horseracing, 62, 120. See also San Beatriz

hospitals, 65, 81, 92, 201
Huallaga River (and valley), 151, 152
Huancayo, 20, 117, 152, 154, 161
Huascar (naval vessel), 22, 41–43, *42*
Huascarán (volcano), 116, 127
Humala, Ollanta, 174–175, 179–180, 185, 195, 196, 197
human rights and human rights organizations, 148, 150, 161, 162, 163, 172, 173, *173*, 174, 189, 205
Humboldt Current, 108, 125

IDL Reporteros (organization), 177
Iglesias, Miguel, 45, 49
immigrants and (overseas) immigration, 21, 38, 75
imports. *See* trade, and specific products
Inca and Inca Empire, 1, 60, 76, 82, 83
Inca Trail (tourism), 177–178
Independence, 4–7, 28–29, 30, 34, 35, 41; centennial celebrations of, 78–79
indigenous peoples (of Peru), 6, 30, 54, 55, 56, 57, 60, 70, 86, 93, *109*, 110, 113m 117, 126,138, 147, 162, 166, 168, 177, 188, 202, 205, 206, *206*, 207, 208; racism towards, 74, 162–163. *See also* tribute and tributary system, Tupac Amaru II, Ashaninka, and other specific names
Indignismo, 98, 138
Infante, Pedro, 106, 140
inflation, 91, 126, 130, 145, 149, 151, 155
Los Inocentes (book), 133–134
Integrated Security, doctrine of, 124
International Monetary Fund, 114, 130, 149, 151, 164
International Petroleum Company [IPC], 123–124, 125
internet, 183, 187, 198, 200, 202–203
Iquique (battle of), 42
Iquitos, 56, 116
Ireland and Irish, 29

Italy and Italians, 29, 32, 66, 78, 81, 85, 89, 90, 91, 97, 100, 108, 128, 131, 134, 181
Ivcher, Baruch, 159, 189
Izquierda Unida. *See* United Left

Japan and Japanese, 57, 75, 91, 114, 125, 165, 166, 168, 173
Japanese-Peruvians, 91, 155, 183
Jaramillo, Julio, 140
jeringa, 134
Jesús María (Lima district), 99, 120
John Paul II, 187–188
Journalism. *See* Media
Joy Way, Víctor, 164
Junín (battle of), 7, 14

Kroehle, Charles, 65
Kropp, Miriam, 111
Kuczynski, Pablo, 174, 179, 195–196,
Kuntur Wachana (film), 138

labor and labor rights, 57, 60, 74, 75–76, 78, 82, 92, 101, 108, 112, 116, 130. *See also* anarchism, communism and Communist Party of Peru, socialism and Socialist Party of Peru, and unions and strikes
land and land ownership, 30. *See also* agrarian reform
Lara, Juan Jacinto, 8
Larriva y Ruíz, José Joaquín de, 31
Latina (TV station/network), 159, 189, 190, 200
Lavoe, Hector, 142
law and lawyers, 71
Leguía, Augusto, 73–74, 76, 77–80, 85, 86, 100, 111. See also Oncenio
León, Melin, 191
Liberal Party [Partido Liberal], 55
liberalism, 6, 19, 30, 37–38, 63, 86
Libertad, Tania, 184
Lince (Lima district), *102*

Lima, 2, 11, 51, 53, 54, 57, 58, 62, 65, 68, 73, 75, 78, 81, 84, 87, 89, 92, 95, 99, 100, 101, 108, 110, 111, *115*, 116, 134, 138, 149, 168, 175, *185*, 186, 187, 188, 197, 198, 199–200, *203*, 204; civic administration in, 57, 149; growth and population of, 128–129, 178, 199; independence and. 1, 5–7, 10; media in, 105, *106*, 136, 137, 140, 166, 168, 189, 191, 200; and Sendero War, 152, 154, 159–161, *160*, 162, *163*; transportation in, 120–121, *121*, 178, *181*. *See also* Limeño upper class, and specific locations, e.g. Plaza San Martín, and districts by name
Limeño upper class, 14, 17–18, 27, 35, 37, 69, 74, 75–76, 79, 80, 81, 86, 89, 94, 99, 110, 117, 134, 155; APRA and, 88, 107, 119; Aristocratic Republic and, 53–55, 58, 73; distrust of popular governments, 124, 130, 175; lifestyles and, 25–26, 61–62, 66, 99, 101, 102, 128, 178, 187; racism of, 85, 148, 185–186, 199, 205, 208; in War of the Pacific, 44–46
Lizárraga, Alicia, 104, 105
Llosa, Claudia, 192
loans. *See* debt and finances
Lobatón, Guillermo, 122–123
Lombardi, Francisco, 138, 184, 188, 190
López Aliaga, Rafael, 201, 202
Lopiani, Juan, 59
Loquibambia (radio show), 137
Los Morunos (band), 141
Loza, Tulio, 137
Lynch, Albert, 66

Machu Picchu, 64, 177–178, 201
Madrid, 68, 149, 197
Magallanes, Ana Cecilia, 162, 164
Malachowski, Ricardo de Jaxa, 99

Malinowski, Ernest, 50
Mantaro River, 114
Maoism, 122, 126, 146, 147
de la Mar, José, 9, *10*
Mariátegui, José Carlos, 81–82, 83, 84, 94, 98, 101, 102, 104, 146,
Marxism, 93, 123, 147. See also communism and Communist Party of Peru, Maoism, socialism and Socialist Party of Peru
Matto de Turner, Clorinda, 70
Matute (stadium), 186
May 2 (battle of), 22–23, 35, 37
media, 126, 131, 136, 154–155, 159, 166, 167, 171, 172, 175, 176, 190, 198, 200, 201, 204, 205. See also Lima: media in, newspapers, radio, television, and specific radio and Television broadcasters
medicine and medical practice, 51, 65, 70, 71, 92, 201. See also hospitals, Unanue, Hipólito
Meiggs, Henry, 38
Melgar, Mariano, 20, 33
Méndez, Josué, 189
Mendoza, Abelardo, 88
Merino, Ignacio, 31–32
Merino, Manuel, 198, 200
Metro. See Tren Eléctrico
Metropolitano (bus system), *121*
Mexico, 78, 82, 99, 104, 106, 119, 134, 140, 157, 184,
middle class, 55, 62, 78, 86, 94, 107, 110, 111, 121, 130, 136, 137, 146, 147, 162, 175, 179, 190, 198, 200, 202
migration (internal), 128, 129, 137
military and militarism, 27, 44–45, 54–55, 85, 89, 110, 112, 120, 124, 130, 150, 152, 155, 157–158, 158, 165, 168, 172, *173*, 174, 189, 204. See also air force, army and army officers, navy, War of the Pacific

mines and mining, 39, 50, 56–57, 79, 101, 108, 113, 172, 177, 179, 181, 182, 188, 207, 208. See also Las Bambas, copper, silver
Miraflores (city and district), 18, 45–46, 46, 67, 68, 70, 87, 105, 128, 159, 160, 166, 178,
Miró Quesada, Antonio, 89
Modernism, 138
Montesinos, Vladimiro, 157–159, 158fn, 160, 165, 166, 168, 174, 189,
Morales, Evo, 174
Morales Bermúdez, Francisco, 130–131, 149
Morales Bermúdez, Remigio, 51
El Morro (battle of), 43–44, 59
El Morro Solar (hill), 45
Movimiento Revolucionario Túpac Amaru. See Revolutionary Movement Túpac Amaru
Un mundo para Julius (novel), 134–135
Muñoz Barrata, Hugo, 137
music, 29, 34–35, 140–143, 184–185. See also specific genres and musicians
Música Criolla, 102–104, 105, 141, 184

National Club, 37
National Democratic Party [*Partido Democrático Nacional*], 76
National Library, 20, 65, 68
National Normal School, 133
National Palace, 69, 76, 85, 99, 168, 202, 203, 204
National Police, 130, 158, 168, 176, 198, 200
National Radio of Peru, 105–106, *106*, 134, 136,
National School of Engineering, 99, 119
National School of Fine Arts, 66, 97, 186
National Stadium, 106, 121–122, 175
National Union, 59

National University of Central Peru [UNCP], 152, 154, 161–162
Nationalist Party [Partido Nacionalista], 180
navy [in modern era], 87–88, 95, 130. See also military and militarism, War of the Pacific, and specific names of battles, officers, and ships
Neira, Hugo, 138
Neo-colonialism (architectural style), 99
neoliberalism (economics), 149, 164, 175, 177, 180, 181, 182, 195
Neruda, Pablo, 102
newspapers, 31, 59, 63, 79, 88, 154. See also specific names
New York City, 18, 28, 79, 138, 141, 149
Nieto, Domingo, 14
Nixon, Patricia, 127
Nixon, Richard, 113, 115
northern coast, 14, 15, 20, 45, 75, 87, 124, 128, 183, 186. See also cotton, sugar, Trujillo
novels and novelists, 69–70. See also specific authors and novels by name
Nuestra Señora de Guadalupe (school), 16, 51

OAX (radio station), 105
Ocenio. See Odría, Manuel A.
Odebrecht, 177, 196, 197
Odría, Manuel A., 107–108, 110–112, 117–118, 149, 150
Ognaes, Juan Carlos, 191
oil and gasoline, 55–56, 114, 125, 176. See also International Petroleum Company, Petroperú
Olaya, José, 34, 35
Oncenio (of the Leguía government), 77–80, 81, 119
Operation Condor, 131
Organization of American States [OAS], 166, 168
Oroya, 79
Ortiz, Beto, 199
Osita de felpa (song), 141
Otiniano, Pedro, 140

El País (newspaper), 51
Paisajes Peruanos (book), 76
Palacio Nacional. See National Palace
Palais Concert (Lima), 101
Palma, Clemente, 68
Palma, Ricardo, 58, 61, 66, 69; writings of, 67–68
La Palma (battle of), 18
Pan-American Highway, 90
Panama, 26, 181
Panamericana Televisión, 136
Pardo, José, 55, 73, 75, 76, 80
Pardo, Manuel, 38–40, 41, 188
Partidos. See specific names, in English
Patria Nueva, 78
Paz, Octavio, 134
Paz Soldán, Mateo, 64
Paz Soldán, Mariano Felipe, 64
Peace Corps, 146
El Peruano (newspaper), 31
Pérez Jiménez, Marcos, 110
La Perricholi (TV series), 189
Pershing, John "Blackjack," 80
Perú Libre (political party). See Free Peru
Peruvian Football Federation, 187
petroleum. See oil
Petroperú, 125, 149, 176
Pezet, Juan Antonio, 21
philanthropies. See charities
photography, 65, 138
Picasso, Pablo, 101
Piérola, Nicolás, 28, 40, 44–45, 51, 69; presidency of, 53–55
Pinglo Alva, Felipe, 103–104
Pinochet, Augusto, 174
Pisco, 15, 100
Piura, 114

Pius IX (pope), 19
Pizarro, Francisco, 1, 65
Plaza de Armas (Lima), 6, 28, 39, 61, 99, 188
Plaza San Martín (Lima), 71, 111, 122, 196,
El Plebeyo (song), 103–104, 105, 141
poets and poetry, 33–34, 58, 69, 84, 101–102, 134, 135, 183–184. *See also* specific names
Polay Campos, Víctor, 152, 153
police and policing, 74, 108, 111, 112, 116, 121, 126, 141, 142, 146, 147, 157, 159, 163, 168, 179, 180, 184, 197, 204. *See also* National Police, security services and SIN
Polo Campos, Augusto, 141–142
Pontifical Catholic University of Peru [PUCP], 76
Popular Action [*Acción Popular*], 112, 115, 116, 117, 131, 154, 198
Popular Force [*Fuerza Popular*], 179, 182, 195, 196, 208
Popular Universities, 81
population, 37, 54, 62, 63, 79, 92–93, 112, 113, 128, 178, 195
Porras Barrenechea, Raúl, 136
Porres, Martín de, 35
Portal, Magda, 84, 89, 94–95
Positivism, 53, 71
poverty, 30, 81, 86, 97, 101, 102, 129, *129*, 130, 142, 146, 155, 177, 178, 182, 188, 197, 199–200
Prado, Manuel, 90–93, 111–113, 116
Prado, Mariano Ignacio, 18, 37, 40, 41, 90
La Prensa (newspaper), 94, 111
Presbítero Maestro Matías (cemetery in Lima), 66, 68, 81, 83, 88, 188
Prescott, William, 32, 65
prison and prisons, 20, 64, 69, 80, 82, 150. *See also* El Frontón
de la Puente y Ramírez, Gaspar, 37

Protestantism, 74, 76, 143, 188, 202, 206
public health. *See* health and also medicine
de la Puente, Luis, 122–123
Puerto Rico, 88, 141, 142
Purple Party [*Partido Morado*], 200
Putumayo, 56

Quechua, 46, 147, 168, 192
Quispe, Flaviano, 191

race and racism, 2, 7, 28, 33, 35, 60, 86, 98, 148, 162, 185–186, 208. *See also* Limeño upper class: racism of
radio and radio stations, 86, 104, 105–106, *106*, 136, 140, 184. *See also* National Radio of Peru, and specific names of networks and stations
Radio Programas del Perú [RPP], 137, 141
Radio Sono, 141
Radio and Television Institute of Peru, 191
Radio Victoria, 142
railroads, 38, 50, 56, 63, 178,
Ramirez, Óscar, 165
ranchero (music), 106
Reconstruction and Rehabilitation Commission [CRYRZA],128
records (phonographs), 141, 142, 143, 184, 185
Red Faction, 126
Regional Workers Federation, 74
Reportaje al Perú (TV show), 191
La República (newspaper), 162, 167
Residencial San Felipe, 120
Revolution of 1895, 52–53, 69
Revolutionary Leftist Movement [MIR], 122–123, 124
Revolutionary Movement Tupac Amaru [MRTA], 152, *153*, 164–165
Revolutionary Union, 90
Reyes, Lucha, 142

Reynoso, Oswaldo, 133–134, 138
Ribeyro, Julio Ramón, 134, 135
Ricardito (saint), 188
Rimac (district), 129, 141, 142
Riva Agüero, José, 8
Riva Agüero, José de la, 76, 77, 89, 93, 100
roads and road construction, 78, 90, 109, 120, *121*. See also Lima: transportation in, Vía Expresa
Rodríguez, Dulante, Laura, 70
Rodríguez Pastor, Carlos, 181
Romanticism, 32, 58, 65, 66
Romero, Dionisio, 158, 179
rondas (civil patrols), 151
Roosevelt, Franklin D., 119
rubber, 56, 79
Russia, Russian Revolution, and Soviet Union, 78, 82, 101, 125, 154, 187

Sabogal, José, 98–99, 138
Sagasti, Francisco, 200–201
salsa, 142, 184
San Beatriz (racetrack), 88
San Carlos (school), 7, 19, 67
San Jerónimo (seminary in Arequipa), 20, 33
San Marcos (university), 3, 17, 31, 39, 54, 59, 70, 76, 82, 84, 90, 100, 120, 135, 137, 138, 158; student militancy at, 74, 76, 78, 80, 87, 113, 162
San Martín, José de, 5–6, 17, 28–29, 33, 34, 203
San Román, Miguel de, 21
Sánchez Carrión, José Faustino, 7–9
Sánchez Cerro, Luis Miguel, 88–89, 90; government of, 85–88
Sánchez, Monica, 189, 191
sanitation, 57, 63, 129
Santa Cruz, Andrés de, 10–11, 13, 86
Santa Cruz, Victoria, 185–186
Santa Rosa (Limeño saint), 28, 32
Santiago de Chile, 98, 100, 137, 140

Saquicuray, Antonia, 162, 163–164
schools and schooling, 16, 17, 18, 30, 33, 39, 51, 54, 55, 58, 74–75, 76, 90, 91, 126, 133, *148*, 199; for girls and women, 69, 70–71, 93. See also specific institutions, including San Marcos
security services and SIN [Servicio de Inteligencia Nacional], 147, 151, 152, 157, 160, 161, 162, *163*, 165, 166, 171, 172
Sendero Luminoso [Shining Path], 126, 145–148, *148*, 150, 151, 152, 154, 159–161, 165, 172, 174, 189, 196, 198, 200, 202, 204. See also Abimael Guzmán
de la Serna, José, 5
Seven Interpretative Essays on Peruvian Reality (book), 82
Seventh Day Adventists, 74, 76, 206
sheep, 57
ships and shipping, 15, 16, 20–21, 40–43, 55, 62, 63, 103, 127. See also navy, War of the Pacific
El Show de Tulio Loza, 137, 141
sierra. See highlands
Sifuentes, Marco, 199
silver and silver mining, 6, 57
SINAMOS [Sistema Nacional de Apoyo a la Movilización Social], 126, 138
slaves and slavery, 5–6, 20, 21, 33, 35
soccer. See football
Social Darwinism, 53, 54
socialism and Socialist Party of Peru, 82, 84, 151
sol (currency), 91, 110, 151
Solar, Pedro Alejandrino, 51
del Solar, Salvador, 190
de Soto, Hernando, 201
Spain and Spanish, 1, 4, 5, 68, 78, 89, 99, 100, 101, 136, 138, 149, 181; war with Peru, 21–23

sports. See specific games
Spruce, Richard, 65
Stahl, Ana and Ferdinand, 74
sterilization program, 162–163
Stevenson, Adlai, 115
Sucedio en el Perú (TV show), 191
Sucre, Antonio José de, 7, 8
sugar and sugar estates, 38, 57, 75, 82, 125, 146
Surco (Lima district), 104, 128, 152, 178, 199
Szyszlo, Fernando de, 140

Tacna, 43, 46, 53, 79–80, 138
Tadolini, Adamo, 66
Talara, 55
tapadas limeñas, 31
tar, 55
tariffs, 21, 54, 57, 113
Tarapacá (battle of), 46, 79
taxes and tax policies, 39, 50, 54, 57, 114, 123, 149, 158, 165, 172, 175, 179, 207–208
television, 136–138, 140, 141, 154, *163*, 166, 168, 179, 184, 189, 190–191, 198, *199*. See also specific networks and shows
terrorism, and fear of, 149, 150, 151, 154, 159, *160*, 161, 162, 166, *173*, 176. See also Sendero Luminoso
theaters, 57, 58, 63, 105, 141, 142, 175
Ticlio Pass, 50
Toledo, Alejandro, 166, 168–169, 171–172, 174, 179, 180, 195
El Tornillo (TV show), 137
de la Torre, José, 34
Torrico, Juan Crisóstomo, 18, 41
tourism, 177–178, 201. See also Machu Picchu
trade, 91, 113, 177
Tren Eléctrico (Lima), 178, *181*
tribute and tributary system, 5, 7, 30, 54, 78, 113

Trilce (book), 101
Tristán, Flora, 31
Trujillo, 5, 7, 16, 82, 108; uprising and massacre at, 87–88
Truth and Reconciliation Commission [CVR], 172–173, *173*, 173fn
tuna, 109, 113, 125
Tupac Amaru II, 1–2, 9, 138
Tupac Amaru (film),138

Ugarte, Alfonso, 44
Ulloa Elías, Manuel, 149
El último Bastión (telenovela), 191
Unanue, Hipólito, 3, 7, 8, 10, 21, 27, 65
unions (labor) and strikes, 82, 87, 93, 94, 110, 111, 114, 116, 126, 130, 130–131, 133, 145, 149, 201. See also labor and labor rights, General Confederation of Peruvian Workers
universities, 122, 126, 146, 147, 175. See also San Marcos and other specific names
United Left, 149–150

United States of America, 21, 28, 57, 67, 73, 74, 76, 77, 79, 80, 82, 88, 93, 109, 110, 119, 137, 151, 155, 166, 168, 172, 175, 202, 205; business interests and, 111, 113, 125, 130, 152, 181, 208; military/security links and, 110, 117, 123, 124, 157, 165, 172; relations with during Second World War, 90–92, 105, 107
Urbina, Melania, 190
Urresti, Daniel, 202

Valcárcel, Mariano, 51
Valdelomar, Abraham, 100–101
Vallejo, César, 101–102, *102*
Vallejo, Henry, 192
Valparaiso (Chile), 22, 58, 73
Vals Criollo, 103, 140
Varela, Blanca, 134, *135*, 140

Vargas, Chavela, 185
Vargas Llosa, Mario, 135–136, 137, 155, 179, 184
Vásquez, (María de) Jesús, 105
Vatican (and Vatican councils), 19, 20
Velasco, Juan, 124–126, 130, 146
Velasco military regime, 135, 137–138, 157, 164, 177, 184
Venezuela, 110
de Verneuil, Adriana, 58
Venezuela, 4
Vía Expresa (Lima), 120, *121*, 128
viceroy, 1, 3
La Victoria (district), 154, 186
Villegas, Micaela, 189
Villa El Salvador, 129
Villanueva, Alejandro, 186–187
Vivanco, Mauel Ignacio de, 14, 18, 40, 41, 101
Vizcarra, Martín, 196, 197–198, 200
Vladivideos, 168
Volcan Mining, 181
volcanoes, 116. *See also* Huascarán

War of the Pacific, 41–47, *42*, 46, 58, 62, 68, 70, 73, 191
Watanabe, José, 183–184
weapons. *See* military and militarism
Willax Television, 182, *199*, 202
Wong Lu, Erasmo, 182
Woodman, Arturo, 175
women, 30–31, 33, 45, 63, 66, 75, 105, 133, 164, 166, 191, 192, 206; in APRA, 89, 94–95, 111; emancipation and, 69–71, 97, 184, 185–186. *See also* specific names
World Cup, 187
World War I, 78
World War II, 90, 91, 94, 104, 107

Yellow Fever, 32
YMCA, 74
Yungay (battle of), 11, 13
Yungay (town), 127

Zamora, Jesús, 190
Zubiaga, Francisco, 9, 100, 101

www.ingramcontent.com/pod-product-compliance
Lightning Source LLC
Chambersburg PA
CBHW060949230426
43665CB00015B/2133